Invisible Gardens

Pepsico Headquarters, New York.

Edward D. Stone, Jr., Landscape Architect.

Invisible Gardens

The Search for Modernism in the American Landscape

Peter Walker and Melanie Simo

The MIT Press   Cambridge, Massachusetts   London, England

This book was set in Gill Sans by DEKR Corporation and was printed and bound in the United States of America.

Library of Congress Cataloging-in-Publication Data

Walker, Peter, 1932–
    Invisible gardens : the search for modernism in the American
landscape / Peter Walker and Melanie Simo.
        p. cm.
    Includes bibliographical references (p.   ) and index.
    ISBN 0-262-23177-8
    1. Landscape architecture—United States—History—20th century.
2. Landscape architects—United States—Biography. 3. Modernism
(Art)—Influence. I. Simo, Melanie Louise, 1949– . II. Title.
SB470.5.W34 1994
712'.0973'09045—dc20   94-16586
                                                              CIP

To our subjects,
beginning in critical interest,
and ending in respect and fond affection.

Contents

In 1975, after almost twenty years of continuous professional activity, I returned to teach at the Harvard Graduate School of Design. The years of practice had been intense in both growth and change. American corporations had returned to peacetime, expanded their power, and consolidated their self-image in a series of great corporate palaces. All levels of government had also built their images into the environment. The domestic environment had expanded, spreading and extending the prewar metropolitan limits geometrically. Housing developments, shopping centers, schools, and neighborhood parks had multiplied, fostered by federal highway expansion, low-cost mortgages offered by the Federal Housing Authority and the Veterans Administration, and state and local bonding. Public and private colleges and universities had quickly outgrown their prewar facilities, and public housing designers and planners had attacked the problems of the inner cities at a scale rivaled only by European and Asian postwar rebuilding.

And yet the modern postwar environmental nirvana predicted by the design teachers and historians of the 1940s and 1950s had not taken visible form. In fact, the 1970s had brought environmental survival itself into question. What had gone wrong? Why had the brave new world failed to arrive?

Teaching is always another form of learning. In the spring of 1977, I offered students of landscape architecture a modest seminar to inquire into the specific works of a group of contemporary landscape architects, artists, and architects who had practiced and taught just before and after World War II. We began to question what these designers had done, the social and artistic assumptions they had made, their cultural influences, and the impacts they had been able to make. Each student would research one or several of these key figures and present the findings. Then the class would discuss the results. The seminar grew, becoming a lecture and discussion class in 1978. Among the key issues reviewed were the artistic context or style that each of our "heroes" represented. In 1979 Melanie Simo joined me in this exploration, broadening the presentations of the artistic references and also deepening the specific historical information on our subjects. Later Melanie developed this material into courses of landscape architectural history that she offered between 1982 and 1989 at the Radcliffe Seminars, the Rhode Island School of Design, and the Harvard Graduate School of Design.

This book is focused on the results of those years of work and our collaboration. Our view of many of our subjects has evolved and changed through discussions both within and beyond the classroom, and our interests have changed as well. From an original intent to inform students (and ourselves) of the works of contemporary designers, we have moved on to a deeper interest in some specific questions. Why is such satisfying, or beautiful, or critically important work not better known? Why has the work had so little currency? In effect, why has it so often seemed invisible?

Many of these designers are still living. Most were alive at the beginning of our investigations. Whenever possible, we have talked with them or their close collaborators. Over the past forty or fifty years, a fair amount has been written by, or about, some of these individuals. As a group, however, they are not well known, and the written record of their work and thought remains uneven—now abundant, now sparse, often inaccessible.

This book is not a collection of short biographies. Rather, we have focused on some aspects of our subjects' lives and traced some lines of development we feel are important to American landscape architecture as a whole. (We recognize that I play a part, though a small part, of this story, and we have tried to balance this obvious advantage and disadvantage in our exposition.) Whatever the redeeming elements of this book, I believe the most significant may be traced to our collaboration, a process of continual, sometimes tenuous, balancing of views.

Most historians freely choose their subject; in the beginning, Melanie did not. Rather, some thirteen years ago, she fell into it as a body of material almost totally new to her: a collection of individuals, ideas, and issues that were exceedingly important to me as a practicing landscape architect and teacher in the field. I was curious about how the pieces of my own education and experience could be put together. I had already constructed a hypothesis and outline and had identified the major figures and issues in the story to be told, from my particular point of view. What I wanted was more information. Who were these figures, after all? What was their contribution to the profession? What did art have to do with it all? And what did it matter? The questions were intriguing. Many years later we agreed to collaborate on a book.

I had sought a coauthor who enjoys probing in odd crannies and undefined places, looking for clues to convoluted problems or enigmas. The time and focus necessary for such probing is not readily available to a practitioner. But as a historian, Melanie insisted that we spend the time, and I agreed. We progressed through joint readings and discussion prior to and during the writing process. In the end, the few moments of modest epiphanies, when suddenly something became clear, have validated the time spent.

We had worked together for quite a while before any problem of defining terms arose. There seemed nothing wrong, for instance, with Norman Newton's definition of landscape architecture (in *Design on the Land,* 1971) as "the art—or the science, if preferred—of arranging land, together with the spaces and objects upon it, for safe, efficient, healthful, pleasant human use."

Problems of terminology arose only when specific instances were called into question. Was Frederick Law Olmsted a "modern" landscape architect, for instance? Insofar as he was responding in fresh, appropriate ways to the conditions—geographical, sociological, technological, political, cultural, and so on—of his site or of the larger environment, he was modern. But in his treatment of pure form and formal relationships—considerations that would become increasingly significant for modern art—he was a fairly traditional, sophisticated designer. Olmsted had a nineteenth-century romantic's love of rich, bounteous, flowing forms (and materials) that were never meant to be perceived in their own right but, rather, generally experienced as scenery and appreciated in their broad social and cultural context.

In contrast, distinctness, often crisp or hard surfaces, abrupt juxtaposition, asymmetrical balance, and acute attention to things—textures, colors, materials, forms—for their own sake, apart from the mass, are among the most recognizable qualities of modernism. Still, the terms *modern* and *modernism* had never been defined to my satisfaction during my years of college, graduate school, and practice of landscape architecture.

For the purposes of this book, we assumed that *modernism* referred to the movement in literature, music, and the visual and lively arts that can be traced to stirrings in Western Europe and the British Isles in the latter half of the nineteenth century; and that that movement first came to maturity, in architecture, in the work of perhaps a half-dozen individuals, including Le Corbusier, Frank Lloyd Wright, Gropius, and Mies van der Rohe. In landscape architecture, if there was no commonly understood modernism, we could assume at very least that "modern" landscapes and gardens were perceived to be somehow fresh, original, and appropriate to the place and the time in which they were laid out. We also assumed that the forms of modern painting, sculpture, and architecture, along with their formal and spatial relationships and sometimes their materials, could be indications of at least a modern expression in landscape architecture.

When the issue of methodology arose, we were reminded of Jens Jensen's belief: that plants, like human beings, have their own individuality. And it is human individuality, more than similarities, that interests Melanie as a historian. Her preferred method of dealing with history is to view a subject through the lens of an individual rather than through the lenses of ideology, morphology, topology, iconography, or any of a number of abstractions ending in -ism. Like my spiritual mentor of many decades, William James, she would rather approach a subject through close examining of pieces—one human being's actions, thoughts, relations, and their consequences—than try to fashion some unified, all-encompassing whole of a period. And like one of her heroes, Thoreau, she considers no small detail in the life of a person unworthy of attention. Our method, in short, has been to have no method but to look, listen, travel, and seek out the facts and insights needed to tell a story. In this instance, the result is a partial history of a period—partial, in that by no means the whole story is told and in that the story's framework has been crafted by one who is indeed partial, engaged, and still interested in that story's expansion, beyond our final page.

A deeper understanding of the achievement of these and other leading landscape architects should follow in time, as individual biographies and critical studies appear. We believe our own efforts will have been worthwhile if this book serves as a catalyst to inquiry and discussion. Among the leading American landscape architects and designers of the twentieth century, which ones (besides our personal heroes) have made outstanding contributions to American art and culture? To what extent have these contributions been visible, generally known, and appreciated? And under what conditions, what motivations, what identities have these individuals flourished—as artists, spokesmen, theorists, educators, visionaries, reformers, leaders, catalysts? These are among the questions that we have tried to answer.

Peter Walker
San Francisco, August 1992

Acknowledgments

It is with great pleasure that we acknowledge the assistance, encouragement, friendly criticism, and wise suggestions of many individuals. It is not possible, here, to mention everyone by name, particularly the many students, teachers, and colleagues who have inevitably influenced us in our quest and in our perceptions. To all we remain indebted.

This book was supported in part by a grant from the National Endowment for the Arts. Melanie Simo received the grant, a U.S.A. Fellowship, for travel, research, and writing. This book was also supported in part by the office of Peter Walker and Partners, which became known as Peter Walker William Johnson and Partners during the later stages of our efforts. We wish to thank particularly William Johnson, Douglas Findlay, Tony Sinkosky, Thomas Leader, Cathy Blake, David Walker, Jane Williamson, and David Meyers for their financial support and patience with the authors.

The authors have had varying degrees of acquaintance with the individuals whose contributions to the field of landscape architecture form the subject of this book. With some, who are longtime colleagues, Peter Walker has shared ideas and enthusiasms as well as differences of opinion. Melanie Simo would like to thank several of these individuals for interviews and conversations, in particular, Garrett Eckbo, Stuart O. Dawson, Kenneth DeMay, Richard Haag, Lawrence Halprin, Charles W. Harris, William Johnson, Dan Kiley, Ian McHarg, Kalvin Platt, Robert Royston, Hideo Sasaki, and Carl Steinitz.

The authors are grateful to Kalvin Platt for allowing some portions of Melanie Simo's unpublished history of The SWA Group to be revised for inclusion in this book and to W. George Waters for allowing some portions of Melanie Simo's articles on Garrett Eckbo and Hideo Sasaki, previously published in *Pacific Horticulture,* to be revised for inclusion in this book.

At our invitation, the following individuals have read all, or parts of, this book: Charles E. Beveridge, Walter L. Creese, Arline Williams Eckbo, Garrett Eckbo, Lawrence Halprin, Charles W. Harris, Peter L. Hornbeck, Dan Kiley, Ian McHarg, William C. Muchow, Robert Royston, Hideo Sasaki, Carl Steinitz, and John Webb. We have benefited from their observations and corrections; for any remaining imperfections, we are responsible.

We are grateful to the photographers—both those known and credited at the end of this book, and those unknown—whose perceptions of certain landscapes and individuals have helped us to tell our story. We thank the principals of firms who provided photographs and color transparencies from their own collections, and we thank Peter and Paul Cirincione, who consistently provided fine transitions from color transparencies to black and white photographs. Others who assisted us in locating and acquiring images include William Howard Adams, Gerald Campbell, Dixi Carrillo, Pam Palmer, Elizabeth Roberts Church, Mick Cochran, Susan Duca, Arline Williams Eckbo, Grace Hall, Amy Hau, Michael Laurie, George Ramirez, Michael Van Valkenburgh, and Stuart Wrede. We thank the staffs of museums, foundations, and libraries, particularly Hinda Sklar, Suzanne Smyrl, and Martha Mahard, of the Frances Loeb Library, Harvard University Graduate School of Design. We also appreciate the genial and constant assistance of Lisa Ganucheau, who coordinated innumerable details of text and image, maintaining communication between the authors, particularly when they were separated by a continent and an ocean.

We thank those at The MIT Press, in particular, Roger Conover, for underscoring some suggestions of the outside readers and deciding, in the end, to proceed; Beverly Miller and Sandra Minkkinen, for their careful, sensitive treatment of the typescript; Mimi Ahmed, for an elegant design of the book; and Ann Sochi, for her gracious assistance on many occasions.

Finally, we are grateful to our dear families, who suffered our preoccupation, our inattention, our anxieties, and our absences: Martha and Brian, and the boys, Chris, Peter, David, Jacob, and Josie.

Invisible Gardens

Over the past 130 years, landscape architects have shaped portions of the American continents no more dramatically than water has shaped the land over geological periods of time. In ponds and lakes of temperate zones lie gentle waters that erode rocks and fell trees along the shore through seasonal freezing, thawing, expanding, contracting. From great rivers and their ancestral glaciers come sterner waters to redistribute soils and change the earth's contours. From oceans and their magnificent storms come powerful waves gathering great force, surging, cresting, breaking, subsiding. The impact of all these waters on the land is profound yet often invisible within the span of two or three human lifetimes.

In America, landscape architects' impact on the land within two or three human lifetimes has been uneven: now pronounced, now subtle, generally invisible—except, perhaps, during the great surges of collective energies, when architects, landscape architects, painters, sculptors, planners, engineers, social reformers, political leaders, and others unite to accomplish some great manifestation of shared values. Inevitably, the human spirit is uplifted and refreshed by the process and product of these energies. In time energies are spent, the great unity is fragmented, and waves recede. The ebb tide carries disappointments along with promise of renewal. Meanwhile, for lack of a chronicler, the more ephemeral achievements of landscape architects slip away, unnoticed, or merge with the larger environment.

The main purpose of this book is to make visible the work of American landscape architects since World War II, that is, from about 1945, to the late 1970s. This period overlaps one great surge of collective energies—the modern movement, an upheaval of traditional values, beliefs, and artistic forms that had evolved over centuries in the Western world. In European painting, sculpture, and architecture, one could find evidence of the modern movement well before World War I. Modern (or "modernistic") gardens appeared in the 1910s and 1920s in Europe, particularly in and around Paris. But in the wider field of landscape architecture, encompassing environmental design at a great range of scale and purpose, the impact of the modern movement was not felt until the 1930s. In landscape architecture, this impact was more gradual and often less striking than in other visual and spatial arts yet no less profound.

In modern landscape architecture, space was rediscovered as the great unifying medium. People, no longer merely spectators, became actors in the modern landscape. Landscape design, suddenly released from dependence on precedent or historic styles and cut off from some of its healthiest roots, became a process of experiment and testing. From crude, bold, and ingenious beginnings came solid achievement. A few successes, described and photographed in the magazines of art, architecture, and design, became icons. But reasoned criticism did not follow, and modern landscapes slipped beyond even the peripheral vision of art historians. Why so?

There is a wide spectrum of tentative explanations. Landscape architecture, a fledgling profession that is barely more than a century old, is made up of too many preexisting fields and disciplines to have a clear focus. Landscape architects typically create settings for more prominent objects—buildings, sculpture, or specimen plants. Landscape architects tend to be reticent, discreet, accommodating, not given to undue publicity. Works of landscape architecture tend to be ephemeral, and their moments of perfection (between long periods of growth and decay) are fleeting. These observations may be valid, even comforting, but they do not explain the invisibility of a still-growing profession. This book offers a closer look at some of the individuals who, by their deeds and words, have defined what modern American landscape architecture is and aspires to be.

For better or for worse, the terms *modern* and *modernism* in landscape architecture have not yet been defined to satisfy all those concerned. The field has had no Nikolaus Pevsner to trace the links among the pioneers of modern landscape architecture. Nor has a team such as Henry-Russell Hitchcock and Philip Johnson ever attempted to enumerate the principles of an emerging modern style of landscape design.[1] Rather, in the absence of a great deal of scholarly and critical attention to their chosen field, landscape architects have tended to be doers rather than critics or philosophers; they have tended to focus on the practical work at hand. Moreover, the broad range of problems that landscape architects are now tackling—from a garden to a toxic waste dump, a regional planning study, or an urban renewal site—tend to draw them away from the physical locations and social, cultural, or educational milieux where their values and beliefs were initially formed. Such dislocations, increasingly common among professionals in many different fields, to be sure, have tended to isolate or radically differentiate landscape architects while eroding what was once believed to be common ground—a core of common knowledge, concerns, and goals.

Our own search for modernism in the American landscape has proceeded with the hope that some common ground can be restored. Rather than impose new definitions of landscape architecture (or of recent practice), we have returned to its beginnings, with a brief review of the career of Frederick Law Olmsted (1822–1903) in this introduction. Although younger than his friend and occasional colleague, land-scape architect H. W. S. Cleveland (1814–1900), Olmsted is generally considered the founder of his profession in America—not so much because of his earlier official use of the title "landscape architect" but because of his extraordinarily prolific achievement.[2] Having been immersed in a demanding, nationwide practice and also deeply concerned about the future of his profession, Olmsted left a body of work, in built projects and writings, that can serve as a measure of all subsequent work in landscape architecture.

Two aspects of Olmsted's work and thought, in particular—his efforts to establish landscape architecture as an "Art of Design" and his dedication to the social purposes of his work—were inextricably interwoven, mutually reinforcing, and generally well balanced. It is to examine these two aspects of landscape architecture under different conditions, with a change of emphasis or balance in the work of later generations, that chapters 1 and 2 have been written. Chapter 1 focuses on the social purposes of Clarence Stein and Henry Wright, as site planners of new communities in the United States; chapter 2 considers primarily the artistic aspirations of Roberto Burle Marx, Luis Barragán, and Isamu Noguchi, as designers of memorable landscapes in North and South America.

The chapters that follow consider major figures and issues of modern landscape architecture in the United States through the late 1970s. Not all of these figures have themselves defined or discussed the terms *modern* and *modernism* in landscape architecture. Rather, they have approached certain problems of the planning, design, and use of land in a way that appears fresh, original, and appropriate to their own time and

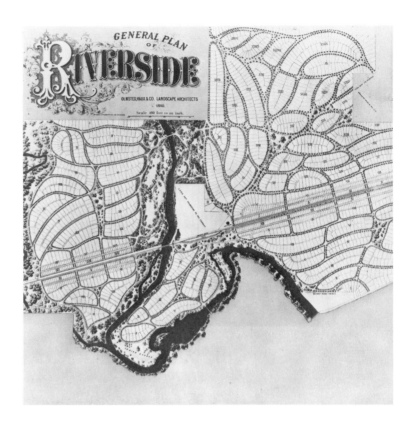

place; in this sense they were as "modern" as was Olmsted, relative to his time and place (figure 1). But they were also modern in another sense. None of these figures, from Thomas Church onward, could practice landscape architecture in isolation from the forces of the modern movement mentioned above—mainly a twentieth-century phenomenon.

Not surprising, our own perspectives on the modern landscape have been influenced by the writings of our subjects—observations drawn largely from practice in the decades immediately after World War II. In 1950, posing the question, "What do we mean by Modern Landscape Architecture?" Garrett Eckbo began by likening the entire modern movement in twentieth-century arts to a stream of tradition; momentarily checked by impediments in its path, that stream would always find new channels and eventually "burst forth with renewed vigor. . . . Thus the serious and intelligent modern artist does not reject tradition, he only rejects imitation of past segments in the stream."[3]

1. General plan of Riverside, Illinois, 1869. Olmsted, Vaux and Company, Landscape Architects and Planners. Prominent in this plan for a new residential community, located nine miles west of Chicago, are the railroad (an essential connection to the city, via modern transportation) and the public park, which Olmsted also considered essential for modern urban and suburban life. The smaller neighborhood parks help to maintain Olmsted's desired balance of community and privacy.

More interested in the continuous flow, Eckbo regarded some of the past segments in the landscape tradition as merely frozen pools, stagnant reservoirs, and controlled locks—apt metaphors for pictorialism, the historic styles, and the old dichotomies of formal-informal design. He also sensed that landscape architecture, "the direct physical expression of the relations between man and nature," was lagging behind the other arts; he believed that the field's thinking was not up to date with the world around it. To try to catch up by employing only the most obviously "modern" devices, however—such as an abstract pattern on the ground unrelated to one's three-dimensional spatial experience—would end in a trap, he warned. More significant were those efforts, however conservative in appearance, where "serious effort is made to understand the nature and problems of our time."

In this essay, a distillation of several issues elaborated in his book *Landscape for Living* (1950), Eckbo's implied definition of modern landscape architecture centered around two main issues: first, the relationship of the landscape to modern architecture, which was then responding to new social concerns and searching for "functionalism and spatial richness," and second, a trio of considerations that Eckbo found consistent in the arts of the modern movement: space, materials, and people. Here, Eckbo offered no methods for practice, only principles: Vitality and productivity lie in solving specific problems in relation to specific local conditions, without reference to preconceived forms. Vitality, productivity, and, ultimately, the expression of harmony between human beings and nature will be found not in the theoretical extremes of formal or informal design but in the rich, fertile ground between the extremes. And, as in any other advanced art form, landscape architecture may expand the boundaries of human experience, "even as advanced science expands the boundaries of human knowledge."[4]

During the 1950s Hideo Sasaki wrote briefly about specific problem areas of the landscape architect, including urban renewal, landscape design in relation to architecture, ecological factors in planning and design, and professional education. He was acutely aware that the landscape architectural profession was in a state of transition, somewhat reluctantly changing its "lethargical" ways in order to address current problems. What intrigued him were the processes of identifying the key issues, asking the right questions, and, in the case of urban design, achieving a "full measure of livability." The solution to a design problem would emerge from a "critical thinking process," through research, analysis, and synthesis. Thus, the resulting form could be "a functional expression consistent with structure and materials used, with little concern as to whether it is 'modern' or 'traditional.'"[5]

Sasaki often used the words *modern* and *contemporary* interchangeably. His interests lay in purpose more than form, in meaningful environments rather than what he alluded to as "some enormous artifact of super modernism." For him, tradition was rich and deep; it included not only the world's great gardens but also folk art and its directness of expression; utilitarian works, such as grain elevators and high tension lines; and vernacular works, such as cultivated fields, where one could study ecological relationships that had evolved over long periods of time. Thus, Sasaki did not set up oppositions between the traditional and the modern. Having identified "the arch enemies of design" as preconceptions and dogmas, he devoted his energies to such concerns as "the questioning and exploration of new ideas," the forging of "new knowledge to meet existing and new situations," and contributing to "social progress in [one's] professional life."[6]

The open-minded, optimistic spirit in these and other writings on landscape architecture in the 1950s was unmistakable. Writing a decade later, however, and imbued with a similarly optimistic feeling about this field and about life in all its strange and splendid manifestations, Lawrence Halprin could not avoid using the term *modern* in negative contexts. "The new man-made landscape is a nightmare community made of rooftops," he wrote in 1961. "Now the bulldozer strikes its terrible blows and overnight the native trees lie dead. The hills flatten down under the impact of carryalls and in all the flat agricultural bottomlands the rich soil is networked with sewer lines and tens of thousands of concrete slabs stretch out mile after mile waiting for 2 × 4's. . . . In this man-made modern landscape, it is important that we take stock and evaluate what we are after and what methods can be used to achieve our purposes."[7]

In the 1960s and 1970s, Halprin, like many of his colleagues, did not precisely define the terms *modern* and *modernism.* He was enthusiastic about modern attitudes and new communities, but he also considered the distant past a measure for the modern world, as in the following, from *Cities* (1963): "Our own modern needs are, it is true, more complex than earlier ones. But are they so different? If we think of the new city as a complete environment for living, then it, too, will achieve the same simple, direct, biological qualities of its ancient prototype."[8] Later, in 1988, Halprin did define his terms: "To be properly understood Modernism is not just a matter of cubist space but of a whole appreciation of environmental design as a holistic approach to the matter of making places for people to live. . . . Modernism, as I define it and practice it, *includes* and is based on the vital archetypal needs of human beings as individuals as well as social groups."[9]

Modernism in landscape architecture has been reconsidered in conferences, symposia, and publications of the 1980s and 1990s.[10] This book is not meant to be definitive but exploratory, even as our subjects continue their own explorations. Tentatively we may conclude that some of the most articulate modern landscape architects have maintained respect for and interest in tradition while searching for ways to ensure that the design process addresses the most compelling issues of our time, including the survival of all life on the planet. "It was as a part of a Modern approach to design that I included Ecology, Psychology, and social values in my process," Halprin reflected recently.[11] For him, modernism in landscape architecture has always implied, among other things, dealing existentially with issues of our times, emphasizing people (*all* people) and their use and enjoyment as the major purpose of design, accepting change and anticipating it, and viewing landscape architecture as an art form interactive with and influenced by the other art forms.[12]

Looking to the next century, Eckbo would not revise what he wrote about modern landscape architecture in 1950; he believes that his earlier views on the importance of landscape design and the design process remain relevant to today's practice.[13] However, in observing that "Economics and ecology may prove to be the chief contending forces in the world of the next century," he now moves closer to a position staked out some thirty years ago by Ian McHarg, our preeminent spokesman for the environment, who has recently regretted not having achieved more in the way of designed and built work.[14] McHarg, Dan Kiley, and many of their colleagues in design, planning, research, and education may never have felt inclined to write about modernism per se, yet they also have defined modern landscape architecture by their individual and collective contributions to the field.

Because we believe that modernism, or at least the finest expression of its ideals, is still unfolding, changing, and adapting to increasingly unpredictable conditions, we offer no neat, conclusive end to our story. However, to reclaim some of the common ground lost through the ideological divisions in the profession during the 1960s and 1970s, we offer instead a reconsideration of the profession's beginnings, in Olmsted's work and thought.

Landscape architecture, as Olmsted conceived its broad scope and mission, had to reflect as well as shape collective values; for among the profession's loftier aims was to create tranquil landscapes in the public domain, where people of diverse backgrounds could relax, intermingle, and develop a sense of community and cooperation, thereby furthering the progress of civilization. Such had been the aspirations of Olmsted's forerunners, landscape gardeners J. C. Loudon, in Great Britain, and Andrew Jackson Downing, in the United States. Both men had recognized important links between aesthetic and social concerns, but no one before Olmsted managed to publicize these aims, fulfill them in built work, and institutionalize the process in a new profession.[15] Altogether Olmsted spent some forty years building the profession of landscape architecture on the foundations of art and design theory, agricultural sciences, engineering, social theory, and the broader environmental context, which has since evolved into specialties of city and regional planning.

Now that Olmsted's private papers, reports, correspondence, and fragments of books are being published in chronological order, this awesome figure in landscape architectural history is becoming better understood, perhaps losing some of his mythical and forbidding aura while gaining sympathy for his human achievements and dilemmas.[16]

There is no doubt of his genius or his great ambition; he struggled to comprehend the big issues of his day: democracy, civilization, culture, art, science, ethics, moral duty, and progress. But his internal struggles and ambivalence are also significant in light of the profession's evolution.

In 1890, for instance, writing to his old friend Elizabeth Baldwin Whitney, Olmsted assessed his life's work in terms of the larger context—the future, the greater physical environment, American civilization, and the growth of a great profession. His public parks, "with perhaps a single exception," were a hundred years ahead of any spontaneous public demand, serving as role models for other parks and clearly manifesting their educative, civilizing effects. For his profession, he had educated "men of liberal education and cultivated minds." Through his efforts, men of influence now recognized landscape architecture not as a trade or handicraft, but as a liberal profession—an "Art of Design." Further, clients recognized him as a counselor, a trustee, someone who would refuse a job rather than yield this professional role.[17]

Despite these achievements, Olmsted made a confession: "Earth gets its price for what Earth gives us, and the truth is that, regarding the price that I have paid, I need all the esteem that I have earned from you to sustain my self-esteem," Olmsted wrote Mrs. Whitney. "I have been selling being for doing."[18] The context of this remark Charles McLaughlin has traced to a sermon that Olmsted had read some fifty years earlier while studying part time at Yale. In James Martineau's sermon, three attributes of great men, "having," "doing," and "being," were assessed for their value to a Christian way of life. Merely acquiring great possessions was of the least value. Doing great things was worthy, but *being* great was worthier still, more Christ-like.[19]

Olmsted's mention of selling being for doing indirectly illuminates the struggles for personal and professional esteem that later generations of landscape architects would experience, under changing circumstances in practice. Perhaps there was no way Olmsted could have ensured that his successors would avoid such dilemmas—apart from his insisting that they be carefully selected and thoroughly trained. And yet there is much to be learned from understanding another's personal and professional difficulties. Ironically, in Laura Wood Roper's meticulously researched biography (FLO, 1973), there is no mention of Olmsted's struggle over being and doing. Instead, Roper strengthens Olmsted's official image as a pioneer landscape architect by quoting at length the accomplishments he mentioned to Mrs. Whitney.[20] Thus, many readers will have received a more generally satisfying, less complex impression of Olmsted's life and work. More recently, with a particular interest in the "being and doing" dilemma, Melvin Kalfus has written a stimulating intellectual and psychological study of Olmsted.[21] No doubt further studies of Olmsted will continue to shed light on Olmsted—the man, his intentions and preoccupations, and our own.

Here, our interest is in Olmsted the artist, a maker of things, and in Olmsted the communicator of social and cultural values. If his practice is to serve as a useful measure of practice today, in a world utterly changed by private automobiles and freeways, jumbo jets, planned obsolescence, computers, and international finance and communication, then we should at least be aware of a few aspects of his world that remain relevant in ours: his social and cultural background, his relationship to the artistically and socially progressive people of his age, and his means of attaining the power to achieve his ends—seeing that his projects were realized, appreciated, and maintained long after their growth to maturity.

The son of a reasonably successful merchant in Hartford, Connecticut, and descendant of one of the original Puritan settlers of that town, Olmsted had inherited a seriousness and sense of responsibility toward one's community and fellow human beings. From his father he had also learned to enjoy the simple pleasures of leisurely travel and unanalytical appreciation of landscape scenery. Olmsted's mother had died when he was three years old, however. His father soon remarried, and apparently a concern for his son's spiritual and secular education induced the father to send Frederick to live in the rural households of a series of ministers while he kept at home his younger, frailer son John. Thus, from ages seven through seventeen, Frederick Law Olmsted learned to live for long periods of time without family nearby and to endure the often severe discipline of God-fearing strangers.

Young Olmsted's release was to venture out into the countryside, read sporadically, and indulge in daydreaming—"the soul of designing," he would later remark.[22] Another release of sorts was the eye ailment, traced to sumac poisoning, that freed Olmsted from the routine of prolonged, disciplined studies in any institution, encouraged outdoor activities, and inclined him toward the life of a gentleman farmer. He spent two years improving the farm his father had bought for him on Staten Island, New York. Then, in 1850, he made a walking tour of Britain and Europe with his brother, John, and their mutual friend Charles Loring Brace, who had studied for the ministry and would later help to found the Children's Aid Society in New York. Olmsted would always share something of Brace's dedication to social betterment, but in 1850, his own path was not yet clear. By chance, the three young men visited Joseph Paxton's new public park at Birkenhead, where Olmsted noticed how "art had been employed to obtain from nature

2. Stourhead, Wiltshire, England. Formerly in private ownership, Stourhead epitomizes the eighteenth-century English landscape garden that served as a prototype for the public park movement of the nineteenth century. Such parks, with their illusion of naturalistic scenery, inspired Olmsted during his first visit to England in 1850.

3. Back Bay Fens, Boston. Frederick Law Olmsted, Landscape Architect, from 1879. In this project, Olmsted's original design solution addressed problems of stormwater storage, marsh restoration, and sanitation while providing for footpaths, bridal paths, and a parkway. The subsequent damming of the Charles River and other developments have left Olmsted's work much altered, but as a recreational and visual amenity, the Fens remain an asset to the Boston metropolis.

so much beauty."[23] Later, walking through a privately owned English park, he reflected, "What artist, so noble, has often been my thought, as he who, with far-reaching conception of beauty and designing power, sketches the outline, writes the colours, and directs the shadows of a picture so great that Nature shall be employed upon it for generations, before the work he has arranged for her shall realize his intentions" (figures 2 and 3).[24]

Years elapsed before Olmsted gave any thought to designing a park in America. Between 1850 and 1858, the year he and Calvert Vaux won the competition to design New York's Central Park, Olmsted had worked as a journalist (notably, reporting on slavery throughout the American South), as a publisher, and as superintendent of the emerging Central Park. Thereafter he began to develop as an intuitive artist, in collaboration with Vaux. The elder by two years, Olmsted articulated their shared artistic vision for the park and anticipated the problems of construction, management, and education of the park keepers and users. As superintendent, Olmsted also understood the park's topography and its relation to the expanding city. Vaux, an architect who had assisted Downing, America's foremost landscape gardener, had the refined skills in drawing, drafting, and design that Olmsted lacked. Moreover, Vaux willingly took a subordinate role to Olmsted, in part because he believed that rank and leadership meant a great deal to Olmsted, in part because he felt that landscape architecture was emerging as a "better" field than architecture.[25] Assessing individual credit and the status of their emerging profession would continue to strain relations between Olmsted and Vaux, long after their formal separation in 1872. But for the record, in 1893, Olmsted wrote to the art critic Mariana Griswold Van Rensselaer, "I hope you will not fail to do justice to Vaux and to consider that he and I were one. I should have been nowhere but for his professional training."[26]

For a detailed explanation of the development of Olmsted's design theory, one must look elsewhere.[27] Here, it is significant that Olmsted's conception of Central Park, an uncommon fusion of social and aesthetic intentions, was only vaguely understood by the park's board of commissioners. In 1861 he informed the board that the park to date was like a new canvas, with merely a few lines chalked on its inert surface, but his mental image of what the park would become was "all alive—its very essence is life, human and vegetable."[28] Articulate and passionate, Olmsted might have fought for his vision on his own grounds, social and artistic, but he was forced to act otherwise by one obstacle: Andrew H. Green, a rising star in city and state politics, comptroller of the park, and miserly lord over all park expenditures.[29] As Olmsted confided to a friend, he wanted to act "with an artist's freedom and spirit" in the finishing touches of his work, but his hands were often tied by comptroller Green.[30] To combat this political enemy, Olmsted needed power.

To get and hold this power at midcentury (without resorting to the usual political maneuvering), Olmsted tended to emphasize not art but administration, for which he felt naturally suited. As superintendent of Central Park he had looked forward to "spending a good deal of [his] life in the park, being with the people in it, watching over it and cherishing it in every way."[31] He cared for the park as if it were his own child. He believed it would civilize people, offering views of naturalistic landscape scenery that would calm the nerves and refine the sensibilities, working its magic over the mind like music, imperceptibly yet per-

4. Central Park, New York. Frederick Law Olmsted and Calvert Vaux, Landscape Architects, from 1858. When Central Park was still being transformed from rough rock outcroppings and wasteland, Olmsted conceived of its value many years hence: as a wooded open space entirely surrounded by urban development and as a foundation for further artistic and cultural development in America.

manently. In 1858 he saw the park as "a democratic development of the highest significance & on the success of which, in my opinion, much of the progress of art and esthetic culture in this country is dependent" (figure 4).[32]

Those pre–Civil War years saw the earliest signs of the waning of American romanticism, that is, the great wave of individualism, passionate emotions, and fascination with the vernacular and the natural world that rose with Rousseau, Goethe, Beethoven, Delacroix, Wordsworth, British garden designers William Shenstone, Uvedale Price, and Richard Payne Knight, and others on the eastern side of the Atlantic. Reaching western shores and a rising new civilization, the wave of romanticism assimilated extraordinary new forces through the writings of Hawthorne, Melville, and Thoreau, Downing's landscapes, and landscape painters of the Hudson River school (figure 5). Olmsted was familiar with the works of Melville and Thoreau. He had met Downing, and, as a member of the Century Club in New York City, he knew a few leading painters, including Albert Bierstadt and Frederick Edwin Church (on whose Hudson River residence, Olana, Vaux was a consulting architect). Romantic artists of whatever medium were Olmsted's natural colleagues; by temperament, background, and inclination, he should have been one of them (figure 6). What distanced him from them—as well as from his own roaming, daydreaming youth—was his drive to build his profession on such solid, pragmatic foundations that America's most aggressive, powerful men of influence would have to recognize the stature and power of landscape architects.

By the time the next great wave of artistic energies rose in America, in the 1880s and 1890s, Olmsted was regularly identified as an artist—and

5. Asher B. Durand, *View Towards Hudson Valley*, 1851. After the death of Thomas Cole in 1848, Durand was considered foremost among the painters of the Hudson River school. This painting, thought to be a view of a landscape near Newburgh, New York, features cows grazing in a meadow by a stream, an iconic image of the pastoral scenery that Olmsted wanted to idealize in his urban country parks, such as Franklin Park, Boston.

6. Franklin Park, Boston. Frederick Law Olmsted, Landscape Architect, from 1884–1885. Olmsted's design for this urban country park took advantage of the existing land forms—low hills and gentle valleys—that offered a range of views, from broad and open to enclosed and intimate. Over the last hundred years, sketches and photographs of this park often suggest the tranquility and reverence for natural landscape evident in paintings of the Hudson River school.

prominent American artists enjoyed more stature than ever before. Not only did they perform many valuable functions—commemorating, edifying, civilizing, communicating, stabilizing, and reinforcing a collective self-image—but museums, symphony halls, theaters, universities, and schools of music, art and architecture were being established, in part for their training and public recognition. Many artists were also being trained abroad, in Rome, in Munich, and particularly in Paris, in highly disciplined ateliers, and at the Ecole des Beaux-Arts. Olmsted's architectural colleagues Richard Morris Hunt, H. H. Richardson, and Charles F. McKim were trained at the Ecole. Painters John La Farge and John Singer Sargent, sculptor Augustus Saint-Gaudens, and etcher-architect-garden designer Charles Platt were at ease with fine art, architecture, and culture on both sides of the Atlantic. Olmsted, too, had gained much from studying the great parks and gardens of Europe and the British Isles. He was familiar with the classical language of art and architecture, but it was not his idiom. He contributed a great deal to the success of the World's Columbian Exposition of 1893, in Chicago; but he was not pleased by the overpowering, rather sobering grandeur and glaring whiteness of that world's fair—the event that brought together, in Saint-Gaudens's view, "the greatest meeting of artists since the fifteenth century" (figure 7).[33]

If art mirrored only the surface of civilization, Olmsted might have more graciously accepted the changes in taste and style marked by the Chicago Exposition. At its Palace of Fine Arts was no work by Bierstadt or Church, but works by Sargent, La Farge, James McNeill Whistler, Winslow Homer, and Thomas Eakins appeared.[34] Richardson, the architect most sympathetic to Olmsted's romantic and pastoral landscapes, had died; however, his spiritual successor, Louis Sullivan, was

7. Court of Honor, World's Columbian Exposition in Chicago, 1893. In this great collaborative effort among architects, painters, sculptors, and landscape architects, the female figure, *Republic,* by Daniel Chester French, gazes along the main axis toward the Administration Building, by Richard Morris Hunt. Memories of this vision of civic order and grandeur continued to inspire American urban planners long after the fair was dismantled. Fragments of some of the buildings and landscape remain to this day.

8. Lagoon with Manufactures and Liberal Arts Building, World's Columbian Exposition in Chicago, 1893. Involved in the site selection and planning of the fair from the beginning, Olmsted conceived of a series of lagoons to serve several purposes. Given the bustling and dazzling aspects of the fair, for instance, he wished to offer a counterpart—a few places of a more poetic and mysterious character.

given the Transportation Building to design. True, Olmsted's romantic lagoons (figure 8) and Sullivan's building were relegated literally to the backwaters. But Olmsted played a major role in selecting the site of the fair and shaping its central Court of Honor, a dazzling spectacle of white neoclassical buildings, sculpture, and peristyle that enclosed the vast canal and offered the beholder a vision of civic order powerful enough to inspire the first city planning movement in America, the City Beautiful. The fair was widely considered a model of collaboration among allied artists. Olmsted admitted it was a "glowing illustration of civilization and communicativeness."[35] It was also one of his finest moments as a doer.

Daniel Burnham, chairman of the multidisciplinary consulting board to the fair and also the fair's director of works, paid Olmsted a famous tribute at a banquet from which the elderly landscape architect was, with poetic justice, absent. Olmsted, the artist who had created so many parks in America, was, "in the highest sense," the planner of the fair, declared Burnham.[36] But absent from that banquet and remote from the fair's brassier elements was Olmsted's own being.

Often ill, exhausted from battles with politicians, emotionally reticent, and struggling with words (for writing did not come easily to him), Olmsted did manage to express his feelings in letters. He wrote Charles Platt's brother William, an aspiring apprentice, that he cared little for the fine and costly gardening of Italy but appreciated the beauty of that country's commonplace gateways, sheds, winepresses, mills, pergolas, seats, and stairways.[37] To William A. Stiles, editor of *Garden and Forest,* Olmsted explained that his rural parks were crucial counterparts to the city; his "enemies," mostly cultivated gentlemen and artists, viewed rural landscapes as secondary, mere interludes within an elegant urban setting. "There is a place for everything," Olmsted conceded.[38] Fairgrounds, in particular, might be splendid, exuberant, colorful, bold. But to the end, Olmsted struggled to create socially purposeful, artful landscapes in which art was so subdued that the mind suffered no distractions and the spirit could breathe (figure 9).

In the later years of his career, Olmsted was generally viewed by his colleagues as an artist. Alongside Burnham's genial tribute one might place the assessment of another colleague, Boston's Arnold Arboretum director Charles Sprague Sargent. Commenting on Prospect Park, in Brooklyn, New York, a work by Olmsted and Vaux of the 1860s and 1870s, Sargent considered it "one of the great artistic creations of modern times."[39] And at that time, works of art were of interest to a fairly broad public. At least since the time of America's Centennial Exposition in Philadelphia in 1876, and in light of the Aesthetic movement that followed, art in America came to be seen as a significant, if somewhat heightened and remote, expression of its civilization. The fact that a growing number of Americans, particularly those in comfortable circumstances, sensed something lacking in their daily lives and sought from art an elevation to some sort of higher plane provided ample subject matter for nineteenth-century novelists; it also allowed men such as Olmsted and their art forms to command respect. Moreover, landscapes remained a broadly popular genre in Olmsted's lifetime; thus, paintings of stupendous and familiar American scenery, Old World landscape masterpieces, and prints by Currier and Ives all helped to explain how a man who painted with "real" trees, water, lights, and shadows could be considered an artist.[40]

9. "The Long Meadow," Prospect Park, Brooklyn, New York. Olmsted, Vaux and Company, Landscape Architects, from 1866. With its illusion of continuous open space, Prospect Park was designed to offer a quiet, pastoral counterpart to the densely built city that now surrounds it. Charles Sprague Sargent, Olmsted's friend and colleague, considered this park "one of the great artistic achievements of modern times."

After Olmsted's time, both his fame and his profession slipped away from the world of art for a number of reasons. In one unusual sense, he was a man ahead of his times. While many of his contemporaries were looking to art for elevation and distance from everyday life, amassing treasures (or reproductions) from antiquity and the Renaissance, Olmsted had already arrived at the stage of civilization when one looks fondly, with perhaps a touch of nostalgia, on the unencumbered loveliness of simple, vernacular forms and spaces. An old footpath in Italy, a meadow along the Connecticut River valley, the profile of a hillside in Panama: these are details that lingered in the memory of Olmsted the designer. So long as he could evoke the power and beauty of nature, as perceived in some vernacular or unaltered landscapes, and thus offer visible counterparts of scenery to the built forms of city and suburb, Olmsted could pursue his social purposes within the world of art. But once triumphal arches, gateways, surface roads, terraces, and other architectural features began to intrude upon, and appropriate, his landscape spaces and views, the social purposes of repose, reflection, and spiritual regeneration seemed threatened. From that time on, Olmsted and his successors had to emphasize a certain kind of art, socially purposeful and subdued.

Another reason Olmsted's profession slipped away from the world of art after his time lies in the divergence of two paths: one toward aesthetic appreciation of purely formal values in art, toward abstraction, and toward the idea that forms of art could have a life of their own, apart from the imaginations of artists, critics, and connoisseurs.[41] This path led, of course, toward works of art that had nothing to do with representational landscape painting. The other path led toward the socially conditioned views of art articulated by John Ruskin and William

Morris in England and by Lewis Mumford in America. This path led to value judgments about art, architecture, and landscape design based largely on the social effect of the work. Along this path, backward glances at the Middle Ages focused on vernacular design, communal or collaborative efforts, process rather than product, and the common denominator rather than genius.[42]

This path also led to the emergence of planning as a separate profession. And as the surge of energies within the City Beautiful movement subsided, planning became more associated with social and economic policy and less with art. The garden city and regional planning movement, of which Mumford remained the most eloquent spokesman, kept alive Olmsted's dual interests in social purpose and aesthetic quality; however, as adviser to Clarence Stein, Henry Wright, and their colleagues, Mumford steered them away from art for the sake of art, toward a primarily social endeavor.

Olmsted's legacy was carried on by his son, Frederick Law Olmsted, Jr., the Olmsted Brothers' office, and their colleagues in the American Society of Landscape Architecture (ASLA), established in 1899. In the early years, as taught in schools and universities around the country, landscape architecture retained the artistic and social goals of its founder (later, the profession would be broadened to encompass new technologies and broader environmental concerns). Planning remained a major component of the profession at least until the founding of the American City Planning Institute in 1917. Landscape architecture as an art of design suffered, however, from a curious compromise. Formal, or clearly man-made, geometrically ordered design was taught along with naturalistic design. Both modes of design were encompassed by the prevailing beaux arts system of design education. Olmsted's attitude, "There is a place for everything," prevailed; but as indicated in the 1917 textbook of Henry Vincent Hubbard (a partner with Olmsted Brothers and professor of landscape architecture at Harvard), naturalistic design was viewed as a higher art than clearly man-made design.[43]

This point of view alone might have doomed the profession of landscape architecture to the backwaters of an era increasingly marked by the qualities of modernity: rational, scientific, industrial, technological, efficient, orderly, pragmatic, specialized, universal, and so on. These are, of course, the qualities that one associates with the modern movement in the visual arts, which had no significant intellectual force in America before, say, the Armory Show of 1913, in New York. There for the first time the reputedly outrageous modern art of Europe was shown on this side of the Atlantic. Two decades later, in 1932, photographs and models of International Style modern architecture (mostly of Europe but also of America and elsewhere) were exhibited at the Museum of Modern Art in New York.[44] Within another two decades or so, the modern movement had become assimilated into the mainstream of American life and culture, a stream through which currents of landscape architecture also flowed.

The following pages trace the rising and subsiding of collective energies, some of which left icons of surpassing beauty and power in the landscape, others, landscape changes for the better, though barely visible. A richer synthesis in fact, image, perception, and critique may follow in time. These pages are merely an early glimpse.

"Art is the beginning of vision."[45]

Chapter 1

**The Garden
as Social Vision**

Between Olmsted's era and that of American landscape architects who came of age just before and after World War II, nearly half a century of transformations had passed. Not only had people and their environments been forever changed by the intervening world wars, economic crises, and the accelerating pace of new scientific, technological, social, and cultural developments; but the profession of landscape architecture itself had also changed, both profoundly and subtly. To trace these changes—including the demise of large, private country residences, the eclipse of horticultural concerns, and the new emphasis on site planning for public and institutional clients—one could examine the careers of such transitional figures as John C. Olmsted, Frederick Law Olmsted, Jr., Arthur Shurcliff, Fletcher Steele, Gilmore Clarke, Beatrix Farrand, and Lockwood de Forest. New project types, such as Charles Eliot's ecological studies of open space reservations in metropolitan Boston (1896) and Clarke's scenic Bronx River Parkway (1913), could be studied. One could note as well the outstanding regional contributions of the elder Olmsted's contemporaries and colleagues, including Jens Jensen in the Midwest and Warren Manning in several regions of the country.[1]

But to explore this intervening terrain is not our interest here. Rather, let us suppose that the two paths identified in the introduction—one toward primarily social interests, the other toward artistic interests—have each led to a bridge that conceptually spans the two eras, linking Olmsted's ideals and aims with those of mid-twentieth-century landscape architects. The first bridge, represented by the garden city movement, springs from a conviction that also motivated Olmsted: the belief that people's lives can be enriched, gently molded, and directed toward socially progressive aims by certain built environments. The second bridge, represented by the work of Burle Marx, Barragán, and

10. Portrait of Clarence S. Stein. Architect, planner, designer of new communities, Stein focused his creative energies not on the design of individual buildings but on the shaping of whole environments for, in his words, "good modern living."

11. Portrait of Henry Wright. Architect, landscape architect, and teacher, intellectually curious and probing, Wright made major contributions to the planning and design of new communities, particularly in site planning and housing design.

Noguchi discussed in chapter 2, springs from another cherished belief of Olmsted: that the design of landscape is a noble art form. Neither bridge is exclusively social or artistic in its essential purposes; each represents a particular set of priorities or balance of emphasis. And balance is absolutely critical to a hybrid profession ever in search of the best combination of elements—of materials, methods, information, ideals, insights—to accomplish the work at hand.

The garden city movement in America, as pioneered by Clarence Stein (figure 10), Henry Wright (figure 11), and their colleagues, was primarily motivated by social purposes: to offer people of modest incomes a range of house and apartment types that were intimately related to the heart of their new community, a shared open space; and ultimately to provide a regional network of moderately dense garden cities as an alternative to the increasingly congested and sprawling metropolitan city. But beauty, too, was an imperative of these planned communities, as Lewis Mumford explained: "The beauty of ordered buildings, measured to the human scale, of trees and flowering plants, and of open greens surrounded by buildings of low density, so that children may scamper over them, to add to both their use and their aesthetic loveliness."[2]

Laid out in the 1920s and 1930s, the landscapes of garden city prototypes such as Radburn, New Jersey, and Chatham Village, in Pittsburgh, became more beautiful as they matured, while the impetus to create them gradually faded. The basic idea of garden cities remained of interest in the popular magazines and professional design magazines through the 1920s; however, the comprehensive vision behind the garden city movement (which presupposed a radical shift in emphasis from private home ownership to collectively owned land framed by dwellings) was never generally understood or appreciated. In the 1930s the Roosevelt administration built only three small greenbelt towns. Thereafter, once depression-era and wartime privations gave way to an explosion of urban and suburban development, the important contributions made by Stein, Wright, Mumford, and their colleagues were all but ignored by the housing and building industries in America. Only a few exceptional entrepreneurs, such as Robert E. Simon, at Reston, Virginia, and James Rouse, at Columbia, Maryland, showed comparable vision in building new communities. It was to uncover the reasons for this relatively small legacy, then, that our research into the American garden city movement began. Could it have been more than just a question of priorities or balance?

12. Radburn, New Jersey, view toward central open space, or "meadow." Clarence Stein and Henry Wright, Planners; Clarence Stein, Chief Architect; Marjorie Sewell Cautley, Landscape Architect. Until Radburn was developed, the luxuriousness of its meadows and playgrounds could be found only on large private estates or in great urban parks, such as Central Park, New York. This represented an earlier vision—that of the New England village green—rather than an image of twentieth-century International Style architecture.

It is land—a designed landscape of open space—that lies at the heart of Stein's and Wright's contribution to modern city planning. Even a brief survey of their collaborative projects, beginning in the early 1920s with Sunnyside Gardens, in Long Island City, New York, reveals how landscape became the medium for both shaping and expressing the values of the community. In the early years, before Sunnyside had any structures or improvised rooms for social gatherings, people met casually in the garden courts. Over time, as the landscape flourished, the vernacular structures receded into the background. Stein observed the same effect at Radburn: "The broad lawns and spreading trees are the center of visual beauty just as much as they are the center of the community. It is this spaciousness that is the keynote of the wholesome, good living of these places" (figure 12).[3]

Located ten miles west of Manhattan's George Washington Bridge, Radburn would seem to owe something to Riverside, Illinois (1869), the fairly affluent suburb nine miles west of Chicago planned by Frederick Law Olmsted and Calvert Vaux (compare figures 1 and 13). The main feature of both communities is central open space—the linear parks. Yet in citing precedents for Radburn, Stein mentioned not Riverside but Central Park, New York, with its separation of pedestrian and vehicular traffic, made possible by sinking the most heavily traveled roads (the crosstown streets) and eliminating crossings at grade.[4] At

13. Plan of Radburn, New Jersey, 1929. As both a design plan and an economic enterprise, Radburn introduced the thinking of European environmental reformers into the United States in a nonsocialistic, nonpaternal form. The plan attempts to deal overtly with the automobile's impact on the suburban community. Though not fully realized, Radburn stands as an important early design effort to deal with the conflict between modern man and his machines.

TOWN PLAN
RADBURN, N.J.

FIG. 15
RADBURN, NEW JERSEY—PLAN OF MODEL COMMUNITY

[134]

Radburn this separation is so carefully preserved that one can still walk along networks of paths, past private gardens, through interior parks and underpasses, without confronting an automobile. In effect, the automobile is accepted without being allowed to dominate one's existence.

Like the living elements of the natural landscape, the garden city was conceived as an organism integrally related to the larger environment. Moreover, for Wright, Stein, and their colleagues, planning new garden city prototypes was theoretically inseparable from regional planning. While new communities were to be built on undeveloped, relatively inexpensive land beyond city limits, the decayed inner cities were to be renewed and rebuilt.

The philosophical roots of this connection—linking regionalism, urban renewal, and garden city development—can be traced to the writings of two British planners, Patrick Geddes and Ebenezer Howard. In 1898 Howard, the founder of the garden city movement in England, envisioned a series of garden cities with their own industries, parks, and social and cultural institutions that would draw population away from the London metropolis. Gradually, as metropolitan land values fell, the depopulated slums of London would be transformed into parks.[5] In the 1920s Stein and Wright, no less idealistic, envisioned the redevelopment of inner-city slums at lower densities, the curbing of metropolitan growth, and gradual decentralization through garden city development in planned locations within a region.

Such comprehensive planning was a revolutionary concept in the United States, where land had been developed largely through the vicissitudes of the market. Even zoning and other land use controls that became standardized in the early twentieth century were initiated mainly to protect long-term private investments.[6] Focusing on public interests, however, Wright emphasized evolutionary change: continual experiment and gradual refinement in each element of the whole, from the design of floor plans to the siting of new communities within a region. In the early 1930s, while he admired the most technologically advanced housing of Europe (in which a modern style was clearly evolving), Wright himself aimed for modern urban housing that would be rooted in the past yet "reach into a more hopeful future."[7] Both Wright and Stein aimed for continuity, then, through visual, psychological, and functional links to traditional communities, the city, and the region.

Stein and Wright viewed the art of planning and building a livable environment as a high art form. In these efforts, their most able spokesman was their younger friend Lewis Mumford, the eloquent humanist, urban critic, and frequent contributor to the *New Yorker, Harper's,* the *New Republic,* and the professional journals of architecture and planning. During the planning stages of Sunnyside, Mumford passed on to Stein and Wright a suggestion from a British colleague, sociologist Victor Branford—that "the town planner needs the aid of the poet." Stein and Wright agreed, Mumford noted.[8] In their own writings, however, Stein and Wright emphasized not art, not poetry, but the social purposes and economic rationales for regional planning. Facts, figures, and floor plans dominated most of Wright's housing and planning studies, intended for an audience of bankers, developers, realtors, and architects. Stein, who outlived Wright by nearly forty years, later wrote about the quiet beauty of their mature communities. Nevertheless, while he and Wright were still struggling to create garden city prototypes and build a consensus for regional planning among political and financial leaders, it was Mumford who located the essential aims and ideals of such planning on the highest levels of cultural aspiration. And it was Mumford who assumed the role of their cultural adviser, their poet.[9]

In *The Culture of Cities* (1938), Mumford recognized the city's powerful roles as nurturer, guardian, and participant in the development of culture. Along with language itself, the city was, for Mumford, the world's greatest work of art. Born in 1895, he had grown up in New York City and knew intimately the streets of the Upper West Side, the dim, stuffy apartment interiors, and the release of walks in Central Park and along Riverside Drive, as well as the great literature, architecture, and works of fine art that were accessible in a world city—not only works produced within and for the city of New York but works that had come from, or been influenced by, other cultures and traditions. In his own contributions to culture, including studies of Melville, Emerson, Thoreau, H. H. Richardson, Louis Sullivan, Olmsted, and Frank Lloyd Wright, Mumford emphasized both local and cosmopolitan influences, both particulars of a single time and place and qualities universally revered.

Mumford appreciated the fresh energy and ideas that continually enriched the best, most life-sustaining cities. With increasing horror, he watched New York succumb to "gigantism," but still he appreciated its accumulating layers of culture. In the 1920s, he noticed that New Yorkers and other metropolitan inhabitants were beginning to migrate outward, for electricity, automobiles, telephones, and radios were beginning to extend the benefits of urban life over a wider area. And he welcomed this migration. By 1938, he could see emerging a fluid, boundary-free civilization, with the urban centers continuing to "focus the flow of energies, men and goods that pass through a region, concentrating them, dispersing them . . . exerting a close and controlling influence over the development of region as a dynamic reality." What was needed was farsighted planning for the region by geographers, sociologists, planners, designers, and others. "The region, no less than the city," he wrote, "is a collective work of art."[10]

Sharing Mumford's high expectations for regional planning were the congenial group of men who came together in New York City, in 1923, to form the Regional Planning Association of America (RPAA): architects Frederick L. Ackerman and Robert D. Kohn, of New York; John Bright, of Philadelphia; E. Henry Klaber, of Chicago; architect and urban planner Frederick Bigger, of Pittsburgh; Alexander M. Bing, a developer of apartment houses and skyscrapers; economist Stuart Chase; Charles H. Whitaker, editor of the *Journal of the American Institute of Architects;* Benton MacKaye, the forester, ecologist, and father of the Appalachian Trail; and Stein, Wright, and Mumford. Some time later, housing experts Edith Elmer Wood and Catherine Bauer were admitted to this circle, which was kept small, Mumford recalls, so as to maintain a consensus among a culturally diverse group.[11]

Born in Kansas in 1878 of Quaker parents, Wright had graduated from the University of Pennsylvania (in architecture) in 1901, and he had served as an architectural draftsman for Root and Siemens, in Kansas City. In 1902, he had helped landscape architect George Kessler plan the landscape for the Louisiana Exposition. Later he became Kessler's chief designer.[12] Among Wright's early independent projects were three subdivisions in St. Louis—Brentmoor Park, West Brentmoor, and Forest Ridge—laid out in 1909 for a group of shareholders. The two-acre lots and substantial brick, half-timbered, and stuccoed houses (some designed by Wright) were conventional; however, the siting of the houses in groups, with their backs to the boulevard and their fronts facing a ravine, was novel. Twenty years later, Wright would provide a similar orientation, with interior parks and minor interior roads, for the humbler houses of Radburn.[13]

The idea of orienting houses away from the street came from Wright's first trip to Europe, at age twenty-four, fresh from architectural school. Visiting friends in Waterford in southern Ireland, he had entered an archway through a blank house wall on the street and found a villa fronting on interior gardens. "That archway was a passage to new ideas which have struggled up through the ensuing years!" he wrote. "I learned then that the comforts and privacy of family life are not to be found in the detached dwelling, but rather in a house that judiciously relates living space to open space, the open space in turn being capable of enjoyment by many as well as by few."[14]

A chess player, intellectually curious and adventurous, Wright enjoyed working out the small details of a scheme. As Mumford recalled, Wright was also a dreamer, independent and flexible, "never rigidly committed to even his own best ideas," nor ever "bribed into submission."[15] During their close collaborations on housing projects, Stein was the driving force, a brilliant organizer and skilled politician. Without arrogance or egoism, both attacked stale, conventional planning. "Henry Wright was like a flame that suddenly lighted up and thus clarified and simplified what seemed complicated problems," Stein wrote of Wright.[16] Stein's own light was steadier, "in contrast with the meteor flashes of our more publicized architects of genius," noted one observer.[17]

Born in 1882 in Rochester, New York, Stein was a frail child whose schooling (in Rochester and, later, in New York City) was irregular. After a trip to Europe in 1902, he thought of becoming an interior decorator and spent a year at the Columbia School of Architecture. Unhappy with the classical curriculum, however, he left to work in a decorator's studio in Paris and then studied architecture at the Ecole des Beaux-Arts.[18] Returning from Europe in 1911, he entered the office of Bertram Grosvenor Goodhue, where he became chief designer and worked on both the new mining town of Tyrone, New Mexico (1915–1917, now destroyed), and the 1915 Panama California International Exposition, in San Diego (figure 14).[19]

Stein found the Spanish-colonial style of the exposition buildings appropriate for the region of San Diego, but he was more interested in planning the fair and its civic focus, which became Balboa Park. In Europe he had enjoyed the contrast of approaching great civic places through narrow streets, where little events of daily life unfolded among the shadows. Dignity, grandeur, and swift movement would be necessary in the modern city; "but we need also the more intimate side of city planning," Stein observed, "the by-ways with their little shops, the occasional drinking fountain at a street corner, the glimpse of some secluded garden through a half-opened gate."[20]

It was World War I that, indirectly, brought Stein and Wright together. Wright, a founding member and secretary of the St. Louis City Plan Association, became director of a St. Louis planning study for the local chapter of the American Institute of Architects (AIA). In 1918 he went east to work under the direction of Robert D. Kohn and Frederick L. Ackerman on defense housing for the Emergency Fleet Corporation. After the war, Kohn introduced Stein to Wright, and the two men be-

14. "Along the Prado," Panama-California International Exposition, San Diego, 1915. Bertram Grosvenor Goodhue, Consulting Architect; Carleton Monroe Winslow, Site Architect. Stein was a gifted architectural designer in the office of Bertram Goodhue (Cram, Goodhue & Ferguson/ New York) before he became a planner and social reformer.

gan a joint study of an industrial workers' community for the AIA's new Committee on Community Planning. Soon realizing that their ideas were incompatible with the social, economic, and physical patterns of urban growth in America, Stein and Wright traveled to England, met Howard, and examined his first garden cities of Letchworth (from 1903) and Welwyn (from 1920), which were planned and built by prominent British architects, including Barry Parker and Sir Raymond Unwin.[21]

Between 1920 and 1923, Wright also served as architect for the St. Louis City Plan Commission. Meanwhile Stein, having served as a first lieutenant in the Army Corps of Engineers during the war, was taking the lead on housing and planning committees—for the City Club of New York, the Hudson Guild (a West Side social settlement), the state of New York, and the AIA. By 1923 Stein had also persuaded the semi-retired developer, Bing, to provide financial backing for the new City Housing Corporation, and brought in Wright to help plan the corporation's first experimental housing projects.

These committees, commissions, and corporations are mentioned to underscore the degree to which Stein and Wright had been working within the establishment when, in 1923, they began their full-time collaboration in the nation's financial and cultural capital and tried to reform its patterns of growth, one small housing project at a time. Through their contacts with Mumford, Howard, Parker, Unwin, Geddes, and others, they would absorb a philosophy of social betterment through physical design and yet remain realists. Reading a draft of Mumford's *Culture of Cities,* for instance, Stein commented, "I do not think you bring out plainly enough the connection between our present form of metropolitanism and capitalism, nor do you explicitly show that the present form of city growth can be changed but to a small degree as long as capitalism exists."[22]

Within the prevailing economic system, Stein and Wright tried to effect whatever beneficial change they could, maintaining their lofty vision of regional planning while they toted up square footages, adjusted floor plans, and tried to make the numbers work. Both world's fair veterans, both dreamers of sorts, they worked without illusion to unite social goals and free-market enterprise—with or without government subsidy.

The first garden city effort, Sunnyside Gardens, was begun by the City Housing Corporation, Bing's limited dividend company, in 1924, when the economy was buoyant and building costs were considered high, having nearly doubled since 1914. Without any experience in large-scale low- or moderate-income housing, the corporation sought a "cautious, safe investment."[23] Some seventy-seven acres of relatively inexpensive, undeveloped land in the Borough of Queens (fifteen minutes from Times Square, by existing rapid transit) was purchased from the Long Island Railroad. Between 1924 and 1928, fifty-five acres of this land were developed into a community of 1,202 housing units. The grid plan of streets, already platted by the borough engineer, could not be altered, despite Wright's exhaustive economic analyses that favored the elimination of a few dead-end streets. Thus, the rental apartments and units for sale were built in parallel and perpendicular rows of two, three, and four stories, and grouped to form larger and smaller courts (figure 15). The planting design for Sunnyside—as well as for the nearby Phipps Garden Apartments; Hillside Homes, in the Bronx, New York; and Radburn, New Jersey—was done by Marjorie Sewell Cautley.[24]

Wright, Mumford, and RPAA member Charles Ascher all lived at Sunnyside for some time. Stein, an occasional visitor, appreciated the courts and gardens, framed on three sides by the rows of brick houses and flats. Mumford, a renter and later a home owner, found the floor plans somewhat cramped but appreciated the spirit of the place. "The neighborliness that only the poor practice in New York became more and more our daily habit," he noted.[25] Wright, with his wife and four children, eventually lived on a farm in the country, in Mount Olive, New Jersey. Stein, married in 1928 to the actress Aline McMahon,

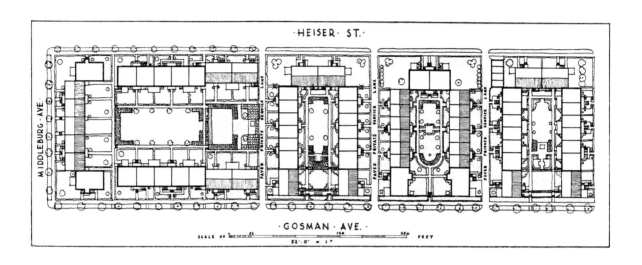

·HEISER· ST.·

MIDDLEBURG·AVE.

·GOSMAN· AVE.·

SCALE OF ⊢⊢⊢⊢⊢⊢⊢ FEET
52'·0" = 1"

15. Sunnyside Gardens, Borough of Queens, New York: part of a block with an inner court and three courts opening off the street, built in 1927. Clarence Stein and Henry Wright, Planners; Clarence Stein, Chief Architect; Marjorie Sewell Cautley, Landscape Architect. Though rigidly rectilinear (a product of constraints maintained by the borough engineer), Sunnyside represented for America the seeds of a revolutionary view of social life in the city.

maintained a Manhattan apartment and a country home. Mumford remained at Sunnyside, his "enclave in the midst of an industrial desert," for eleven years before moving permanently to an old farmhouse in Amenia, New York. But that enclave would always hold poignant memories.

Sunnyside was, for Mumford, a kind of suburban Greenwich Village, where people of different means, interests, and backgrounds mingled. Privacy was respected, yet one could avoid the "overpowering impersonality and loneliness" of the overgrown metropolis. Mumford relished the intellectual companionships, the vivid discussions, and even the politics of running the nursery school. After a party one winter, he and his friends threw snowballs in the snow-drifted courtyards, pausing to "take in the muted rosy beauty of the night sky over Manhattan,"

16. Sunnyside Gardens, an inner court built in 1926. This was the first collaborative attempt of Stein and Wright to deal with urban community through the conscious design of open space within the city.

laughing, shouting, embracing one another, embracing the world. Once the community was completely built, he could walk along paths for nearly half a mile, past rear gardens outlined in trimmed privet hedges and greens filled with Breughel-like scenes of children at play.[26] This was a genuine neighborhood, he felt—not a complete garden city but a beginning. "So, though our means were modest," he concluded, "we contrived to live in an environment where space, sunlight, order, color—these essential ingredients for either life or art—were constantly present, silently molding all of us" (figure 16).[27]

Radburn never had a chronicler of Mumford's eloquence, nor did it ever become a true garden city by Howard's definition: a town large enough for housing, industry, and social life, its size limited by a greenbelt, and all of its land publicly owned or held in trust for the community.[28] The City Housing Corporation's purchase of two square miles of farmland was not sufficient for a complete greenbelt. Construction began in 1928. Then came the stock market crash of 1929 and the Great Depression. Radburn attracted no industries. The corporation went bankrupt in 1934 and was forced to sell off land after less than half the plan was completed. Speculative development gradually filled in around the original development, and Radburn became, like neighboring subdivisions, a bedroom community for New York City. In 1985, Radburn contained 149 acres, with 2,800 residents (rather than the projected population of 25,000).[29]

In 1929 Radburn was proclaimed "a town for the motor age."[30] Yet nowhere in the community is motoring celebrated. Stein and Wright wanted to minimize human contact with the automobile, which, ideally, would remain at the back of the house, tamed among the laundry lines, while residents would walk from front doors and gardens, through paths and parks, to school and to shops. In reality, the automobile and other forms of modern technology were indispensable, not only in Radburn but within the larger region. Why, then, did Stein and Wright neglect any clear, memorable expression of technology in their planned communities?

By 1925, Stein considered New York and other great metropolitan areas to be "dinosaur" cities, doomed by their own congestion. His ideal solution to congestion, regional planning, was rooted not in technological means but in sociological needs. He felt the "spirit of cooperation" was being "crushed by the machinery of the modern industrial city." Rather than celebrate modern technology, then, Stein focused on communal interests—the common land—and let the lawns, trees, and shrubbery quietly dominate. He offered what he believed people most desired: "a beautiful environment, a home for children, an opportunity to enjoy the day's leisure and the ability to ride on the Juggernaut of industry, instead of being prostrated under its wheels."[31]

Wright's attitude toward the machine and industrial technology was different. He was impressed by European advances in housing since World War I, particularly by the quantity and quality of German housing. As if to wrest some independence from England's aesthetically conservative garden cities, Wright noted that "Germany originally took the lead in community planning even before the advent of the English garden city in 1904"; moreover, Germany's development of advanced,

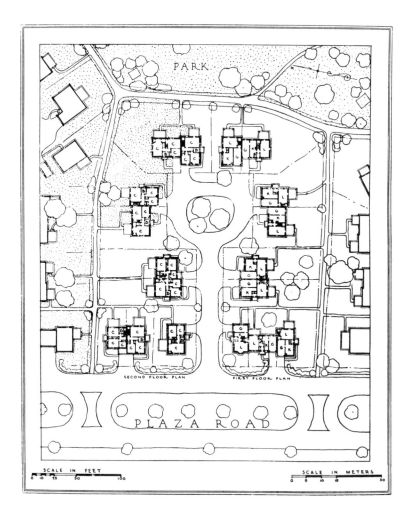

17. Radburn, New Jersey, plan of Burnham Place. The exquisite economy of these cul-de-sac plans produced the generous open areas that characterize the whole community. Even with larger cars, the culs-de-sac work well to this day; they have always provided a remarkable social focus for these mini-neighborhoods.

modern design was linked with that of Holland, the first country to start housing on a large scale immediately after World War I.[32] Eager to move on from past solutions to new and better ones, Wright became increasingly interested in the technical and formal innovations of European modernism. Meanwhile Stein would continue to attack the urban menace, congestion, by promoting the "Radburn idea."

Stein explained this idea as a novel interweaving of five elements: the superblock, the specialized roads for single purposes, the separation of pedestrians from automobiles, the houses with their backs to access roads and their fronts facing private gardens and parks (figure 17), and the park as backbone of the neighborhood. Unfortunately, these elements of planning were never realized in memorable form. Offering no bold expressions of twentieth-century technology nor any landscapes that might transcend the vernacular with something clearly inspired by a new vision, Stein rejected some powerful means of attracting the next generation of young modernists to his revolutionary cause. Like Howard, Stein counted on the power of humane instincts and common sense to bind his coalition of followers.[33]

In 1934 Stein and Wright had a falling out. Mumford was aware of the reasons but mentioned in public only their disagreement over modern design.[34] The effects of the depression, on Radburn and on the whole building industry, may have exacerbated personal tensions. But for whatever reasons, that rift between two of the four central figures of the RPAA (MacKaye and Mumford were the other two) virtually destroyed the association's influence. Mumford sided with Wright, and his protégée, Catherine Bauer, who had been Stein's research assistant and adviser, moved on. She and other members of the RPAA were drawn into middle-level management posts in the Roosevelt administration, and Stein became a consultant on the greenbelt towns. These developments, however, left the former RPAA activists no independent base from which to lobby for fundamental changes in urban development. Nor was any of them sufficiently powerful within the administration to set policy. After World War II, the RPAA was revived, then disbanded. As Mumford noted, the dynamism of original group could not be regenerated.

After breaking with Stein, Wright joined Mumford, Albert Mayer, Henry Churchill, and Carol Aronovici in forming the Housing Study

Guild to explore housing issues with a new generation of architects and designers. Wright also taught briefly at the Columbia University School of Architecture and served as a part-time consultant to Robert Kohn's Housing Division of the federal Public Works Administration. Together with Mayer and Churchill, Wright helped plan Greenbrook, New Jersey, a greenbelt town for the Resettlement Administration, but the plans were scrapped for political reasons.[35] Suddenly, in 1936, Wright died at age fifty-eight.

In 1933 Wright had written to Mumford, "I'm not too fond of what we did at Sunnyside or Radburn; but whatever it was, the important accomplishments were social rather than technical."[36] Indeed, these garden city prototypes, along with Chatham Village, in Pittsburgh, and Baldwin Hills, Los Angeles, remain socially cohesive, their property values secure, and their identities distinct (figures 18–20).[37] Still, their planning principles have not guided mainstream American home builders. Some fragments of the garden city have been reproduced—curvilinear roads, culs-de-sac, neighborhood parks, and other amenities of planned-unit developments—but Mumford's concept of regional planning for a series of garden cities has never caught on. Why not?

Perhaps people never really saw the essential ingredient of landscape in the garden city. It may not have occurred to Wright that his innovations in site planning could slip into obscurity without a visually powerful, memorable landscape.[38] Perhaps informed by Jens Jensen's regionalism in the Midwest, Cautley used native plants at Radburn—birch, viburnum, shrubby dogwood, wild azalea, sweet fern, and high bush blueberries, many of them brought in from the nearby woods. She hoped to preserve something of the natural vegetation that was fast disappearing in urbanizing northern New Jersey.[39] But her achievement,

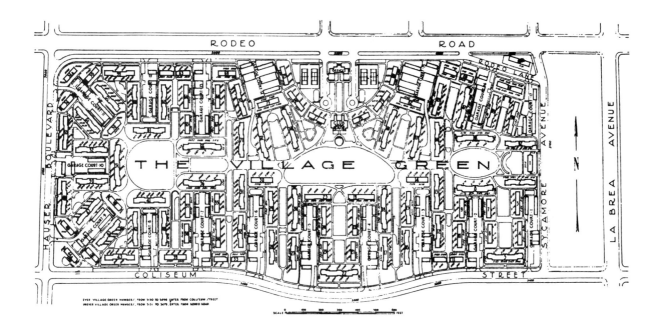

18. Chatham Village, Pittsburgh, Pennsylvania, 1930–1932. Clarence Stein and Henry Wright, Site Planner and Consulting Architects. Ingham and Boyd, Architects. In America, whether for economic or artistic conservatism, the revolutionary idea of the garden city was expressed in familiar vernacular forms. In time, the garden city prototypes would be viewed as simply suburban, even antiurban, in character.

19. Pierre-Auguste Renoir, *Monet Painting in His Garden at Argenteuil,* 1873. In the garden city prototypes of Stein and Wright, plain vernacular buildings are complemented—even obscured—by luxuriant vegetation. Such visual effects can also be found in paintings by Renoir, Monet, and other French impressionists, in which buildings and the landscape are often visually fused into a single impression of felicity.

20. Baldwin Hills Village, Los Angeles, California: Plan, 1941. Clarence Stein, Consulting Architect. Reginald D. Johnson and Wilson, Merrill and Alexander, Associated Architects. Only in 1941 did modern architecture briefly combine with the modern planning ideas of Stein and Wright.

too, could remain unnoticed by a public grown accustomed to the naturalistic landscapes of Olmsted and his contemporaries.

In 1950 Stein was delighted with the merging of landscape and buildings at Radburn, where time had mellowed the two into one. "Harsh lines are subdued and enveloped by the verdure," he noted. "It is almost what happens in a primeval forest to rock and tree bark when they have lived together for a long time—they seem to reflect each other's color and texture."[40] In effect, Cautley's unobtrusive landscape treatment may have served not only as screens for undistinguished vernacular buildings but as veils for Stein's and Wright's revolutionary ideals of community development. One is reminded of the handsome stone service buildings along Gilmore Clarke's state-of-the-art Bronx River Parkway, the intricate floral designs on nineteenth-century typewriters and sewing machines, and other examples of ornament applied to a utilitarian object after the functional requirements had been met. (Not that every beholder or resident would consciously reflect on the appropriateness of form to function; rather, the familiar materials of stone or vegetation and references to the familiar natural world would tend to dispel some people's innate resistance to the new, however functional the object or place might prove to be.)

Mumford explained such disparities between form and function in the design of machinery as the reincorporation of the "human factor." He appreciated aesthetic expression in both the craft traditions and machinelike industrial forms. But he could not view the garden city—a "town for the motor age"—as merely a complex machine for living. Over a lifetime he struggled to promote an ideal of equilibrium between "technics" and art, toolmaking and symbol- or myth-making, pragmatism and idealism: "The great problem of our time," he wrote, "is to restore modern man's balance and wholeness: . . . to bring back, into the very heart of our culture, that respect for the essential attributes of personality, its creativity and autonomy, which Western man lost at the moment he displaced his own life in order to concentrate on the improvement of the machine."[41]

In search of balance, Mumford would often rail against one excess or another—even against a "merely" beautiful object. In 1927, commenting on the English garden city movement, Mumford asserted that the garden city had become a kind of "rare and isolated *objet d'art*." More effort, he argued, should have gone into the comprehensive regional planning of many garden cities; the prototype was useful "only as a concrete objective in a complete scheme of regional cities."[42]

Mumford wrote these words while consulting on the plan for Radburn and serving as "poet-in-residence" for the RPAA. He worked best with words, crafting literary monuments to civilizations he admired or envisioned. Having never seen a real garden city that deeply moved him, however (Welwyn, for example, he found too suburban), Mumford may have underestimated the power of a beautiful, modern garden city to delight and inspire. In a somewhat analogous situation, Siegfried Giedion noted a similar flaw in Henry Cole's efforts to unite the fine arts with industry in the mid-nineteenth century: that Cole and his circle were unable to offer a new artistic vision.[43]

Community participation was another road not taken by the RPAA, a fact that Bauer underscored in a letter to Mumford in 1934. Having begun to learn from day-to-day struggles in housing and community planning in Philadelphia, she believed Stein and Wright had placed too much faith in the training of "experts" to design better communities for, not with, people.[44] Meanwhile, the issue of urban design expression remained unresolved. If the decentralization of the metropolis were ever to be accomplished along the lines drawn by the RPAA, would anyone miss the old densities, sights, sounds, smells, and chance encounters? Despite the great city's ills, some people would always be drawn to it. Mumford recalled his own youthful enthusiasm as he crossed the Brooklyn Bridge one windy day in March, heading for Manhattan: "Here was my city, immense and overpowering, flooded with energy and light . . . challenging me, beckoning me, demanding something of me that it would take more than a lifetime to give, but raising all my energies by its own vivid promise to a higher pitch."[45] Stein could be moved to ecstacy in great urban settings—in Rome, in Liège, even in sunset-softened New York. And yet the RPAA's vision did not extend to the riveting extremes of intensely urban experience.

The RPAA's vision was influential, nevertheless, in planning theory and practice. By 1950 Stein recognized traces of the Radburn idea in Polish planning and in many English and Swedish new towns, as well as in the New Deal's greenbelt towns and defense housing for World War II. The RPAA had also had an indirect influence on the New Deal's Tennessee Valley Authority. In 1954, after twenty years of chronic ill health and underemployment, Stein was named director of planning for the new town of Kitimat, British Columbia. In 1956 he received the AIA's Gold Medal for his service to society and his vision, which led beyond individual buildings to the total environment. Accepting the award, Stein emphasized community architecture and noted that the technological revolution had led to some fresh, contemporary architecture that expressed feeling as well as function.[46] He died in 1975.

Had Stein been given a more prominent role in the Roosevelt administration, the American urban landscape might have developed somewhat differently. But it is not clear that Stein and Wright could ever have significantly changed American patterns of urban development. Without a dramatic, sustained shift in American values, hardly any individual of this century could have assembled and coordinated all the talents required to change the way Americans wanted to live or even dreamed that they might live. In addition to Mumford's grasp of the Western world's cultural heritage, MacKaye's environmental awareness, Bauer's sociological insights and political skills, Bing's experience in real estate development, Wright's blend of practical and dreamy imagination, and Cautley's sensitivity to the natural landscape, others would be needed, including some poet-craftsman-artist of enormous vision and skill. Assuming no major catastrophes, Americans would have to be shown some captivating environment where the "spirit of fellowship and cooperation" clearly overwhelmed the memory—or dream—of possessing a free-standing house in one's own private domain.

Chapter 2

The Garden as Art

Three of the most provocative landscape designers of our time have come to the field without formal training in landscape architecture. Born in the Western Hemisphere at the dawn of the twentieth century, Roberto Burle Marx, Luis Barragán, and Isamu Noguchi pursued a range of arts and sciences that led them to shape environments of extraordinary freshness, power, mystery, and beauty. Whether haunting or exhilarating, these environments may seem to have been conceived deep within some fantastic imagination, unconstrained by tradition, precedent, or utilitarian purpose. They may appear to be new creations, sprung from the earth and stone of the New World.

And yet few other landscape designers have been so profoundly engaged in lifelong efforts to understand and draw sustenance from tradition and culture, both the refined and the vernacular, cosmopolitan and regional. Barragán's gardens owe as much to the rough wooden aqueducts of old Mexican villages as to the fine runnels at the Alhambra or a fountain in a Mediterranean villa. Burle Marx first began to appreciate the rich flora of his native Brazil while studying art in Germany. And Noguchi felt compelled to reconcile the traditions of both hemispheres, East and West. Having studied with skilled Japanese gardeners, he observed, "The Japanese tradition allows for the greatest latitude. It is in rising above the easily recognized that the great tradition asserts itself."[1]

Tradition and culture, in the broadest and deepest sense, lie at the heart of each of these designers' achievements. Noguchi, Burle Marx, and Barragán were all uncommonly educated, highly cultivated individuals who, in our age of increasingly narrow specialization, should be considered Renaissance men. But to examine their work and aspirations in the context of modern American landscape architecture is to do more than celebrate a Leonardo-like approach to one's life work. First, it is to recognize the kinship of all the Americas—North, South, and Central—and to focus on a truly New World landscape architecture, informed by some social and cultural traditions not yet attenuated by global forces of modernization. Second, it is to consider a way of grasping experience, known as surrealism, which runs counter to the logical, rational modes of thinking on which the profession of landscape architecture was founded. Though vastly different in their expression, Burle Marx, Barragán, and Noguchi all produced surrealist work—surreal not only in its forms and spaces but in its implicit commentary on the discontinuities and chance occurrences of modern life.

Other movements in European art—cubism, constructivism, and expressionism—also influenced the work of these three American artists. Moreover, their awareness of these movements was central to their art, not merely a stimulus. Thus, although none was integrated within the profession of landscape architecture as established in the United States, each maintained strong connections not only with artists and architects in their native lands but also with arts and architecture abroad. Their clients and peers were often similarly connected, through museums, other cultural institutions, and their common interests in poetry, philosophy, music, film, theater, and dance.

Without formal training or apprenticeship in landscape architecture, these artists developed their craft along different paths. For Burle Marx, training as a painter, apprenticeship to a botanist (in the midst of the world's richest botanical resources), and lifelong pleasure in both gardening and drawing led him to an exuberance in design and planting. Quickly growing to maturity in tropical climates, however, his works are exceedingly difficult to maintain. Apprenticeships with sculptors

21. Portrait of Roberto Burle Marx. Painting, botany, and garden design are combined in the modernism of Roberto Burle Marx.

and craftsmen led Noguchi to work with stone (both carved and cut) while developing little knowledge of horticulture. For Barragán, training in civil engineering and experience in building led to constructivist composition; and, intrigued by both surrealist painters and the dreamlike, intensely private gardens of a writer in the south of France, Barragán was drawn to natural landscapes and plantings of a wild, sometimes bizarre character, rather than to meticulous gardening or agricultural practices. If such diverse training and experiences have distanced these three artists from landscape architects in the United States, their works have also attracted great interest and even emulation.

In 1954, concluding his talk before the American Society of Landscape Architects, Roberto Burle Marx reminded his audience, "Through art there are no barriers: we speak the same language" (figure 21).[2] Thus, through vivid colors and bold forms, reminiscent of paintings by Jean Arp, Joan Miró, and Vincent Van Gogh, his gardens and landscapes became comprehensible to those North American designers who may have been unfamiliar with many of the plants and the environmental conditions of Brazil. Thereafter, Burle Marx has been praised—and sometimes dismissed—as someone who "painted with plants" (figure 22 and plate 3).

In that talk, Burle Marx emphasized artistic concerns: color, harmony, structure, space, form, volume, and expression. But he also emphasized the ephemeral and seasonal qualities of plants, the value of native plants, and ecological groups of plants that served as metaphors for their native habitats. And he defined the main purpose of a garden: "to give Man pleasure in the shapes and colors of the growing plant."

How Burle Marx came into contact with the world of European modern art is well known. Born in São Paulo in 1909, he grew up there (and, from 1913, in Rio de Janeiro) in a cultured environment, where the parents fostered in their six children a love of art and music. His mother, a Brazilian opera singer, gave him music lessons at home. His father, a German Jewish businessman, not only provided the material foundations for a broad, rich development in the fine arts but also sent Roberto to Berlin to study art and music in 1928–1929. The school was small and academically oriented. Toward the end of his stay, however, Roberto became acquainted with contemporary art and was most impressed by the work of Pablo Picasso, Paul Klee, and Wassily Kandinsky.[3] An exhibition of Vincent Van Gogh's works also made a deep impression.

On his return to Rio in 1930, Burle Marx enrolled in the National Academy of Fine Arts, where he came under the influence of painter Candido Portinari, artist Leo Putz, and architect Lucio Costa, then director of the academy. That Burle Marx won the academy's Gold Medal for Painting, in 1937, indicates his achievement in that medium, having explored the possibilities of several movements within modernism: cubism, geometrism, concretism, and, clearly, surrealism.[4] The influence of these movements is clearly detected in the colored and monochrome plans of his gardens, plazas, and parks (figure 23). But once realized, Burle Marx's designed landscapes are never still; they are planted carpets seething with life.

One early roof garden (1938–1939), now destroyed, remains in photographs as a study in contrasts between crisp modern architecture and languid vegetation; between a metaphorical arrangement of earth, stone, and water and the natural, heroic landscape of water, mountains,

22. Odette Monteiro garden, Rio de Janeiro, 1948; current residence of Luis César Fernandez. Roberto Burle Marx, Landscape Architect. Bold masses of *Coleus* cultivars and other plants form part of the larger three-dimensional composition, a continuous interplay of sinuous lines, swelling contours, and mysterious natural forms.

23. Plan of a garden around and under an apartment house on pilotis, São Paulo, Brazil, ca. 1947. Rino Levi, Architect. Roberto Burle Marx, Landscape Architect. Burle Marx's garden plans are virtual paintings that are often utilized as foregrounds for dramatic urban or primeval vistas beyond. Here, plants were selected for their color contrasts, as well as for their adaptability to deep shade, temperate light, or brilliant sun.

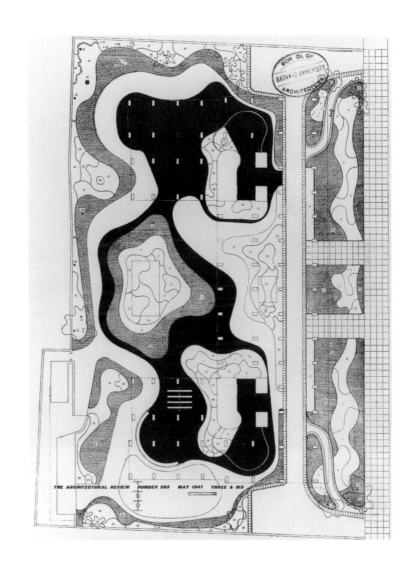

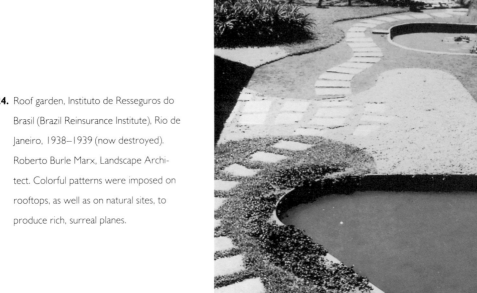

24. Roof garden, Instituto de Resseguros do Brasil (Brazil Reinsurance Institute), Rio de Janeiro, 1938–1939 (now destroyed). Roberto Burle Marx, Landscape Architect. Colorful patterns were imposed on rooftops, as well as on natural sites, to produce rich, surreal planes.

and sky in the background; between a surreal juxtaposition of plants on a rooftop and mental images of the plants' natural habitats. This garden was created for the Brazil Reinsurance Institute in Rio, overlooking the bay (figure 24).[5] Not a picture or a fragment of nature, it was a surreal composition of sinuous lines, taut planes, and swaying volumes of vegetation. The shock of recognition that Burle Marx felt in the late 1920s, discovering the glory of Brazilian plants in the Dahlem Botanical Garden in Berlin, was thus recalled in Rio, where splendid native specimens flourished in an unexpected setting.

Discussing this garden, Burle Marx has compared it to both an abstract painting and the configuration of Brazilian rivers, as seen from an airplane.[6] Similar observations about art and context have been made about Thomas Church's Donnell garden, of 1948. But rural Sonoma County, California, site of the Donnell garden, is a world apart from cosmopolitan Rio, and a wide gulf separates the sensibilities of Church and Burle Marx. For each, surrealism was a tool for different ends.

To appreciate Burle Marx's achievement, one must be aware of Brazil's Victorian flower gardens, full of exotics; the imitations of French Baroque gardens in the older public parks; and the French engineer Glaziou's introduction of English landscape gardening, to which Burle Marx was sympathetic. Also, as Frederick Gregory observes, one must experience the unaltered Brazilian landscape in all its variety, including the mysterious Amazon and its tributaries, flora, and fauna; the surrealistic, isolated east-central plain of Brasilia; the Atlantic coast; and the Pantanal. In 1981 Gregory noted that roughly 20 percent of the earth's species of flora could be found in Brazil.[7] Since then, the continual devastation of the rain forests has attracted international concern, along with Burle Marx's efforts as an environmental activist. But equally threatened may be his native culture.

Burle Marx's inherited place within the cosmopolitan, once-colonial culture of Rio de Janeiro is privileged; however, Brazilian culture is not immune to assault from modern industrial capitalism, multinational interests, and urbanization. These very forces, which sustained his parents' relative affluence and his own livelihood, are also a constant threat to the diverse professional practice and idiosyncratic way of life that Burle Marx has enjoyed. Confronting the forces of modernism in a different country and time, Clarence Stein retreated, artistically, to an earlier, pastoral aesthetic. Roberto Burle Marx, who came of age between the two world wars, found his own voice in the expressive lan-

25. Santo Antonio da Bica, Burle Marx's country home, Guaratiba, near Rio de Janeiro. Roberto Burle Marx, Landscape Architect. Tropical plants, tiles, gravels, and water are used in painterly and romantic ways, in combinations with sculptural constructions of architectural fragments and found archaeological objects. Over time, the robust richness of the tropical plantings modifies the precision of the planar forms. While Burle Marx has a profound interest in nature (especially in botany and horticulture), the forms of his gardens lean toward surreal and constructivist paintings.

guage of contemporary artists. The fact that his works seem to express much greater optimism than, say, Salvador Dalí's, does not deny traces of melancholy in Burle Marx's surreal juxtapositions of biomorphic or cubist forms of lawn, irrepressible succulents and palms, and deteriorating fragments of stone or wood from an old mission—as melancholy as any Mayan ruin, where fecundity and decay are rampant (figure 25).

Burle Marx is not always paid for his work, and the artists and craftsmen who work with him cannot always add up billable hours. Some small Brazilian towns, too poor to pay cash for his park, plaza, or garden designs, give him their "junk"—stones, plants, and architectural fragments from demolished buildings. These items are then recycled in his own garden or that of another client.[8] The results, romantic or haunting, add another layer of meaning to surreal juxtaposition. In Burle Marx's hands, surrealism becomes a way of acknowledging contradictions among the overlapping realities of modern civilization, indigenous culture, and Amazonian wilderness. Centuries ago, the native Indian perhaps showed some hostility toward nature, in burning down the jungle round his hut for a bit of cropland. Such hostility increased exponentially with colonialism, then nationalism. Over time, fear and awe of nature gave way to contempt of nature—despite modern science and ecological awareness. In effect, we have been more irrational than our ancestors.

Burle Marx was not always outspoken about environmental issues. Some forty years ago, however, a visit from Walter Gropius provoked him into action. Offended by the sight of billboards along a mountain road, Gropius asked if Burle Marx had tried to get them removed. His host had not, he said, because protest would not have done any good. Gropius replied, "But it is the thinker's obligation to protest, even if it doesn't change anything." This lesson was never forgotten. Still defending the rain forests and protesting intrusions into his parks, exploiting all the media, including television, Burle Marx explains, "I detest indifference."[9]

Exuberant and somewhat enigmatic, Burle Marx remains the towering artistic figure in twentieth-century landscape design. For over fifty years the leading voice for a new modernist vocabulary, he has been developing a robust personal style through continual experiment and formal exploration. Without vigorous maintenance, some of his early gardens quickly went from their original, refined compositions through a rich, rough, expressive period, to years of decay, then overgrowth into obscurity. From the 1950s onward, however, his more rectilinear gardens seemed to suggest a paring back, using metaphoric tools of clearing and simplification. He has used the flatness of the parterre, plaza rooftop, or lawn, both as a metaphor for the earth and as a surreal plane that magnifies the objects placed on it and the distant objects, buildings, or land forms that enter into the larger composition. As did Le Corbusier, he places objects on a plane not to glorify the object but to express the plane itself. And however enriched with patterning and planting, the plane remains taut. In this he is the first modernist to extend the greatness of Le Nôtre.[10]

Perhaps inevitably, Burle Marx has been followed by landscape designers who could not distinguish the wheat from the chaff of his prolific formal and theoretical output. But more important, over many years of sustained efforts in the office, the cultural community, the public realm, and the fragile wilderness, he has shown that formal and artistic invention can be combined with a passion for ecology and the environment.

26. Portrait of Luis Barragán. Solitude, serenity, beauty, joy, and silence were of profound importance to Barragán. He once spoke of perfection in a work as joy—"silent and serene joy."

A comparable artist (but wary of publicity and temperamentally unsuited to activism) lived until recently in the drier, sunnier climate of Mexico (figure 26). Relatively unknown when he was awarded the Pritzker Prize for Architecture in 1980, Luis Barragán had created houses, gardens, and residential subdivisions that offer what residents of modern cities rarely find: refuge, serenity, mystery, drama, and a beauty attainable only by reduction to essentials. Familiar features of European modern architecture were present in his buildings and landscapes: unbroken planes, unframed glass, and cubist compositions. But he had also achieved that rare quality, emotional and spiritual resonance, which he considered as essential as light and air (figure 27).

Drawing from the dramatic color and sparsity of Mexican and Spanish landscapes and buildings, Barragán created scenes that appear to be caught at a perfect, still moment. These scenes are exceedingly photogenic, haunting. Craft is no longer an issue, nor is permanence. The scenes are intended less for the eye than for the mind. Even in a deteriorating state (to which many have succumbed), they are compelling, for it is precisely this absence of reality that produces the great art of these spatial compositions. A few useful buildings give way to the abstraction of walls, planes, and spouts of water. Rows of ancient trees and expanses of brilliant color define a foreground, while exploding and heightening the raw sunlight of a perfect sky. Through contrast, abstraction, and magnification, this color intensifies one's sense of the out of doors, its nature and its quiet wonder.

Like Burle Marx, Barragán had lived and traveled in Europe, learning from European gardens, designers, and writers. Both had been impressed by Le Corbusier's thinking, for instance, yet they retained deep

roots in their native lands and cultures. Barragán's memories of childhood, focused on his family's cattle ranch in the mountains of Jalisco, remained vivid: the nearby pueblo village of Mazamitla, with its tile roofs and generous eaves; the tree forks and gutted logs that formed aqueducts, running freely over the roofs of the village; the moss that grew on the dripping logs; the walled patios; and the wide-open valleys where horse and rider were silhouetted against mountain and sky. These elements of vernacular building and a traditional rural way of life informed Barragán's houses and gardens of the post–World War II era. In addition, a knowledge of contemporary art and building techniques helped him to make a connection between the ancient and modern worlds.

Barragán was born in 1902 in the countryside of Guadalajara, a provincial capital. After studying civil engineering at the university there, he passed through Mexico City for the first time in 1924, en route for Europe, where he traveled for two years. That sojourn turned his interests from engineering to art and architecture. He became enchanted by the walled gardens of the Alhambra, with its Spanish-Moorish fountains, runnels, and series of enclosed spaces. He also came upon the writings of Ferdinand Bac, a poet and novelist whose villa on the French Riviera, Les Colombières, contained a sequence of gardens, from intimate enclosures to vistas of wild vegetation, sea, and sky.[11] Returning to Mexico, Barragán began to design and construct houses while helping to administer the family's ranch and farm properties. On a second trip to France, in 1931–1932, he lived in Paris and attended lectures by Le Corbusier, frequently escaping to Bac's gardens of memory on the Riviera.

Barragán's first exposure to surrealism could have come through painting, photography, cinema, or other art forms available in Mexico in the
1920s.[12] Then, too, in *La Volupté romaine* (1922) Bac describes scenes
of the Roman campagna that could have been painted by Giorgio de
Chirico or Ives Tanguy, scenes of desolate plains, with rust-colored
arches in ruins, a few sheep, a shepherd on a black horse, an immense
horizon, an immense solitude.[13] This is the kind of austere melodrama
that Barragán's residential subdivisions would later evoke, although the
architectural forms at El Pedregal and Los Clubes would be abstract
and the rider would lead his horse toward rust-colored fountain walls
or a mirror-still water trough in a grove.

Some observers have linked Barragán's buildings and landscapes to the
dreamlike paintings of European surrealists, particularly de Chirico and
René Magritte (figure 28).[14] A photograph of blank walls and empty
spaces, animated by deep shadows or billowing white clouds, may even
recall a specific painting—just as Burle Marx's plan for the Odette
Monteiro garden, of 1948, a fluid composition of biomorphic forms in
vivid colors, may recall one or two works by Miró. If some designers in
the United States find these linkages between art forms unconvincing,
then a word about culture and professional practice in Latin America is
in order.

Although all the Americas were once colonial, dominated politically and
culturally by European nations, most of the Central and South American countries long retained their cultural ties to Spain and Portugal,
where vivid color and rich, imaginative embellishments are traditional
in all the arts. These ties, reinforced by the aesthetic inclinations of the
native Americans and former slaves from Africa, remained strong even
after the Latin countries won their independence, and the dominant

cultural influence began to come from France. Transmitted through academic institutions, French influence would include rational thought and methodical training, but it could not suppress the Latin American's delight in sensuous, intuitive, and spontaneous qualities in art.

In Mexico, Brazil, and other Latin nations, where a large middle class and bourgeois values were slow to take hold, intellectual milieux remained small and vibrant. As Paul Damaz observes, artists, writers, architects, and other intellectuals knew one another, maintaining social contacts and often deep friendships.[15] Trained in the same schools, architects and other artists in the Latin countries have not been accustomed to our professional barriers and specialization. One result, in Damaz's view, is that in Latin America, more than in any other part of the world, architecture is regarded as an art. The same could be said of gardens.

This explanation may help to illuminate why modern architecture was generally accepted sooner in the Latin nations than in the United States. If political leaders, intellectuals, and the public at large expected significant buildings to be works of art, then the experiments in modern European poetry, painting, photography, and sculpture, centered in Paris during the early twentieth century, would soon attract the interest of Latin American architects and at least some of their clients. Damaz also notes that architecture is a relatively new profession in Latin America (and landscape architecture is still not yet well established). Thus, even among more academically minded designers, there could be little institutional hindrance and much cultural encouragement to follow the lead of modern European artists in Paris.

The modern movement in Brazil can be traced to three major factors: the Modern Art Week in São Paulo, in 1922; Lucio Costa's artistic leadership in Rio; and Le Corbusier's visit to Rio in 1929, which had a decisive influence on the development of the new capital, Brasilia, by Lucio Costa, Oscar Niemeyer, and others, including, eventually, Burle Marx. In Mexico, the Revolution of 1910, a popular uprising, had created a highly charged atmosphere that favored social and artistic experimentation. Out of that fervor, in the late 1920s, came Mexico's first modernist buildings, including the Institute of Hygiene in Popotla (1925) and the Tuberculosis Sanitorium in Huipulco (1929–1936), both by José Villagrán García.[16]

These buildings by Villagrán García were functional and socially responsible, almost devoid of architectural ornament. The sanitorium offered patients a common patio-garden and spacious wards from which they could look upon the surrounding countryside through large windows of industrial glazing. Photographs of this building complex in the 1930s reveal austere courts and façades flooded with sunlight: a bold precedent for Barragán's later gardens and walls, where functional concerns would be lightly overshadowed by aesthetic ones. Not surprising, in 1967, Villagrán García reflected on nearly five centuries of cultural influence from Western Europe and still asserted the particular "accent" of Mexican culture—where "the innate inclination of our people toward the esthetic, in everything we do and the manner in which we try to live, is perhaps our chief characteristic."[17]

One facet of Latin American culture that intrigues outsiders is the quality of public life and its counterpart, the intimacy of home. Both public places and the home reveal deep currents of aesthetic emotion and religious or spiritual feeling beneath the surface of evolving material culture in Latin America. And both public and private life are served by the best work of Barragán and Burle Marx, yet each will be remembered for the brilliant achievements suited to his own temperament. Burle Marx has offered festivity: in a mass of plants; on the facade of his chapel, where his workmen and their families gather to celebrate St. John's Night, June 24; at a Carnival Ball in Rio; and in the great sweep of Botafogo gardens that gives human scale to Rio's sublime urban shore. Barragán offered refuge, a quiet space walled against the assaults of modern civilization: the noise, the crowds, the pollution, the soulless buildings, the telephone. A devout Catholic, he also offered serene, uncluttered space for the soul.

After World War II, in search of a site for residential development, Barragán took a wasteland of petrified lava formations, El Pedregal, and transformed it into a surreal landscape of walls, concrete planes, lawns, pools, and fountains among the rocks, still somewhat hostile yet beautiful (figures 29 and 30). His astute handling of real estate ventures later provided Barragán the financial means to focus, as an artist, on a limited number of intriguing projects (figures 31 and 32, plate 4). Among them

29. El Pedregal (The Rocky Place), entry to
the residential subdivision, Mexico City,
1945–1950. Luis Barragán, Architect and
Landscape Architect. The delicate, scrim-
like steel gate dramatizes the rugged lava
outcrop of the site of El Pedregal. This artifact, juxtaposed to the rugged site, produces a dreamlike expression.

30. El Pedregal, garden gateway, 1945. The
heavy geometry of wall and gate both engage and give way to the rocky site—the
primary drama. Planting serves as coun-
terpoint to this drama.

31. San Cristobal, Los Clubes residential sub-division, Mexico City, 1967–68. Luis Barragán, Architect and Landscape Architect, in collaboration with Andrés Casillas, Architect. This is one of the surreal outdoor "stage sets" that influenced a generation of modern American architects and landscape architects.

32. Las Arboledas, entry to the residential subdivision, Mexico City, 1958–1961. Luis Barragán, Architect and Landscape Architect. This powerful composition of existing and added elements combines reflection, shadow, and linear and planar elements to produce one of the most memorable surreal images of modern landscape design.

33. Roof garden, Barragán residence. Walled emptiness, rising to the endless sky. contrasts with the borrowed view of a single tree. This garden of emptiness is perhaps rivaled only by the Zen gardens of Japan.

was the entrance to Ciudad Satellite, a large subdivision north of Mexico City. In 1957, with his friend, the artist Mathias Goeritz, Barragán designed five prismatic towers, ranging in height from 100 to 165 feet. Horizontally striated, rising up from a gridded concrete plane, the enigmatic towers announce the entrance to Satellite City and perhaps succeed in putting human beings in scale with their environment, one of Barragán's lifelong quests.[18]

In later gardens for other architects, such as the Camino Real hotels in Ixtapa and Mexico City, by Ricardo Legorreta, Barragán used many more plants. These gardens express the raw power, even the chaos, of nearly unattended plant growth—as in a jungle—in contrast with the great colored planes of the buildings. In La Jolla, California, Barragán's great sense of the ethereal and serene returned in his advice to Louis Kahn on the Salk Center: to leave the central court unplanted, quiet, and surreal. In the end, given the many layers of artistic and cultural references in Barragán's work, one still feels the overpowering privateness of these places, of their art, and of the man (figure 33). Luis Barragán died in Mexico City in November 1988.

A month later, a sculptor with some similar inclinations and ambitions died in New York City—Isamu Noguchi (figure 34). To put human beings in scale with their environment, to escape from the fragmentation that modern civilization demands of people, to recapture the essence of ritual, ceremony, myth, and drama, both inside the theater and out of doors, to offer a new synthesis of sculpture and space, to make of a playground a beginning world, to supply the poetic and artistic meaning of our existence: these are among the ambitions that drove Noguchi to the artistic achievement that, still fresh and elusive, remains awesome (figures 35 and 36).

Early in his career, Noguchi received some encouragement, fellowships, honors, and commissions but not the recognition that most serious artists usually crave. Still, he discounted worldly success and hated the business of art. From 1948, after the suicidal death of his friend, the painter Arshile Gorky, he also refused to strive for the art world's recognition, which by then appeared to him as superficial and cruel. Thereafter, as told in his moving autobiography, he considered each day an undeserved gift. "Somehow," he wrote, "I have sought to express myself more fully, to make contact with a larger world, more free and more kindly than the one that had killed my friend."[19]

In 1948 the desolate landscapes that surrealist painters had envisioned were already a threat; the war had shown that atomic annihilation was possible. Both the art world and the larger world fed Noguchi's depression. Then, with the instincts of a survivor, he broke free and set out on a personal and artistic journey to discover a larger, nobler purpose for sculpture. He wanted to find out how, in the past, in different parts of the world, sculpture had been related to people and to space.

34. Portrait of Isamu Noguchi. Noguchi stands by one of his works in his studio, now the Isamu Noguchi Garden Museum, in Long Island City, New York.

This search entailed a personal quest for his roots in both Western and Eastern traditions. Along the way he encountered some of the world's greatest works of landscape architecture, including the gardens of Italy, Gaudí's parks in Barcelona, sacred sites in Greece and Egypt, and the temple gardens of Japan. In the eyes of his friend Buckminster Fuller, he was an "intuitive artist precursor of the evolving, kinetic one-town world man," inherently at home everywhere.[20] Noguchi, however, described himself as a wanderer in a world growing increasingly small: an "artist, American citizen, world citizen, belonging anywhere but nowhere."[21]

Born in Los Angeles in 1904, Noguchi inherited at least a genealogical claim to three continents. His father, the Japanese poet Yone Noguchi, was living in New York when he met Isamu's mother, Leonie Gilmour, a writer, schoolteacher, and translator, whose father was an Irish immigrant and whose mother was part American Indian. The year of his son's birth, Yone Noguchi returned to Japan and to a traditional culture that did not normally welcome children of racially mixed parentage. By the time Leonie and her son arrived in Japan in 1906, Yone had married a Japanese woman.

The events that followed help to explain both Noguchi's resourcefulness and his sense of belonging anywhere and nowhere: childhood with his mother in a Japanese seaside village, early adolescence at a French Jesuit school in Yokohama, emigration to America at age thirteen while his mother stayed in Japan, his school in Indiana abruptly converted to a truck training camp during World War I, informal adoption by a Swedenborgian minister, apprenticeship to sculptor Gutzon Borglum (who finally told Noguchi he would never be a sculptor), medical studies at

35. Stage set for Martha Graham's dance
performance, *Errand into the Maze,* 1947.
Isamu Noguchi, designer. This surreal
stage set, one of a series of designs for
Martha Graham's performances, predates
Lawrence Halprin's choreographic ideas
of poetic movement through space.
These sets also anticipated Noguchi's later
gardens, composed of surreal and occasionally constructivist pieces of sculpture.

36. Isamu Noguchi, *Contoured Playground,*
1941. Model, not built. Composed of
what Noguchi called "earth modulations,"
this playground was to be a fresh, new
world appealing to a child's imagination:
simple yet mysterious, inviting the child to
explore without fear of physical danger.

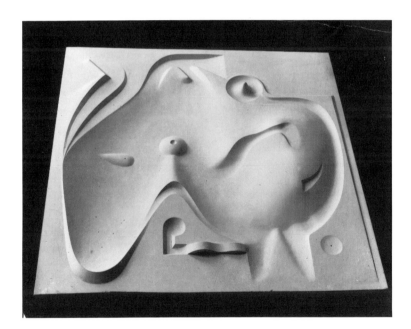

Columbia University, one-man shows of his sculpture by age twenty, a Guggenheim fellowship to study in Paris, apprenticeship to Rumanian sculptor Constantin Brancusi in Paris, the death of his mother in 1933, voluntary internment in 1942 at Poston, Arizona (where he made plans for the Niseis' parks and cemetery), and the death of his father in 1947, after having been "swept up in the nationalism of the war."[22]

Noguchi clearly had mixed feelings toward his father, who had rejected him in infancy: a blend of bitterness, independence, and admiration. Just as his father, the poet, author of books on Japanese art, and professor of English at Keio University, had created a bridge between Japan and the West, so Noguchi would make his life work a bridge between the two cultures. This involved new kinds of synthesis, including a fusion of sculpture and space that, traditionally found in the Japanese garden of contemplation, would also be enjoyed in public spaces for play, work, and relaxation. In Japan, these efforts at synthesis began immediately after World War II, when the rubble was not yet cleared and the materials available to Noguchi were ephemeral—bamboo, wood, plaster—rather than enduring, like stone.

Reflecting on those efforts in 1950, Noguchi saw the interdependence of nations and cultures as inevitable, and yet he had cautioned the Japanese against copying: "The new Orient must come fresh born of itself, and that in turn, is necessarily involved also with us." In the midst of reconstruction, the Japanese had asked him for direction. "I found a kind of envy without bitterness; envy, for instance, of our American energy and imagination, our efficiency and drive. . . . I said they should work for each other to develop their own communal life in which the arts would have their proper contribution to make. . . . I told them that many Americans were not at all sure about mere progress being such a good thing. . . . Even though we are very adept at [the practice of materialism], our best ideals lead elsewhere. It might even lead to concepts of space and living not unlike their own."[23] Among Noguchi's lasting contributions to their landscape were the two concrete bridges he designed for the approaches to Kenzo Tange's Peace Park at Hiroshima. One, evoking the rising sun, was named *Tsukuro,* "to build." The other, resembling a boat, was named *Yuku,* "to depart."

Noguchi's remarks on materialism were hopeful. A year before, he had alluded to a moral crisis brought on by two world wars and exacerbated by mechanization, specialization, fragmentation, privatization, modern concepts of power, and meaninglessness—a loss of spirit. His response to the crisis was twofold: to urge the reintegration of the arts toward some purposeful social end (ultimately, to fill the spiritual void) and to make sculpture for public enjoyment.[24] In 1968, he again asserted the artist's purpose in society: to make life interesting, worthwhile, and rich. These were his purposes in creating sculpture—not to make *"objects d'art"* for museums.[25]

Sharing some of the social and cultural values of Lewis Mumford, Noguchi might have been a brilliant, if temperamental, collaborator on the garden city efforts of Stein and Wright. In fact, among Noguchi's portrait sculptures of artists, writers, and family members was one of actress Aline MacMahon, Stein's wife, done in 1937 as the return of a favor she had done for him in 1930.[26] Did Noguchi and Stein ever move in overlapping circles of acquaintants? Both men were critics of modern civilization. But Noguchi's response to its contradictions was to work with abstract form and new materials as well as with ageless stone and wood; to use technology to comment on, and perhaps triumph over, a technologically controlled world; and to create sculptural environments, strangely beautiful and surreal, that belonged to a world of forms remote from those found in landscapes by Stein and Wright.

As an artist, Noguchi faced a classic dilemma: that of the sculptor who tries to create an object in space with sufficient intrinsic energy to command that space—yet also yearns to make the space itself energetic and memorable. Just as in great architecture, his work must be both sculptural and spatial—particularly spatial. In most of his environmental and stage works, however, Noguchi's intuitive inclination seems to have been toward sculpture. In speaking of Zen gardens, he often referred to the stones as the "bones" of the garden, the permanent, substantive form giver. He felt uncomfortable dealing with plants, for instance, when he tried to use them as objects, as filler materials, or as decoration. Perhaps only in stage sets for the dancer Martha Graham and in two later gardens—one for the Sogetsu school of flower arranging, by Kenzo Tange, in Tokyo, and one for the Domon Ken Museum, by Yoshi Taniguchi, in Sakata—has he escaped this dependence on the object, singular or composed, as focus.

In these two gardens, completed toward the end of his life, Noguchi's great mastery and range of craft (carving, building, placing, and fabricating) has been subordinated to the sense of place as significant space rather than as mere setting. This is no small achievement, for the Corbusian dependence on objects to command space is still perhaps the supreme strategy of modern Western design. At the Domon Ken Museum, as in an early painting by de Chirico, the great sloping slabs of stone, with their elegant sheen of moving water, direct the eye down the surreal stepped plane from the sentinel stone to the mirror of the lake below. At the Sogetsu school, within Tange's glass prism of a tower, Noguchi's white stone slabs form a stepped plaza for display and sitting—an elegant, intricate piece of public furniture. When empty, however, the plaza exudes a primitive power, like that of a ruined acropolis. A place seen from below, above, or within, it is both a dream stage and an environmental sculpture in its full physical reality.

Some of Noguchi's early gardens were equally compelling, in strikingly different contexts of architecture and landscape. The Connecticut General corporate headquarters, or CIGNA, near Hartford, Connecticut (1956–1957), was a product of Noguchi's collaboration with Gordon Bunshaft, of Skidmore, Owings & Merrill (SOM), and SOM's landscape architects, notably Joanna Diman. Here, the specific contributions of each individual may never be known.[27] CIGNA nevertheless remains a masterpiece of building setting, courtyard, terrace, and sculptural objects in nature (figures 37 and 38). The spatial composition and landscape development rivals all of the other landscape work of the postwar era in the United States. It also set the stage for the Pepsico headquarters in Purchase, New York, designed by Edward Durrell Stone, Jr., and, later, Russell Page; Upjohn's headquarters in Kalamazoo, Michigan, by Sasaki, Walker and Associates; and much of the corporate work to this day.

At CIGNA, the materials are simple: grass, gravels, groundcovers, clipped hedges, trees, a few walls, concrete reflecting pools, a small lake, and occasional stone, either carved or laid as paving. The spaces function as places for informal congregation, relaxation, and contempla-

37. Connecticut General Life Insurance Company (now CIGNA) headquarters, Bloomfield, Connecticut: Terrace, 1953. Skidmore, Owings & Merrill, Architects; Gordon Bunshaft and Isamu Noguchi, Principal Designers. Isamu Noguchi, Sculptor. Joanna Diman, Landscape Architect. The first of the great postwar corporate villas, CIGNA incorporated International Style architecture and modern art with an Olmstedian landscape, pictorial and naturalistic. The terrace is both useful (for dining and sitting) and demanding of visual attention. Here, paving, pool, and bench are formed sculpturally and composed architecturally.

38. Courtyard garden, CIGNA. Isamu Noguchi, Landscape Architect and Sculptor. The garden is a purely visual, spatial object, to be viewed from several levels within the glass box of the building.

39. Sculpture garden, viewed from Reading
Room, Beinecke Rare Book Library, Yale
University, New Haven, Connecticut,
1960–1964. Skidmore, Owings & Merrill,
Architects. Gordon Bunshaft, Principal
Designer. Isamu Noguchi, Landscape Architect and Sculptor. Layered with mysti-
cal and symbolic meanings drawn from
both Eastern and Western cultures, the
white marble garden is like a landscape
on another planet: surreal, seemingly endless, and physically inaccessible. One enters through the mind.

tion. Small details of carved stone and moving water provide intimacy.
The partially sculpted stones placed on a rolling lawn across the lake
both focus the view from the terrace and ennoble it. Throughout is the
strong, expressive shadow of surrealism, rendered less chilling than a
work of Dalí or de Chirico by the oddly cheerful, anthropomorphic
stone figures on the rise of lawn.

The Beinecke Rare Book Library at Yale University (1960–1964), also
in collaboration with Bunshaft, contains one of Noguchi's masterpieces:
a small sunken court, or garden of stone. The surreal space is mysterious, nearly empty, predicting by many years the success of Maya Lin's
Vietnam memorial in Washington, D.C. This garden, however, recalls
not the fact of nations clashing with nations but a mythic drama played
out beyond human intervention. The cube, the pyramid, and the sun
enigmatically represent chance, earth's past, and energy, respectively.
Seen from above or from the reading room through walls of glass, the
garden can be entered only in the imagination (figure 39). In polished
marble, totally white, it is at once perfect in scale and endless in
dimension.[28]

California Scenario, in Costa Mesa, perhaps Noguchi's most famous garden, is also his most literary (figure 40 and plate 5). Seen from the periphery or from within, the series of formal objects and settings appear
to have allegorical meanings. Bold specimen plants, along with sculpted
benches, lights, and furniture, are all subordinated to a few mysterious
objects, including a wall, a stream, and a coffin. The stone base plane is
subtly separated from the earth and from the stream. Though slightly
less abstract, this garden recalls the sunken gardens of the Beinecke Library and the Chase Manhattan Bank, in New York City (1961–1964).

40. California Scenario, Costa Mesa, California, 1980–1982. Isamu Noguchi, Landscape Architect and Sculptor. A collection of sculptures are composed into a garden. Here, as in Noguchi's garden at UNESCO, in Paris (1956–1958), plants are used for visual richness, while the stones form the space.

All appear to be allegorical, yet their precise meaning for Americans may forever be open to speculation.

If Burle Marx will be remembered for his landscapes of festivity and Barragán, for his landscapes of refuge, Noguchi will be remembered for his landscapes of the mind, dependent on stone: rough or smooth, barely carved, machine-cut or hand-hewn, heavy as the earth from which it emerged, or light as a spectral presence, magically levitating, as the stone seems to be doing in the sunken garden of the Chase Manhattan Bank. To stand there, in benign sunlight or in a storm of rain or snow, and look down upon heavy, dark stone that seems openly to defy all laws of gravity in the heart of the financial capital of the United States is a surreal experience. Noguchi considered this garden "an unnatural thing of will, as is our whole technological age—like going to the moon."[29]

Chapter 3

The Modern Transformation
of Thomas Church

By the middle of this century, Thomas Church and his gardens had be-come an irresistible topic for the print media (figure 41). Talented, in-ventive, admired by his colleagues, and sought after by a burgeoning middle- and upper-middle-class clientele, Church was also a genuinely likable person who could put others at ease. From the 1930s in San Francisco, he built up a landscape design practice that included tiny ur-ban backyards and tract house lots, as well as larger gardens for subur-ban and rural places. Although he also did some public housing, campus planning, and commercial and corporate work, his finest work was in garden design—small scale, attentive to individuals' needs, with plenty of scope for improvisation and unannounced visits to gardens in evolu-tion. Each garden was to be unique, appropriate to the particular client, site, program, and budget (figure 42). Satisfying on all these counts, many of the gardens became, as is widely recognized, works of art, re-calling cubist and surrealist paintings of the early twentieth century.

Honors and awards accumulated. In 1951 Church received the Fine Arts Medal of the AIA. In 1967, *House Beautiful* featured "Three Tow-ering Men of Today," with articles on Otto Klemperer, Thomas, Church, and Marcel Breuer. In the professional journals of America and Britain, writers discussed Church's gardens in the context of ideas, the-ories, and other works of art.[1] But this likable, brilliant designer did not care to theorize and had little to say about art. Toward the end of his life, when asked about his philosophy of design, he replied after some hesitation, "My philosophy is that the client is usually right."[2]

To give long-lasting pleasure to some two thousand home owners in Northern California and beyond would be gratifying in itself. But Church also attracted to his office some of the most promising young landscape designers in the United States, particularly in the years imme-

41. Portrait of Thomas Church. Church designed through personal drawing, site inspections, and discussions with clients. The office was kept small intentionally, so that Church could have direct contact with all aspects of the design.

diately before and after World War II. Lawrence Halprin, Robert Royston, Garrett Eckbo, Douglas Baylis, Jack Stafford, Casey Kawamoto, Theodore Osmundson, and architect George Rockrise were among the designers who worked briefly or for years in Church's office at mid-century, before setting up their own practices. In time they and other landscape architects throughout the country considered Thomas Church the founder of the modern garden—not only in California but for the whole United States. What impressed them was his consistent body of fine built work: sure in scale and proportion, simple in materials, and apparently effortless in fitting into a given site and social milieu.

One of the first outsiders to recognize Church's ability in design was an idiosyncratic easterner, trained at Cornell and Harvard, landscape architect James Rose. In 1941 he saw in Church's gardens "an uncommon understanding of form, an appreciation of material combinations, and a sound knowledge of construction" that, along with a playful ingenuity,

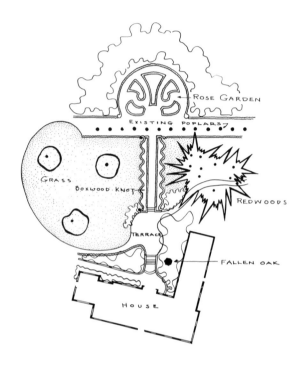

42. Keator Garden, plan, Hillsborough, California, 1941. Thomas Church, Landscape Architect. Drawing by Thomas Church. Church's early gardens followed the formal, neoclassical organizations he had encountered through his education and his southern European travels.

would endear those gardens to both professionals and the general public.[3] The tradition that was built on these foundations can be traced in a succession of gardens by Church, his former apprentices, and his distant followers. Less accessible are the thought processes that led Berkeley- and Harvard-trained Church to synthesize lessons learned from great Mediterranean gardens of the Renaissance, opulent estates in California, constructivist design, the furniture and glassware of Alvar Aalto (for which Church served as U.S. distributor), works of art by Miró and Arp, the sinuous streams of Sonoma County flowing into San Pablo Bay, and more (figure 43).

Church published a great deal—two books and many short articles for magazines, such as *House Beautiful, Sunset,* and *Bonanza.*[4] The latter two were regional. *Bonanza* was a Sunday supplement to the *San Fran-*

43. Joan Miró, *Landscape (The Hare)*, 1927. With a minimum of objects and the mere suggestion of earth, sky, and a journey, Miro created an image of a landscape beyond time and space. Such a painting could have informed any number of garden designs that Church offered his clients, for their own release from worldly cares.

cisco Chronicle, and *Sunset* is still a popular guide to western living. Focusing on houses, gardens, food, and travels in California and the American West, *Sunset* introduced readers of varying interests and backgrounds to the idea of living on just about every square foot of their property. This pragmatic what-to-do and how-to-do-it magazine featured photographs of contemporary West Coast gardens, along with construction details and costs, but it deliberately avoided allusions to taste and class. In a similarly egalitarian spirit, *Sunset* routinely credited the garden designers, thereby giving a boost to lesser-known designers as well as to Church, who became the magazine's unofficial garden editor.

Church's amusing comments on overstuffed garages, compost bins, lines, curves, space, time, and ease stop short of revealing the designer's mind. One garden editor, Joseph Howland, at *House Beautiful,* later casually mentioned that he himself had written some articles that carried Church's byline, and in the rush to get the text and photographs to the press, there had been no time to get Church's approval.[5] This fact should reinforce the maxim, "Don't rely on a magazine; go and see the built work."

In Church's case, the advice is particularly apt. The greatness is in the work, not the words. Church was an intuitive designer, unusually responsive to the demands and daydreams of each client, yet responsive, too, to his own instincts for reaching the "right" solution, one that would appear inevitable, timeless. Sometimes a particular form—the biomorphic shape of a pool, a sinuous line between path and lawn, the shadow of an eave slicing across a gridded concrete terrace—would recall a surrealist painting. But all sense of foreboding, melancholy, or dark mystery is absent. It is as if Church had been open only to the more appealing aspects of dreams and the unconscious and remained free of the ideological and sociological burdens shouldered by many artists between the two world wars. It was not his mission to change society, but if he could make life richer, more satisfying, and less harried for some individuals, he would.

A feeling of relaxation was what most people wanted in a garden, Church noted in 1971.[6] Having worked on gardens throughout the continental United States, he may have found that desire common to most Americans. The majority of his clients, nevertheless, were Californians, some newly arrived in the Golden State and some whose families had settled there generations earlier. Both newcomers and natives tended to be aware of their exceptional environment and benign climate. On weekends and holidays, they sought out the coastal forests and beaches, the snow-capped mountains, the wine country, the gold country, the ranches and farms, the old missions and the desert, each with its characteristic beauty and wonder. Some natives knew these areas intimately and were able to establish roots in a particularly favored place. And newcomers came to these landscapes with perceptions heightened by the intensity of the dreams that had brought them to the far edge of America: dreams of abundance, superior health, opportunity, a fresh start in life, and freedom, perhaps, from the constraints of older, ingrown societies left behind in Boston, Peoria, Tokyo, or wherever.

Church understood these dreams and offered his clients—mainly middle-class Americans of Northern European background—spaces for leisurely outdoor living, long known to Hispanic and Mediterranean cultures through the patio, the courtyard, the villa, and the hacienda. His product—a gift, really—was not so much sybaritic as remedial, for it was becoming increasingly evident that mainstream American culture exacted a psychological price for progress. By the mid-twentieth century, novelists and sociologists had minutely depicted, and advertising agencies had brilliantly exploited, the cultural demands for conformity in America. What had begun on the East Coast—corporate culture, government regulation, and innumerable other demands for conformity, with or without the gray flannel suit—were soon established on the West Coast as well. Church's remedy, a garden, lifted or suspended those demands. It was a place to wind down from the tensions of the day, a private world shaped and molded to one's own needs, desires, whims. For some, the garden was also a gift of culture, filling a void or adding another layer to a long-cultivated existence.

Church was a successful garden designer, in part because he understood his clients' ambivalent desires: for relaxation and stimulation, for the comfort of tradition and the adventure of innovation, for conformity and individualism. The demands and incentives to conform may have been less numerous on the West Coast than elsewhere in America, but the demands were all the more stressful where expectations (or recollections) of freedom and fulfillment were higher. As Kevin Starr characterized the Golden State in the decade before World War I, "California yet ached with promise" (figure 44).[7]

44. Meyer and Kuhn Garden, Aptos, California, 1948. Thomas Church, Landscape Architect. In this garden on Monterey Bay, bold geometry plays dramatic contrasts of sunlight and shadow, hard and soft materials, against the white sand and bay.

Born in Boston in 1902, Church was reared in the Midwest and in California. His father was the inventor of the first commercially successful washing machine. His mother, an elocutionist, became a teacher of English, a drama coach, and a character actress on the radio. The marriage was brief. Divorced, Mrs. Church took her daughter and son westward—first to Ohio, then to Southern California, in the Ojai Valley, where her father, a retired Ohio State Supreme Court judge, was enjoying his avocation, gardening. At thirteen, Tommy moved with his mother and sister to Berkeley. There, at the University of California, he first studied law, then switched to landscape architecture after his interest was piqued by a course in landscape design history. He earned a bachelor's degree from Berkeley in 1923 and a master's from Harvard in 1926.[8]

Church's training in landscape architecture on both coasts was grounded in the French beaux arts design tradition, with its emphasis on an analytical, systematic approach to design, clear spatial structure and composition, rather than details of style. At Berkeley, however, where landscape design was housed in the College of Agriculture, students took several science courses and learned to recognize some 2,000 plants.[9] At Harvard, landscape architecture was initially taught under the auspices of the Department of Architecture; there, form, function, scale, and site planning were emphasized, and plants were considered "materials."[10] At both schools, courses in landscape design history introduced great gardens of the Western world and, at Berkeley, Japanese gardens, as well. Church had an excellent preparation, then, to design country places in the period styles popular during the years of economic boom that followed World War I. But three events altered his course.

First, he met Fletcher Steele, formerly an apprentice of Warren Manning and, by the mid-1920s, a leading practitioner in Boston. "It was from Steele," Church recalled, "that I learned you can take the wall around the tree—that the tree is more important than the axis. This was my first insight into what landscape architecture could become. From then on, for me, the Beaux-Arts rules of symmetry were dead and gone."[11] To imagine some of Church's finest gardens minus their great live oaks (*Quercus agrifolia*), around which the designs revolve is to appreciate Steele's influence.

Second, Church was awarded Harvard's Sheldon Traveling Fellowship, which he used in 1926–1927 to study the gardens of Spain and Italy. His purpose, to discover how to adapt such gardens to the climatic and social conditions of California, was inspired by the bad examples back home. Unimpressed by rows of orange tiles and stuccoed surfaces that were meant to be "Spanish" or "Mediterranean," Church sought an understanding of principles and techniques: how to achieve a subtle transition between the formality of the house and the natural or agricultural landscape beyond and how to conserve and recycle water during California's long, rainless summers. Among the weeds and grotesque grottoes of neglected old Italian gardens, Church also recognized limits to the intellect, for those melancholy gardens possessed "an underlying beauty, impossible to describe and hard to analyze—a spirit of poetry and imagination which we sense rather than understand."[12]

In 1927 Church returned to America, taught landscape architecture at Ohio State University for two years, then moved to San Francisco just before the third fateful event occurred: the stock market crash in October 1929. Demand for large country places all but dried up, and traditional practices declined. Church spent two years working for Oakland landscape architect Floyd Mick before opening his own office in San Francisco. He also found ways to supplement his income while jobs were scarce. He made tiny outdoor rooms out of urban backyards and passageways between houses. For the magazine *California Arts and Architecture,* he edited plant lists and also wrote a series of articles on small gardens, including one entitled, "A New Deal for the Small Lot."

Published in May 1933, this article is the closest thing to a manifesto that Church ever wrote—a nonpolitical invitation for landscape architects to build upon a new design tradition, perhaps even to stand on an equal footing with architects. The key to this status was the new intimacy between house and garden—new, that is, to Anglo-American culture, however venerable its tradition in Egypt, Greece, Rome, and Renaissance Italy. The landscape architect was now being called in to collaborate on projects at an early stage. Both architect and client could appreciate outdoor living in an age of scarcity. Lots were smaller. Houses were down off their stilts. Doors were replacing windows. Front lawns and foundation planting were obsolete. Hedges and fences gave new freedom to live as one pleased. The smaller the lot, the more one needed privacy—as well as proper scale, neatness, function, beauty, adaptability, convenience, and economy of upkeep. "This is a new era in garden-making," Church concluded, "because, while many things have entered our life to make the problem complex, our ideas and requirements tend toward simplicity of solution."[13]

Working with William Wurster at Pasatiempo Estates, a golf course–oriented community north of Santa Cruz, California, Church had already earned one prominent architect's respect. Among their projects at Pasatiempo was the design of a modest wooden honeymoon cottage/studio (1931) for Church and his new bride, Betsy. Wurster and Church, both trained in Berkeley, shared an interest in simplicity, integrity of materials, function, adaptation to the site, and uninhibited, un-self-conscious form. These were the qualities of comfortable, older wooden houses by Bernard Maybeck, Julia Morgan, Ernest Coxhead, and other Bay Area architects. Houses built among the Berkeley hills, clad in weathered brown shingles and sheltered by pitched roofs and generous eaves, were often so well fitted to their sites that the life within could easily spill out into the garden. To Maybeck and his friend, the poet Charles Keeler, hillside architecture was "landscape gardening around a few rooms for use in case of rain."[14]

These turn-of-the-century houses were the roots of what Lewis Mumford called the Bay Region style, an expression of the topography, the climate, the materials, including rot-resistant, beautifully weathering redwood, and the relaxed way of life on the Pacific coast.[15] By 1947, when Mumford first described this style (now also known as Bay Area style), houses by Wurster, Gardner Dailey, Joseph Esherick, and others in and around San Francisco were modern in spirit, yet no one would mistake them for products of European or International Style modernism. Buildings of Bauhausian or Corbusian influence had, for instance, flat roofs, smooth white or cream-colored stuccoed surfaces, ribbon windows, pilotis, flowing interior space, and outdoor rooms elevated above the ground, on rooftops. Ideally, European modern houses were sculptural objects in space, best revealed against a neutral background, a woodland, or a meadow. Inevitably, the object in space stood *on* the earth, detached, and best photographed without a human being in sight.

But the Bay Region house, like a distant cousin of Frank Lloyd Wright's prairie house, was *of* the earth, visually and functionally rooted to its site by gently pitched roofs, deep overhangs or trellises, and outdoor spaces terraced, decked, embanked, or otherwise built into the earth. Wright and Maybeck had often designed outdoor spaces themselves, calling in a planting designer if necessary. Wurster and his colleagues, however, recognized Church's rare talent for siting and orienting a house, fitting it to the site, and making subtle transitions so that life could flow more freely than ever before, through walls of sliding glass, out onto terraces and beyond. And as architects and clients increasingly recognized the value of such outdoor spaces, the gardens and their designers became indispensable. On these gardens was built a new tradition of modern garden design.

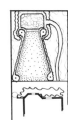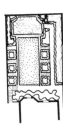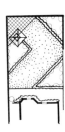

45. Sullivan Garden, San Francisco, California, ca. 1937: Four alternative plans. Thomas Church, Landscape Architect. Drawings by Thomas Church. Through discussions with clients and further studies, Church would quickly produce many sketches and variations. Both traditional motifs and modern forms were included in his studies, and classically inspired forms would return, in whole or in part, throughout the modern period of his career.

46. Sullivan Garden. Many of Church's gardens were appealing in both two and three dimensions. From above, they could be perceived as paintings; as one entered, one recognized the effective spatial compositions. The crisp, original forms were often softened by rich, luxuriant planting.

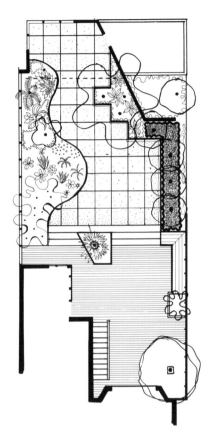

47. Kirkham Garden, San Francisco, California, plan, 1948. Thomas Church, Landscape Architect. Drawing by Lawrence Halprin. The purity and economy of the expression of pattern, texture, and line mark Church's high period of revolutionary modernism.

The depression years demanded ingenuity and flexibility of landscape architects, but even long afterward, Church built gardens in unconventional ways. After figuring out the spatial relations of a terrace, a fence, a pool, a tool shed, he might have a load of plants trucked in and then complete the design on the spot. He used ordinary materials—wood, concrete, brick, gravel, asphalt, turf, and groundcovers—and experimented with corrugated asbestos, redwood bark, and, for paving, redwood blocks and rounds. He found a contractor he could trust, Floyd Gerow, and considered him a partner in the design process; he listened to Gerow, often took his advice, and shared his concern for craftsmanship. Church also listened to the workman on the job, watched him and learned from him. Walking onto a lot, Church might know within ten or fifteen minutes what ought to be done with it, yet he would spend considerable time in the office, over the telephone, and at the site, trying to make something of the client's ideas.

For some of his more exacting and challenging clients, such as Mrs. Jerd Sullivan, in San Francisco, Church would revise designs over and over, replanting and rebuilding if necessary, until the clients were satisfied (figures 45 and 46). He would cheerfully tackle a remodeling job, and he liked to compare the before-and-after effects (figures 47–49). In fact, the puzzle of a site and an intricate program kept him working many nights and weekends. He would not delegate this careful process, for his design process was like a conversation, or a series of conversations—purposeful, amiable, expansive, and intimate, bringing out the best in everyone involved. He used to remark that he loved to work with the gardening ladies who wore those big flowered hats. They and their husbands would become family friends whom he was welcome to visit anytime, even with pruners hooked into his back pocket. In this

48. Kirkham Garden, section. Drawing by
Lawrence Halprin. This brilliant section
demonstrates Church's complete understanding and control of the three-dimensional aspects of a site.

49. Kirkham Garden. The small garden becomes spatially rich and extended
through the artful use of opposed lines.

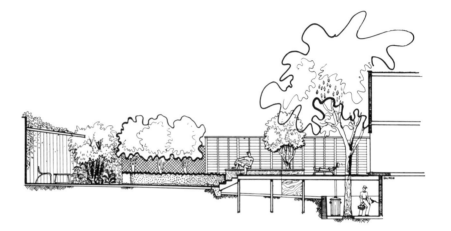

way, though Church would not impose his ideas on clients, their gardens became partly his own.

When built, each garden had to be ready to use. Some gardens would have to accommodate "forty people after the Big Game, or once a year a hundred for cocktails"—yet not feel empty after the party was over.[16] On city lots, the challenge was to make the garden appear larger. For Mr. and Mrs. Sullivan, Church oriented the backyard garden on a diagonal, so that lines and planes appear to slip beyond the walls. There, within a dynamic space, the sitting area is a corner of repose.[17] Details of animated lines and curves, photographed at just the right time of day and juxtaposed on a page, were arresting. A reader or a guest might not feel the space pulling him into the scene—but he would remember some fine detail, in dappled or blazing light, edged by shadow.

Gardens were Church's life, Halprin recalls.[18] They were also invitations to a way of life. Jean Wolff, a keen gardener and grateful client, noted that San Francisco backyards were once dull places no one ever bothered with, particularly in foggy, windy, cool weather. But by building a deck just outside the living room and by terracing a hilly waste into levels for walking, gardening, and lingering, Church offered her a "constant joy." To Wolff and others less initiated, Church provided a "culture of gardening, the idea that gardens were beautiful living monuments of our lives."[19] They remain artifacts of a new regional culture beginning to emerge just before and after World War II, when standards of living were rising and California accommodated tremendous in-migration. Nowhere else, except perhaps in Florida, had so many uprooted middle-class Americans settled so quickly in a developing region. Never had there been such a cultural void to be filled.

And yet that developing region, the San Francisco Bay Area, had a relatively well-established artistic and cultural milieu through which Church moved easily. Many of its members had been drawn to other artistic centers during the 1920s and 1930s—New York, Paris, London, Rome, Florence—and returned to the Bay Area with developed skills and strong inclinations toward certain modes of expression, particularly surrealism, synthetic cubism, and the modernism of Northern European architecture. Some, including the Howard family (John Galen Howard, the eminent campus architect at Berkeley, and his sons Henry, Robert, Charles, and John Langley, who pursued careers in architecture and the fine arts), Adaline Kent (Howard), and William Wurster, were also family friends of Elizabeth (Betsy) Roberts Church.[20]

Reared in Berkeley, Betsy was one American in Paris whom Thomas Church did not happen to meet during his year abroad, in 1926–1927, but after they were married, their lives together in San Francisco became rooted in a physical place and a cultural community that would seem remarkably intimate and vital by any standards, particularly those of today. Sculptor Jacques Schnier has recalled the area around Montgomery Street, San Francisco, as "home to a small, well-knit group of artists, poets, and writers who worked, entertained, and exhibited in this neighborhood."[21] During the depression and for many years after World War II, this area at the base of Telegraph Hill remained sufficiently affordable for Church and follow designers and artists to maintain offices and studios there. Occupying an office in the same building as Wurster, Church welcomed his friends—architects, artists, photographers, designers, and others—to drop in for morning coffee and, in many ways, to share in a camaraderie born of a quiet dedication to one's work, whatever the medium. As recollected, those impromptu encounters were joyous, unforced, and memorable—like the gardens that were then taking shape on Church's drafting board and in his mind's eye.[22]

Some gardens, lovingly maintained, suggest the finest domestic aspirations of that postwar culture. At the garden for William Wallace Mein, Jr., (1951) in Woodside, California, the glass doors of Gardner Dailey's two-story vine-clad house open directly onto a plane of brick pavement that merges, without change of level, into curving paths leading past live oaks to the pool or the guest house.[23] The pool, a synthesis of lap pool and wading pool, angles, curves, and a circle, is the most dynamic two-dimensional form in an otherwise calm, nearly level setting. Low wooden retaining walls along straight brick paths offer seating in sun or shade. Beyond the flat expanse of irrigated lawn, above one low retaining wall, is a hill covered with wild grasses, golden brown in summer, and framed by a tangle of distant shrubs and trees. All is in balance: the cultivated and the wild.

The Dewey Donnell garden in Sonoma County, north of San Francisco Bay (1948–1951), is better known—a dream of turquoise blue water, floating free-form in pale, gridded concrete, high above the golden brown marshes that turn misty white beneath the hot September sun (figure 50 and plate 6).[24] Here, a pleasant stroll up from the main house, lawn is reduced to a free-form island of turf with rocks and grasses. Wooden seat walls line the oak-punctured redwood deck (figure 51). A lanai is formed where a single-pitched roof hovers over movable walls of glass. Another wooden seat, backed by a high stone retaining wall, runs uninterrupted from outside to inside the lanai. One is sheltered yet free. Nothing, not even the free-form white sculpture

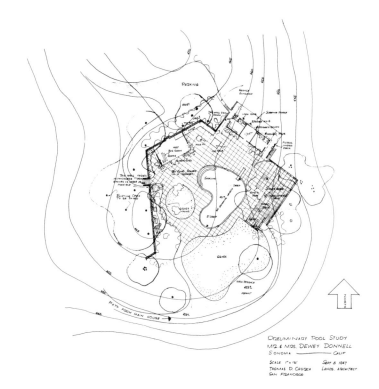

50. Donnell Garden, Sonoma, California: Preliminary pool study, September 5, 1947. Thomas Church, Landscape Architect. Drawing by Thomas Church. George Rockrise, Associate (for architecture); Lawrence Halprin, Associate; Adaline Kent, Sculptor. Whatever the genesis of the form—surreality or distant salt marsh—there was here a fusion of form and setting that became the most powerful, defining icon of early landscape modernism. In its fluidity, simplicity, and directness, this garden influenced a generation of designers and clients.

51. Donnell Garden, live oaks growing up through wooden deck. The trees and their shadows bring drama to the simple wooden deck. The result is at once constructivist and surreal.

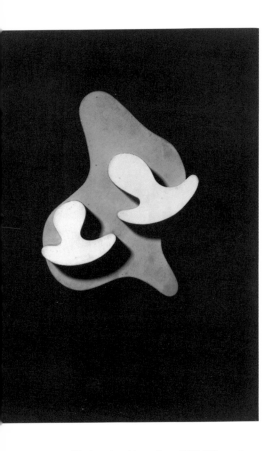

52. Jean Arp, *Vase—Bust,* 1930. This small relief, of carved and painted wood, only 12 × 8 1/4 inches, seems to be without scale, without weight, free of constraints and conventions. These are the qualities that one also senses at the Donnell Garden.

in the pool, appears to have any weight. One thinks of Jean Arp—or the mother and child with dog, photographed near this pool and featured on the cover of *House Beautiful,* April 1951. Church, who took many of his own photographs, understood the power of the image, humanized.

Several individuals contributed to this garden, including Donnell, the contractor-client. Adaline Kent designed the pool sculpture and Rockrise, the lanai. Halprin laid out the approach road that gradually ascends along the contours and, in effect, initiates the sequence of movement that culminates in the garden—a continuous kinesthetic experience. (Such choreography of movement was one of Church's strengths as a designer, Halprin notes.)[25] Fascinated by Miró and Arp, and intrigued by relationships, though not direct transfers, between art and garden design, Halprin also had a powerful influence on the pool garden (figures 52 and 53). He had left Church's office, however, before the main house was built and its adjacent gardens were designed.[26] As the Donnell residence evolved over the years on a portion of an old ranch, Church brought all the elements into a synthesis that today seems wonderfully fresh and rooted in the land, with sinuous forms that relate to the streams in the salt marsh below.

Apart from its context, the Donnell pool garden also has the universal appeal of an icon. Its seductiveness was prefigured in "Holiday," an elegant garden fantasy submitted by Church and Wurster to the exhibition of contemporary landscape architecture at the San Francisco Museum of Art in the spring of 1937, just before their European trip, when they met with Alvar Aalto. A curvilinear abstraction of planes and volumes, "Holiday" suggests mass and weightlessness, contain-

53. Donnell Garden, sculpture, pool, live oak. Although scaled for a range of human uses, the pool garden can sometimes seem scaleless, weightless, a realm of the imagination where one feels free. The sculpture by Adaline Kent not only invigorates the recreational life of the pool but also lifts the level of garden sculpture to that of an icon.

ment and freedom. "It might be a pavilion and beach in some mirage," noted the two designers, "with thought released from actualities and needs."[27]

With minimal form and few words, "Holiday" embodies the soothing, healing qualities of the Donnell garden, the Charles O. Martin garden, at Aptos, California (figures 54 and 55), and a few others built about that time—a high point in Church's career, Halprin believes.[28] These gardens offered a respite from the little annoyances of modern life that, by 1955, Church knew were accumulating. In *Gardens are for people* he casually refers to the bumper-to-bumper traffic, the particles of dirt and dust in the air, and the endless monotony of tract houses built a few feet apart. A quiet man, however, dedicated to the kind of work over which he could exert some control, Church rarely ventured beyond certain limits—typically, the retaining wall against the golden brown hillside or the lovely distant view.

One large-scale project, the campus master plan for the University of California, Santa Cruz, did hold Church's interest—mainly because of his deep feeling for the land. He was committed to preserving the character of the site: the old Cowell Ranch, where magnificent redwoods covered the upper slopes and cattle once grazed on the lower slopes that command sweeping views of Monterey Bay. The master

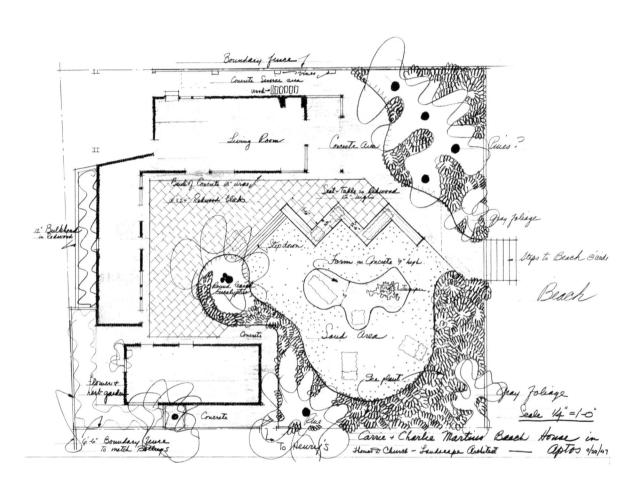

Boundary fence

Concrete Service area

Living Room

Concrete Area

Pines?

Bank of Concrete 18" wide
6×6" Redwood Blocks

Seat-Table in Redwood
12" high

Gray foliage

12" Bulkhead
in Redwood

Step down

Steps to Beach 6 risers

Beach

Round Canopy
Eucalyptus

Farm in Concrete 9" high

Concrete

Sand Area

Ice plant

Gray Foliage

Flower +
herb garden

Scale ¼" = 1'-0"

Concrete

Pine

6'-6" Boundary fence
to match Buildings

To Henry's

Carrie + Charlie Martin's Beach House in
Homer T. Church – Landscape Architect —— Aptos 9/29/47

54. Martin Garden, Aptos, California. One of Thomas Church's original sketch plans, in pencil on yellow tracing paper, dated September 29, 1947.

55. Martin Garden. In the small gardens for beach houses at Aptos, Church offered the privacy, the relaxation, and the directness and simplicity of construction that characterized the Bay Area style, an embodiment of the "California dream" of outdoor living. Constructivist and surreal forms are combined to create cheerful, memorable family environments. These gardens also reveal a certainty and clarity of means rarely found in Church's larger, public work.

plan that Church and architect John Carl Warnecke developed in the early 1960s tucked the roads, buildings, and small surface parking lots in among the redwoods, leaving the meadows and views open.[29] Although some buildings have since encroached on the meadows, that campus still bears evidence of Church's skills as a site planner. But he was less successful in design at the large scale—as in Michigan, at Eero Saarinen's General Motors Technical Center, in the 1950s. Where the site lacked character, where gardening was not possible, where the program was abstract and the client was a board of directors, apparently there was no scope for the relaxed, intimate conversations essential to stimulate Church's great creative drive.

By staying for the most part within the limits of the private garden, Church was able to focus on small-scale built work—useful, tidy, naive and playful, or restrained, knowing, often very beautiful. In so doing, he won such respect for his profession that landscape architects on the West Coast were, for a while, no longer invisible. That alone was a major contribution to his profession, often acknowledged.

In artistic terms, Church's great contribution was the seemingly effortless transformation from classical and neoclassical design to that of twentieth-century artists—cubist, constructivist, and surrealist. Wurster, Aalto, and several others had accomplished this formal and spatial transformation in modern architecture. In the modern garden, only Christopher Tunnard, in England, and Roberto Burle Marx, in Brazil, made comparable breakthroughs. Beginning in the late 1930s, Church led the way for hundreds of young landscape designers in the United States and abroad. Only years later did it become problematic that his real accomplishments were small in scale, domestic in character, and of limited, humble construction. Nevertheless, the strong artistic impact of his deceptively simple gardens virtually silenced the old formal-informal debates and allowed the next generation of landscape architects to work with the second generation of modern architects on larger, more complex problems of the postwar era.

Finally, the social significance of Church's gardens should be considered. His gift to each client, a livable garden of one's own—however small its territory—was generous. As much as the house to which it was related, the garden marked one's place in the world. In a milieu of flux and change, where people packed up and moved every few years, the garden offered roots and slow growth. One could be, or become, what one wished, effectively shutting out the world. Or, through the gentle persuasion of curving paths and distant views, the eye could be led toward the larger world. Church was a master of transitions. But how many clients followed those transitions outward with more than an idle gaze and thought about the neighborhood, the city, the metropolitan area, the region, and the primeval earth, water, and sky? For how many clients did the gift of a garden lead to concern for those successive transitions? Visiting Church's well-preserved gardens today, one feels that they still ache with promise.

Chapter 4

**Beyond the American
(or California) Dream**

On October 24, 1929, a day of unprecedented panic on Wall Street, Garrett Eckbo was eighteen years old. Robert Royston was eleven and Edward Williams, fifteen. On December 7, 1941, the day Pearl Harbor was attacked, Eckbo was thirty one years old, Royston was twenty three, and Williams, twenty seven. The aftermath of the two events—the Great Depression and America's involvement in World War II—separated these landscape architects from their elders in the profession. Whatever affinity they may have felt for Church or the Olmsteds, Eckbo, Royston, and Williams had to make their own way in a world that had been profoundly altered in their adolescence and early careers. Although Eckbo and Royston each passed through Church's office, and Williams was exposed to Church's work at the University of California, Berkeley, none could slip comfortably into Church's way of living and working. Combat duty, defense work, educating the public about planning, and designing communities for migrant agricultural workers were experiences that shaped these younger men's sensibilities and ambitions.

After the war, however, when most Americans turned wearily away from international conflicts and longed for tranquility at home, garden design became the focus of most California landscape architects, including Eckbo, Royston, and Williams, who formed their partnership in San Francisco, in 1945 (figures 56, 57, and 58). Soon they and their contemporary, Lawrence Halprin (who had spent about four years in Church's office before opening his own office in 1949), became Church's heirs and closest competitors. The early work of these designers appeared alongside Church's work in *House Beautiful, House and Garden,* and *Sunset.* By the early 1960s, however, responding to social and economic changes in America and following their own inclina-

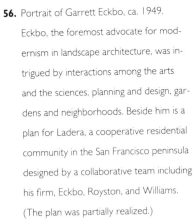

56. Portrait of Garrett Eckbo, ca. 1949. Eckbo, the foremost advocate for modernism in landscape architecture, was intrigued by interactions among the arts and the sciences, planning and design, gardens and neighborhoods. Beside him is a plan for Ladera, a cooperative residential community in the San Francisco peninsula designed by a collaborative team including his firm, Eckbo, Royston, and Williams. (The plan was partially realized.)

57. Portrait of Robert Royston. A kindred spirit who shared Eckbo's intellectual and artistic interests, Royston had worked for Thomas Church before joining Eckbo in practice in 1945.

58. Portrait of Edward A. Williams. A congenial man with deep concern for the growth of younger people in his firm, Williams expanded the partnership through his management skills and his direction of large-scale planning for natural resources and open space.

tions, these designers had moved on to larger projects of a public, commercial, institutional, and corporate nature.

What follows is a study of the work and thought of Eckbo, Royston, and Williams from 1945 through the mid-1960s, focusing on design at the scale of gardens and neighborhoods. This period incidentally overlaps the partnership's split into two separate firms in 1958. With good reason, one could end there, in 1958. But a few more years were needed to bring into sharper focus the complementary talents of the three original partners. Although each was unquestionably capable of running his own firm—Eckbo and Williams had each practiced independently for brief periods before the war—the three achieved greater strength and flexibility in partnership. Eckbo, the preeminent theorist and reformer, not only led the firm intellectually but also had a broad vision of the potentialities of the field—perhaps broader than any other practitioner at the beginning of the postwar era in the United States. Royston, a gifted designer with a fascination for formal exploration, remained deeply committed to the social purposes of his built work, particularly the private gardens, neighborhood parks, and playgrounds. Williams, an effective manager with a patient, gentle manner and a lively interest in people, became the partner in charge of much of the firm's large-scale planning work from the 1960s onward.

In the 1960s, as opportunities for landscape architects expanded and new financial and technological tools came to be used, partnerships began to be restructured in ways that allowed the growth of more hierarchical, multidisciplinary, corporate firms. In retrospect, one might view the partnership of Eckbo, Royston, and Williams as an embryonic form of these larger organisms. Whatever the differences between the present-day firms of EDAW, Inc. (from Eckbo, Dean, Austin, and Williams) and Royston, Hanamoto, Alley, and Abey, both firms grew and developed internal specializations that reflect the complementary strengths of the three founding partners and the opportunities of the American West on the brink of development.

Flying over the San Francisco Bay Area in a helicopter in the early 1970s, Robert Royston was dismayed by the chaos he saw below: ubiquitous roads, freeways, interchanges, and large-scale developments overlaying, apparently without plan, the creeks, watersheds, older communities, and agricultural fields of a naturally beautiful, varied landscape. Looking more intently, however, Royston observed signs of hope and opportunity that reinforced his innate optimism: here and there a wooded canyon, a marsh, a farm, a regional park had been preserved, and he delighted in some clearly man-made landscapes, including parks and playgrounds, residential communities, roof gardens, and amphitheaters designed by his own firm. Design at the large scale, he concluded, was the exciting opportunity for a new breed of landscape architects—those who would see far beyond property lines and find ways to deal effectively with the chaos.[1]

Through practice and teaching, Royston, Eckbo, Williams, and their partners emerged among this new breed of planner-designer. And as the most prolific writer among them, Eckbo became their spokesman, noting the good built work amid the chaos, as well as a few flaws in the American way of life. "This is the richest country in the world," he reminded his architecture students at the University of Southern California (USC), just after World War II. The expression of that richness lay in perhaps 14% of American homes, some prosperous rural areas, and a few parks, public buildings, and splendid natural landscapes, but the general physical environment that most Americans experienced daily, Eckbo considered impoverished. Even the private lawn was merely insulation, "a greenbelt—between home and an unplanned, unpredictable, chaotic world." The importance of that lawn (or of a garden) was not thereby diminished, but Eckbo insisted that the neighborhood was the "minimum home unit," that is, the minimum unit for rational planning and design analysis. To avoid endless, formless suburbanization, then, he told students to seek the controls of neighborhood planning through democratic participation.[2]

While developing their practice, Eckbo and Royston gave considerable time to teaching in both landscape and architecture departments— Eckbo at USC from 1948 to 1956 and Royston at the University of California, Berkeley (1947–1951), and at Stanford University in the 1950s. The timing was critical. California and the West were being developed at an unprecedented pace; students, including older, mature war veterans, were eager to learn; and there were few precedents for the scale of development these students would later face in practice. At Berkeley Royston assembled teams of architecture and landscape students and assigned them problems in community planning on thousand-acre parcels of land. And, before Eckbo's *Landscape for Living* (1950) was available, Royston had his students read *Planning the Neighborhood* (1948; U.S. Department of Health and Safety), as well as works by Le Corbusier, Gyorgy Kepes, Siegfried Giedion, Laszlo Moholy-Nagy, Frank Lloyd Wright, Erno Goldfinger, and others (who would be discussed in Eckbo's text.)[3]

Eckbo and Royston offered a new way of looking at the environment, relating studies of color, form, space, massing, and movement to the social and psychological issues of community building. Royston built a "model box," a large, shallow drum covered by an opaque dome, and through its peripheral viewing holes, students studied and photographed their models at eye level—an exercise that anticipated by decades Berkeley's more complex Environmental Simulation Laboratory.[4] By this and other means, Royston influenced a number of outstanding designers. Some became his partners and associates, including Asa Hanamoto, Francis Dean, David Mayes, Robert Cornwall, Eldon Beck, and Harold Kobayashi; and some moved on, including Donald Carter, Satoru Nishita, Richard Vignolo, Jean Walton, Robert Reich, Jon Enerson, Howard Troller, S. William Bridgers, Dirk Jongejan, and Terry Gerrard. Perhaps Eckbo's best-known student was Frank Gehry, an architect whose inventiveness and unconventionality remind one of Eckbo's own unusual story.

Born in Cooperstown, New York, in 1910, Eckbo first experienced the American dream in reverse. His well-born parents, an American mother who had attended Vassar College and a Norwegian father too gentle for the business world, became incompatible—and poor. Obtaining a divorce in Reno, Nevada, Eckbo's mother took four-year-old Garrett to California, found a place to live in Alameda, on the eastern shore of San Francisco Bay, and took on menial jobs to support the family, which eventually included her mother.[5]

Eckbo's memories of impatient stepfathers, a kindly teacher who brought him to a farm on weekends, poling a homemade raft in the mud flats of Alameda, camping on rain-soaked Mt. Tamalpais as a Boy

Scout, and copying Viking ships and animals in a school library do not add up to inspiration toward a career in landscape architecture. Unmotivated in school yet identified as a gifted child by a professor of education at Stanford University, Eckbo now believes he would have drifted without any particular direction in life had he not visited his prosperous uncle, an attorney in Oslo, and his extended family, who welcomed him with unfamiliar warmth.

Six months among his spirited Norwegian relations in 1929 changed Eckbo's life. Returning to America just after the stock market crash, he found odd jobs, studied at Marin Junior College, and graduated from the University of California, Berkeley, in 1935. After spending a year designing about a hundred gardens at Armstrong Nurseries, in Southern California, he won a scholarship to Harvard, where he received the M.L.A. degree in 1938. In the worst years of the depression, then, Eckbo had an unwonted sense of being part of society. Yet as he acquired skills and self-confidence, supporting himself, his mother, his wife, Arline and, in time, two daughters, Eckbo remained critical of self and society and repelled by commercialism.

At Berkeley, where he met his future partner and brother-in-law, Edward Williams, Eckbo absorbed a beaux arts approach to landscape design, adapted to depression-era conditions in California. Thomas Church dropped in on occasion, and Church's yound friend, H. L. Vaughan, from Ohio State University, was Eckbo's design instructor: open-minded, somewhat aloof, yet encouraging. What Eckbo learned in their midst can be summed up in two artifacts, both of 1934: his prize-winning project, "An Estate in the Manner of Louis XIV," elegantly rendered in the proper sepia tones and subtly asymmetrical at the core of the scheme, and his hefty volume of typewritten notes, "A History of

Landscape Design," which looks at gardens in a broad social, economic, and political context and mentions contemporary needs for low maintenance and functional space.[6]

While a student at Berkeley, Eckbo visited Filoli and a half-dozen other stately houses and gardens in the Bay Area, each of them freely adapted from Western European garden traditions, and he assumed that there were no rules in design. But at Harvard he ran up against other assumptions. Coming from summer-dry California, where garden design normally entailed irrigating, terracing, and a good deal of construction as well as planting, Eckbo was shocked to learn that gardens of a frankly man-made character (formal gardens) were somehow inferior to informal gardens—that is, imitations of someone's ideal of nature! And so, scribbled in the margins of his Harvard textbook, Hubbard and Kimball's *Introduction to the Study of Landscape Design* (1917), is Eckbo's challenge, "Why is nature more perfect than man?"[7]

Rejecting dichotomies and clichés, Eckbo further scribbled, "Why must we be naturalistic *or* formal? What about all the gradations in between? . . . Pictures, pictures pictures. What about environment? How about three-dimensional space experience? . . . The fallacious nature vs. man concept. . . . Isn't it time to put man and nature back together again? . . . No wonder they insist man's work is unnatural, when they refuse to allow it to be anything else."

James Rose and Dan Kiley, Eckbo's fellow students at Harvard, shared his questioning, iconoclastic attitudes in the landscape design studios. For inspiration they turned to the latest journals of architecture and books on modern art, the cubist paintings of Picasso and Georges Braque, the constructivist sculpture of Moholy-Nagy, as well as older artifacts—the pyramids, Stonehenge, and the anonymous work of farmers and craftsmen.

In 1937 Walter Gropius arrived at Harvard, bringing Bauhaus views of society and art that gave Eckbo, Rose, and Kiley more incentive to experiment. Christopher Tunnard, the Canadian-born garden designer and planner, had not yet arrived at Harvard, but his articles in *Architectural Review* in 1937 and 1938, later published as *Gardens in the Modern Landscape* (1938), had a strong influence on the three students.[8] Another voice, less optimistic and more sharply critical than Tunnard's, was that of Elbert Peets, the Harvard-trained landscape architect-planner who denounced the complacency of his profession in "The Landscape Priesthood" (1927).[9] Here Eckbo found not only a wry assessment of Harvard's reverence for the Olmstedian pastoral landscape but also an appreciation of folk art and the indigenous, anonymous landscape. This respect for the vernacular would reappear in Eckbo's later writings. In isolated regions of America, in Italy, and especially in Japan, he would appreciate (without nostalgia) the coherence of the built environment, dependent on vernacular forms and spaces.[10]

In 1937 *Pencil Points* published Eckbo's first manifesto: a call for gardens expressive of the new technological age, accompanied by designs for a block of urban backyard gardens.[11] Given the typical constraints—row houses on lots 25 feet by 125 feet, a minimum of space and time, the accelerated pace and stresses of modern life in the city—Eckbo personalized each garden with dazzling formal invention. The ramps, spiral staircases, and trees growing through holes in a roof recall Le Corbusier's designs of the 1920s as well as Church's prize-winning scheme for a 25-foot city garden, exhibited in San Francisco earlier in 1937 and published in the April issue of *Landscape Architecture*.

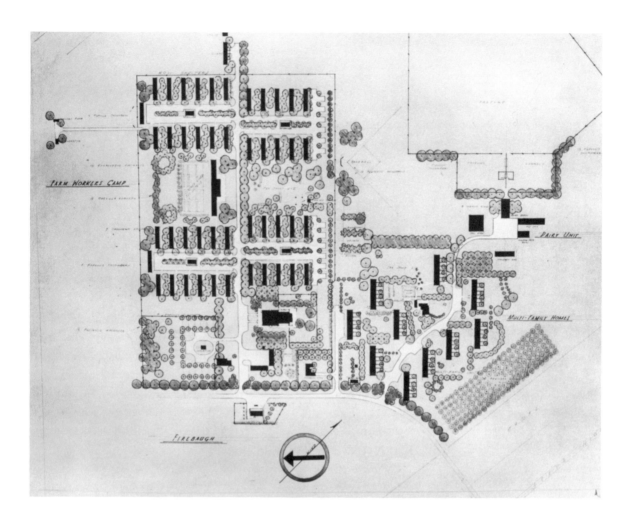

59. Farm Security Administration, multifamily housing, Firebaugh, California, plan, 1939. Garrett Eckbo, Landscape Architect. Burton Cairns, District Architect. Vernon De Mars, Architect. Eckbo believed that modern form and social purpose could be integrated in the design process. In his view, the real product would then be the people—not the space or the setting.

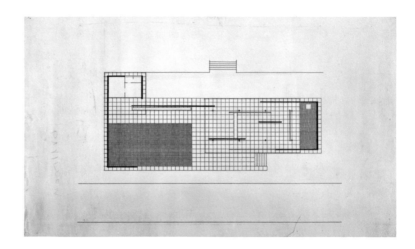

60. Ludwig Mies van der Rohe, plan, Barcelona Pavilion, 1929. Long after adapting this plan for the community center in his thesis project at Harvard, in 1938, Eckbo continued to explore the plan's spatial implications for landscape design.

Eckbo does not recall having been aware of Church's scheme at the time; in any event, the differences between his gardens and those of Church are significant. Temperamentally at home in calm, balanced, beautifully proportioned spaces, Church had to stretch to create a dynamic, energized place. In contrast, Eckbo, who was uneasy in an atmosphere of too much balance, as if smugness and complacency lurked in every shadow, had to reach beyond his own rich inventiveness to achieve a degree of calm.

In January 1939, Eckbo worked two weeks in Church's office—long enough for both to recognize their differences as designers. Moving on to the Farm Security Administration (FSA), Eckbo worked with architects Vernon de Mars, Burton Cairns, and others, designing camps and housing for migrant farmworkers in the western states. Face-to-face contact with the Dust Bowl refugees from Oklahoma, Arkansas, and other states radicalized Eckbo; he was shocked that such destitution was allowed to exist in America. In his spare time, he began to lecture on housing and planning at the California Labor School in San Francisco.

The functional elements of Eckbo's FSA site plans—row housing, detached houses, playing fields, drought-resistant trees and shrubs—are all laid out in straight lines and curves, which, on paper, recall constructivist sculpture and Kandinsky's works of the 1920s (figure 59). The immediate inspiration for these spatial relations was the architectural

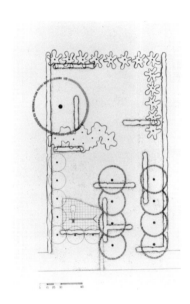

61. Farm Security Administration, plan of a park near Gridley, California, 1939. Garrett Eckbo, Landscape Architect. Influenced by the Barcelona Pavilion, this park was more elegantly architectural, more constructivist, and less surreal.

space of Ludwig Mies van der Rohe, whose Barcelona pavilion Eckbo had adapted for his M.L.A. thesis project the year before (figure 60).[12] A cerebral, Miesian calm, however, was not so important to those bleak, windswept FSA sites as a Miesian flow of space—to suggest the freedom and relaxation that Eckbo and his colleagues hoped to communicate (figure 61). Looking back on this work for the FSA, Eckbo now views it as his most satisfying collaboration with architects. Egos suspended, working together with limited resources, the designers aimed to provide migrant and resident laborers a decent, cheerful, livable environment.[13]

Meanwhile, a war was going on in Europe, and American priorities shifted. The FSA was phased out, and other agencies to erect temporary defense workers' housing were created. Kept out of the armed services by a leg weakened in an auto accident, Eckbo worked in a shipyard as well as on temporary housing. That housing has since been demolished, but one war housing project, begun initially as public housing and slum clearance, remains in remarkably good shape: Valencia Gardens, in the Mission District of San Francisco (1939–1943). William Wurster and the U.S. Housing Authority were the architects; Church, the landscape architect; Beniamino Bufano, the sculptor; and young Robert Royston, Church's job captain.[14]

Royston, who had worked for Church since his junior year in college (1938–1939), was intrigued by the Valencia Gardens project. Despite the low budget, cramped rooms, and lack of privacy, there is a feeling of permanence and dignity in the 246-unit project. Deeply overhanging roofs, entrance balconies, and (originally) expanses of contrasting color helped to scale down the project. The two U-shaped service courts are separate from the three U-shaped garden courts. In each garden court, brick retaining wall/seats (a hallmark of Church's private gardens) protect the trees and islands of raised lawns from the foot traffic that spills onto the paving of diagonally gridded exposed agregate. And Bufano's abstract sculptures of rotund, crouching animals on pedestals add a touch of humor to the space.

Working with Church on some twenty temporary war housing projects and on Parkmerced, a larger, permanent project of towers and low-rise housing in San Francisco, Royston saw how Church made transitions from private spaces to common grounds. He appreciated that relatively small scale of work and enjoyed working for Church—"a very free spirit," he recalls. Then came war in the Pacific. Royston enlisted in the navy, rose to first lieutenant on a ship, saw action in the Aleutians, Saipan, Okinawa, and elsewhere, and made sketches and models of gardens in his spare time. "I have always loved life," Royston sighs. "That's what made it so hard to experience World War II."[15]

Royston was born in San Francisco in 1918. His parents had come from England to California with a love of gardening and rural life, which they continued to nurture in rural Bay Area counties—Marin for a few years, then Santa Clara County, south of Morgan Hill, where the family lived on a ranch and maintained a walnut orchard. Their genial, well-rounded son Robert graduated from San Jose High School and went on to the University of California, at Berkeley. There, John Gregg, chairman of the landscape architecture department, welcomed this young man who loved music, theater, drawing, and nature. A basketball player and an actor as well, Royston became one of Berkeley's most promising students of landscape architecture.

Both Church and Eckbo had hoped to have Royston join them after the war. Royston accepted Eckbo's offer, in part because Eckbo had written him letters overseas, in part because Royston shared Eckbo's interest in theories of art, the avant-garde, and the broader issues of planning and design.[16] In 1947, for instance, Royston assessed the needs of the profession, including a coordinated federal, state, and local program of public information about planning; stronger links with architecture and engineering; analysis of planning legislation; continuing education for practitioners; the exposure of students to practitioners and fine built work; and an adequate text to reveal the broader possibilities of planning and design.[17] In 1950, the last of these goals was realized in Eckbo's first book, which benefited from the financial support and shared intellectual inquiries of all three partners.

Landscape for Living (1950) was to the small body of landscape architectural theory what Church's Donnell garden was to garden design—an expression of the age, a ground-breaking effort, embodying a set of standards by which current and succeeding work (and thought) would be judged for years. Although much of the built work in this book was done by a single firm, Eckbo, Royston, and Williams, the ideas were far-ranging and the graphic techniques expressive of contemporary West Coast landscape design: uninhibited, constructivist, jazzy. Students might be puzzled by the seeming lack of connection between the juxtaposed quotations—from Le Corbusier and Lewis Mumford to Carl Sandburg and Luther Burbank—but the visual material was clearly modern, leaving the world of Hubbard and Kimball far behind.

Informed by an egalitarian, hopeful vision of modern life, Landscape for Living was an attempt to bring all the social, aesthetic, theoretical, and practical aspects of landscape architecture together in a grand synthesis. Perhaps its closest model was Le Corbusier's *Vers une architecture* (1923), which was equally insistent that design reflect the spirit and tempo of the age. Unlike Le Corbusier and many of the other European modernists, however, Eckbo placed less faith in technology than in science. Modern technology had expanded communications, raised living standards, and influenced the designed objects and spaces of everyday life. But technology explained only the pieces, science, the *whole;* technology yielded useful products, science, the means of understanding. By 1950, the scientific method had profoundly informed both aesthetics and sociology. Moreover, science was akin to the sort of art Eckbo most admired. "The scientific method," he noted, "takes nothing for granted, accepts no precedents without examination, and recognizes a dynamic world in which nothing is permanent but change itself."[18]

Eckbo expected great social benefits from science and art, but he noted that landscapes are also shaped by people who control or manipulate political and economic forces. He criticized the entire system of modern urban development, with its parcels, subdivisions, and "arbitrary pigeonholes" all designed in isolation. What should have been a continuum of planning and design was so fragmented that both parts of the creative process became sterilized. Society was a "raiding preserve for those most enterprising"; government was "the police power which prevents those raids from going to extremes." To design within this system, Eckbo offered two broad strategies. First, reinforce the basic cooperative instincts of people, without which society could not exist. Second, let the planner and designer recognize the true product of their efforts—not "magnificent space and beautiful enclosure, but the people who expand and grow and develop within it."[19]

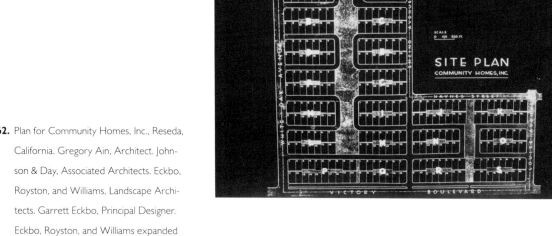

62. Plan for Community Homes, Inc., Reseda, California. Gregory Ain, Architect. Johnson & Day, Associated Architects. Eckbo, Royston, and Williams, Landscape Architects. Garrett Eckbo, Principal Designer. Eckbo, Royston, and Williams expanded their practice beyond backyards to site planning for neighborhoods and for the parks, schools, and shopping centers that complemented the houses.

These were not the musings of a sage but reflections of a busy landscape architect who spent his evenings and weekends at the typewriter, mulling over ideals, theories, and realities. In the Bay Area during the early 1940s, Eckbo had spent countless evenings discussing art, politics, and society with Telesis, a group of architects, landscape architects, planners, and graphic designers, including Vernon De Mars, Francis McCarthy, T. J. Kent, John Funk, Francis Violich, Edward Williams, Corwin Mocine, and Walter Landor. These idealistic young professionals, supported in principle by Church, Wurster, and other elders, were committed to informing the public about planning, design, and development—initially in the Bay Area and later in the Los Angeles region as well. Beginning in 1940, the Telesis group mounted a series of exhibitions on planning and design at the San Francisco Museum of Art. After the war, Telesis ideals were absorbed in the actual projects of members, including Eckbo, Royston, and Williams's work on the 260-acre Ladera planned community, with architects John Funk and Joseph Allen Stein; and the firm's Southern California planned neighborhoods, with architects Gregory Ain, Whitney Smith, A. Quincy Jones, and others (figure 62).[20]

In 1946, Eckbo opened a second office of the firm in Los Angeles and moved there, drawn to the south for its more benign climate, larger scale of landscape, and the greater opportunities offered by a less developed region. Personally liberating, that move also brought Eckbo into a cultural environment of greater extremes—more provincial and unpolished but also more cosmopolitan and progressive. Since the 1920s and 1930s, leading artists and intellectuals from elsewhere in America and abroad had settled in Los Angeles, some drawn by the movie industry, some escaping from an imminent war in Europe. By the late 1940s, Los Angeles had become a center of cultural ferment far removed from entrenched institutions. Rudolph Schindler, Richard Neutra, Thomas Mann, Arnold Schoenberg, Josef von Sternberg, Igor Stravinsky, Henry Miller, and Man Ray, among others, were living and mingling there.

The cultural ferment of Los Angeles was stimulated by John Entenza's superb magazine, *Arts and Architecture,* a forum for discussing modern art, including music, drama, and landscape design. Eckbo and Richard Haag each designed a garden for Entenza's series of "Case Study Houses," featuring prototypes by Neutra, Charles Eames, Eero Saarinen, Ralph Rapson, Wurster and Bernardi, Rodney Walker, Don Knorr, and others. And as Esther McCoy recalled, "What was exciting at the time about the landscaping was that it looked designed."[21] The colors and textures of plants were boldly juxtaposed. Building materials such as metal, concrete, wood, and plastic were used as elements of a common artistic language. And space, scale, structure, transparency, and tenuous balance were common concerns, whatever the art form.

Eckbo's move to Southern California expanded the firm's opportunities (and also gave each partner more breathing space) while the partnership was held together by quarterly meetings and shared interests. As Williams noted, "Although we work as individuals, there is a complete exchange of ideas."[22]

Born in Pittsburgh in 1914, Williams grew up in East Liberty, then one of Pittsburgh's middle-class urban-suburban neighborhoods, where substantial townhouses of brick and stone mingled with ample single-family Victorian houses on small lots. Both in the neighborhood (the reputation of which has since faded) and within the family circle, standards of unassertive, gentlemanly behavior were upheld. When a promotion for Williams's father entailed a transfer to the San Francisco Bay Area, the family moved to a comparable neighborhood in North Berkeley. By then, Williams's mother had died many years earlier, and his father had remarried.[23]

After graduating from the University of California, Berkeley, in 1935, Williams worked for landscape architects E. L. Kiler, in Palo Alto, and, later, for Butler Sturtevant, in San Francisco—men whose practices included private gardens, subdivisions, and campus planning and design.[24] On his own, Williams served as consultant to the San Mateo County Planning Commission on park design and public works. Finally, in 1940, he joined Eckbo in a partnership that survived the war, when Williams became head of mechanical engineering in a steel company. A skillful designer, Williams had placed second in the national competition that sent Eckbo to Harvard. But as their firm grew, Williams assumed more responsibilities in management and planning. For his partners and younger associates, he remained a stabilizing influence—a rock of integrity in a fluid, changing world.[25]

Although each partner would naturally recognize his own tendencies in design, the early gardens were generally viewed as the work of the firm, somewhat in the manner of Church or in the Bay Area style.[26] By 1950, however, the perceptive visitor (or reader) would recognize in these gardens a constructivist complexity in both the ground plane and

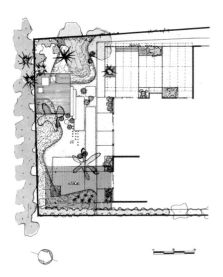

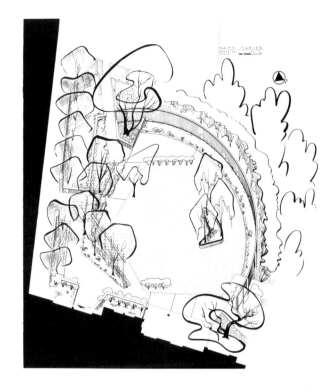

63. Muller Garden, plan. Eckbo, Royston, and Williams, Landscape Architects. Robert Royston, Principal Designer. This dynamic plan, indicating diagonal movement through space, also suggests rich textures and shadow patterns.

64. Muller Garden. The spacious garden, luxuriant in planting, is slightly Oriental in character.

65. Naify Garden, Woodside, California, axonometric plan. Eckbo, Royston, and Williams, Landscape Architects. Robert Royston, Principal Designer. Drawing by Robert Royston. Here the landscape architects explore the spatial dynamic in an original way. The common elements of the garden are placed in a purposefully exuberant composition.

the juxtaposition of materials (figures 63 and 64). Fences, arbors, sunscreens, and walls became bold and witty—clearly objects to be seen (figure 65). Refinement began to appear not in the proportions of a space (as in Church's gardens) but in lighter, finer materials, such as aluminum and steel. In the early 1960s, for instance, experimenting at the request of the Alcoa Company, Eckbo used expanded sheets of aluminum, in vertical and horizontal planes supported by wooden frames, to filter the sun and protect the privacy of his own south-facing patios (figure 66).

Other garden elements were adapted from works of art. Piet Mondrian's paintings of the 1920s and 1930s, with their delicate balance of line, form, and color, are recalled in the A. B. Chinn garden, in San Francisco, of the early 1950s.[27] In other gardens, the paintings and sculptures of Kandinsky, Naum Gabo, Moholy-Nagy, and Aalto are likely formal sources for transparent and semitransparent fences and screens arrayed in overlapping layers and planes (figure 67). Church's own innovative gardens, influenced by spatial and formal qualities in Aalto's architecture and the paintings of Miró and Arp, provided

66. Alcoa Garden at the Eckbo residence, Laurel Canyon, Hollywood Hills, Los Angeles, California, ca. 1960. Garrett Eckbo, Landscape Architect. Engaged by the Alcoa Company to experiment with its products in the garden, Eckbo used new materials—aluminum and steel—not only for their durability but also for their expressive qualities.

67. Laszlo Moholy-Nagy, *Construction,* 1923. Teaching at the Bauhaus, in Weimar and then in Dessau, Moholy-Nagy freely experimented with geometric forms, spatial relationships, and materials, in both two and three dimensions. Aware of these earlier efforts, Eckbo, Royston, and Williams aspired to a similar refinement and elegance in planar detail, going well beyond previous carpentry construction.

sources of inspiration, too; but over time the gardens of Eckbo, Royston, and Williams represented a departure from Church's work. The simple directives and rhythms of carpentry and humble masonry gave way to more sophisticated formal modulations. Occasionally, as in Church's work, a garden would be oriented around an ancient, indigenous tree, but planting design was typically more adventurous. Herbaceous borders and raised beds for vegetables gave way to exotic trees, such as *Eucalyptus citriodora* or a row of *Jacaranda mimosifolia*. Traditional gardening and references to agriculture were eliminated, while sculpture and artful, self-conscious detailing became more prominent.

The San Francisco arts community had fostered connections between art and design at least since the Panama-Pacific Exposition of 1915, and earlier, craftsmen, artists and gardeners had informally gathered around Bernard Maybeck and Charles Keeler at the Hillside Club in Berkeley.[28] In 1929, while architect Arthur Brown, Jr., presided over the San Francisco Art Association, a "Federation for Art" was proposed to strengthen the alliance of artists and designers in that city.[29] Later Grace McCann Morley, director of the San Francisco Museum of (Modern) Art, strongly supported the museum's three exhibitions of modern landscape design, in 1937, 1948, and 1958. In that museum, in 1949, Eckbo, Royston, and Williams set up an exhibition that featured pottery by Edith Heath and Eunice and Antonio Prieto, abstract sculpture by Stephen Novak, and redwood patio furniture and a large, curving, redwood-and-canvas wind screen, all by Eckbo, Royston, and Williams (figure 68).[30]

Two years later, in 1951, an A-frame weekend cabin by architects John Carden Campbell and Worley K. Wong occupied the center of the San

68. Sunbreak, or wind-screen, among other patio furnishings, on exhibition at the San Francisco Museum of Art, 1949. Eckbo, Royston, and Williams, Designers. Robert Royston, Principal Designer. Florence Alston Swift, Sculptor (for decorative panels of concrete and black iron, within vertical Redwood screen/fence). Eckbo, Royston, and Williams participated in housing and planning expositions, art exhibitions, and fairs, using cultural and political channels for their design ideas.

Francisco Art Commission's fifth annual festival at the Palace of Fine Arts, along the marina. Much publicized locally, this cabin was set in a landscape constructed by Eckbo, Royston, and Williams and complemented by Tom Hall's sculpture, Mary Lindheim's ceramics, and Louise Bakewell's interior decoration. At this festival, among some 3,000 other exhibits in painting, sculpture, photography, weaving, and ceramics, was architect Mario Ciampi's project for San Francisco's Corpus Christi Church, with landscape design by Lawrence Halprin and sculpture by Elio Benvenuto and Ernest Mundt.[31]

If these and other events represented truly collaborative efforts among like-minded artists and designers, when did the work of these California landscape architects become invisible to the art world? In later work of a larger scale, friendly, impromptu collaboration might have been difficult. Certainly the pace, the complexity, and the risks of landscape architectural practice intensified. But a fundamental cause may lie deeper, among the factors that led to the demise in 1967 of Entenza's *Arts and Architecture.* Call it functionalism, commercialism, acquisitiveness, or just plain materialism: clearly something in American culture, heightened in the California of Lotus Land myth, began to repel artists and designers of the late 1950s and 1960s. Forsaking the museums, some went to the desert, some to inner-city streets, some to environmentalism; many would have nothing to do with the jewellike objet d'art.

In the worlds of both art and science, old unities were giving way under pressures of scale and speed. As physicist J. Robert Oppenheimer noted in 1954, contemporary scientists and artists faced a similar predicament. "One thing that is new," he said, "is the prevalence of newness, the changing scale and scope of change itself, so that the world alters as we walk in it, so that the years of a man's life measure not some small growth or rearrangement of what he learned in childhood, but a great upheaval."[32] Anticipating some of these changes, the Bauhaus teachers had placed their faith in the unity of art and craft and in the replacement of handicraft by artful machine production—in the service of humanity. Then, on the heels of a worldwide depression, machine production was put in the service of war. For a few years after the war, it may have seemed that beauty and function could be reunited. Machine production, however, was clearly in the service of private profits above all else. Inevitably, the Bauhaus ideals of unity and collaboration faded. Appalled by preoccupations with function, marketability, and social and political conformity, some artists looked elsewhere for spiritual content. And appalled by artists' preoccupation with self-expression, some designers gave up any pretensions to "art."

For landscape architects, however, artistic aims could survive the gentle rise in scale from gardens to neighborhood parks. In the 1950s, before the appearance of M. Paul Friedberg's urban playgrounds and, later, standardized play equipment, Royston experimented with biomorphic forms and constructivist play sculptures in tot lots for neighborhood

69. Standard Oil Rod and Gun Club, Point Richmond, California, ca. 1955. Eckbo, Royston, and Williams, Landscape Architects. Robert Royston, Principal Designer. Fascinated by the child's world, Robert Royston explored the physical and imaginative dimensions of children's play, along with the artifacts that could stimulate a child.

parks, such as Krusi Park in Alameda, California; for the Standard Oil Rod and Gun Club, in Richmond, California; and for Mitchell Park, in Palo Alto (figures 69, 70, and 71). His slides, chutes, and sandboxes, faintly evocative of Mondrian, Arp, and Miró, make adults smile while children go about the serious business of play—on, around, and inside the structures. As a child living on a ranch, Royston had built his own imaginary mountains, cities, roads, and airports. And he still loves the freedom of designing a child's world. "You become one with the space and the child for a while," he says.[33]

By 1960, the design of neighborhood parks and gardens was no longer the mainstay of the leading landscape architectural firms in California. Between 1960 and 1965, the population of California doubled,[34] bringing demands for whole new communities, schools, college campuses, civic centers, and mixed-use projects with parking garages and roof gardens, such as the Kaiser Center roof garden in Oakland, by Osmundson and Staley (1961). As the scale of projects increased, landscape architectural firms became more involved in site planning, resource planning, urban systems analysis, and environmental studies of whole regions—far surpassing the scale of neighborhood and community design pioneered by Royston's and Eckbo's teaching and practice of the late 1940s. By 1965, the "Urban Metropolitan Open Space Study" for the State of California, prepared by Eckbo, Dean, Austin & Williams, would indicate the scale of projects to come.[35]

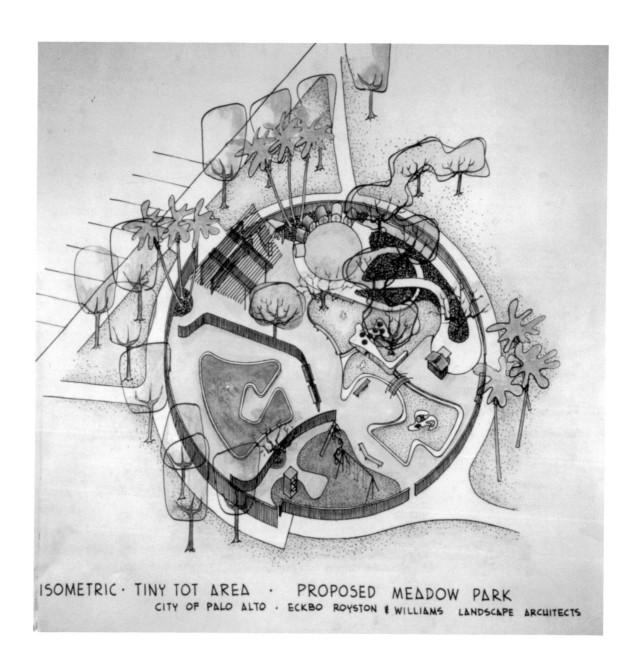

ISOMETRIC · TINY TOT AREA · PROPOSED MEADOW PARK
CITY OF PALO ALTO · ECKBO ROYSTON & WILLIAMS LANDSCAPE ARCHITECTS

70. Mitchell Park, child's playground, Palo Alto, California, ca. 1957: Axonometric Plan. Eckbo, Royston, and Williams, Landscape Architects. Robert Royston, Principal Designer. Drawing by Robert Royston. Using constructivist forms, Eckbo, Royston, and Williams developed a new formal expression of their social commitment that went beyond merely functional satisfaction. They were dedicated to change, reform, and the new—in form, purpose, expression, materials, and institutions.

71. Mitchell Park. Royston developed many original pieces of play equipment, such as this climbing construction, which allows a child to climb without fear of falling.

Pressures for large-scale land development in California have continued to be severe, with some recessionary pauses, ever since. Perhaps no single individual or profession could have given visual coherence and structure to vast, rapid development determined mainly by economic and technological forces that were themselves in flux, never quite predictable, ever in search of the freedoms for which California (and America) have been celebrated.[36] Facing these vaguely understood forces, nevertheless, Eckbo, Royston, and Williams, along with their colleagues and students, yearned for some sort of visual, spatial coherence in the larger environment. Having endured depression and a world war, they remained idealistic and optimistic, even as ruptures and expansions in their office practices required increasing attention to management and finance. Today, their faith in spatial design, artistic expression, democratic processes, and basic human decency appears heroic. As if summing up the impact of all their efforts since World War II, Eckbo's recent words salute the honorable, ongoing struggle: "Landscape architecture is potentially the ultimate art, because the landscape, social as well as physical, is the home, and the source of inspiration, for all other arts. When human society achieves comparable coherence and harmony the landscape as art may become reality. . . . In the meantime those of us who have some inspiration and aspiration do what we can with the jobs that come to us."[37]

Chapter 5

**From Backyard
to Center City**

A sequel to Lewis Mumford's *The Culture of Cities* (1938) appeared more than twenty years later, his equally awesome *The City in History* (1961). By then, a second world war had shown the magnitude of power that man could wield against his fellow man and the environment. "The end of our whole megalopolitan civilization is all-too-visibly in sight," Mumford noted, and if nuclear holocaust was not to wipe out urban civilization entirely, he warned, other forces at work would effect that end through slower means.[1] The dream of a truly life-enhancing regional city had been dimmed by fifteen years of postwar expansion without the planned decentralization that Mumford considered essential.[2] By then, the Regional Planning Association of America had long since disbanded, and some members, including Henry Wright, had died. Still, Mumford had cause for hope. Clarence Stein's book, *Toward New Towns for America* (1951), his recent work on the planning of Kitimat, in British Columbia, and his Gold Medal from the AIA (awarded in 1956) had kept the vision of regional planning alive and in the media. Moreover, in the spatial and technological linkages within the metropolis, Mumford saw the potential for an Invisible City of ever-expanding communication, interaction, and self-realization.

The landscape architect whose urban work of the 1960s and 1970s is our focus here, Lawrence Halprin, followed his own bent, not necessarily Mumford's (figure 72). But for the coincidence of having some friends in common, notably Catherine Bauer and William Wurster, Mumford and Halprin could be viewed as inhabiting quite separate worlds—the New York–born sage, dwelling in a farmhouse in upstate New York, writing and theorizing about the big issues of his time; and the New York–born designer and man of action, living in Northern California, taking part in the creation of urban environments around

72. Portrait of Lawrence Halprin. Reared in New York City, trained in upstate New York, Wisconsin, and Cambridge, Massachusetts, Halprin has spent most of his adult life in San Francisco, on the North Coast, and in the mountains of his adopted home state, California.

the country and abroad and, in so doing, redefining the big issues of his time. Mumford was, and Halprin remains, a towering figure against whom others will inevitably be measured. A reason for bringing them together, briefly, is to consider the unexpected ways in which Halprin managed to bring into existence one of Mumford's ideals—if not "the city as a work of art," then the city as a place for people to realize their own creative potential.

Mumford saw the city as a great center of linkages, in spite of the inherent urban contradiction that he identified in 1961. This contradiction, he explained, springs from the dual origin of the city and the ambivalence of its goals. From roots in the village, the city had traditionally offered its residents some degree of security, stability, ecological balance, and quasi-democratic interaction. But the city owed its very existence and growth to concentrations of power—man's attempts to control other men and dominate the environment. "Release and enslavement, freedom and compulsion, have been present from the beginning in urban culture," Mumford noted.[3]

From these inherent tensions had come creative expression, Mumford realized, and concentration encouraged the assembly, the criticism, the distribution, and thus the ever-widening influence of cultural artifacts.

The museum, a quintessential urban institution, was the epitome of this cultural diffusion. But Mumford went beyond André Malraux's notion of a "museum without walls," the composite of visual and spatial information that was rapidly being diffused by photographic and electronic means.[4] Mumford viewed every historic city as a museum in itself, a rich concentration of human activity, association, and invention. In 1961, then, he was not disturbed by urban concentration per se but by its excesses and by the lack of a truly public-spirited direction to the process of concentration. Disdaining merely economic or political rationales, Mumford saw the modern city's raison d'être as the magnification of all the dimensions of life, including consciousness, action, participation, creation, and communion.

A few years later, in an urban design report prepared for Mayor John Lindsay and Housing and Development administrators, Halprin identified another key issue facing New York City and, by extension, other great metropolitan centers. "We do not seem to be able to structure the process of change," he noted in *New York, New York* (1968). "On the one hand we need citizen participation; on the other the magnitude of the physical needs of rebuilding are enormous."[5] Change is, of course, necessary for cities, as for any biological organism. But in continual change Halprin saw an opportunity that many landscape architects were not yet ready to welcome: the re-creation, perhaps even the transformation, of their own built work in the process of being lived in and used.

"All joy wants eternity," Nietzsche once wrote.[6] Art, too, traditionally yearns for the eternal—as fixed form, comprehensible for generations (if not millennia) to come. But as Halprin confronted problems of urban landscape design in cities and metropolitan areas, he began to focus on process rather than immutable product. One of his consultants on the New York study, George Rand, had observed, "Designed environments which are thought out, formalized, and complete are usually 'lifeless' and unapproachable because (a) they do not invite interaction and modification to suit immediate human needs; (b) they are unable to grow, develop and become extended through human use. . . . Oddly enough, many environments which 'work' well for people meet few, if any, aesthetic criteria ordinarily employed by designers."[7] For most designers this was a bitter pill to swallow, Halprin added.

In *New York, New York,* an analysis of six completed or ongoing projects of the metropolis, with recommendations for renewal or redevelopment, Halprin came to a number of conclusions. Some he found surprising; others clearly mirrored his own previous assumptions: People live in New York largely because they want to. Though far from satisfied with their environment, New Yorkers generally prefer to deal with the city and improve it rather than move away. They want New York to remain urban, lively, complex, diverse, exciting. They do not want solitude, isolation, simplicity, or similarity. They fear alienation and rejection. They want to be involved in the process of change. "They" include people of different economic, ethnic, and racial backgrounds, including the black communities of Harlem, Bedford-Stuyvesant, and elsewhere. For African Americans, whose complex needs lay beyond the scope of his study, Halprin listed a few fundamental requirements: open occupancy, opportunities for jobs and economic advancement, and increased ability to own property. For all New Yorkers, he identified common needs: self-determination and complete participation in the planning process.[8]

73. "Bentley Wood," Halland, Sussex, Chermayeff residence, 1937–1938. Serge Chermayeff, Architect. Christopher Tunnard, Landscape Architect. Tunnard's book, *Gardens in the Modern Landscape* (1938), with its designs for such gardens as "Bentley Wood" and its unconventional views on landscape architecture, profoundly influenced the young Halprin.

In 1968 Halprin was looking at that metropolis as a self-confessed renegade New Yorker, with roots in Manhattan's Lower East Side because his grandfathers—Russian Jewish immigrants—had lived there. Three decades' absence from New York had given him a perspective on the city's vast changes and opportunities. With a concentration of the best and worst qualities of the United States, New York remained, he believed, the nation's center and most exciting city. San Francisco, on the other hand, was "the most beautiful of American cities," his port of embarkation during World War II and his place of work thereafter, like that of countless other postwar immigrants to the West Coast.

Halprin was born in the Bronx, New York, in 1916. His father was president of Landseas, a scientific instruments export firm. His mother was national president of Hadassah, the women's Zionist organization, as well as chairperson of the American branch of the Jewish Agency for Palestine. Growing up in Brooklyn, Larry played competitive sports—baseball, basketball, football, and tennis—and went to summer camp on Mount Greylock in the Berkshires, in western Massachusetts. Then three years on a kibbutz near Haifa, Israel (1933–1935), intervened between high school and college, enabling him to live and work in an intensely cooperative, mutually supportive environment. In 1939 he received a B.S. degree in plant sciences from Cornell University and went on to the University of Wisconsin at Madison, where he received an M.S. degree in horticulture, in 1941. There he met Anna Schuman, whom he married in 1940.

It was Anna who, indirectly, led Halprin into the field of landscape architecture. She had suggested they visit Taliesin East, Frank Lloyd Wright's home in rural Wisconsin, and after they had walked through the house and grounds, Halprin left thinking, "That's what I want to be." Afterward, looking up "Architecture" in the university library, he found a cross-reference: "See Landscape Architecture." Under that heading was listed Tunnard's *Gardens in the Modern Landscape* (1938).[9] The book was a revelation—"like a bolt of lightning," Halprin recalls. In it he found a whole world of interests, brilliantly interrelated: the design of gardens, communities, and the larger landscape, art, science, new forms, new materials, new methods, and new concepts of human settlement.[10]

Calling for simplicity and the integration of aesthetic, functional, and social purposes in land planning at any scale, Tunnard was sympathetic to many of the ideals of Le Corbusier, Walter Gropius and other European modernists. By 1938, in England, he had collaborated with architects Serge Chermayeff and Raymond McGrath on the design of a few modern (International Style) houses and gardens, photographs and sketches of which he included in *Gardens in the Modern Landscape* (figure 73). What distinguished Tunnard from his modernist colleagues, however, was a pragmatic, unsentimental interest in historic gardens and landscapes. He appreciated the qualities of order, unified composition, and artistic expression in great gardens of any era and culture. He also believed in the sort of progress—artistic, scientific, technological, and social—that was based on an understanding of both past achievement and present opportunities. Even centuries-old historic landscapes could be preserved nearly intact *and* intensely developed, Tunnard believed. For Halprin, such views were enlightening, and he came away from his first reading of Tunnard with a wealth of new ideas, among the most enduring of which would be these: A garden is a work of art, and it remains a vision for guidance as one tries to extend the garden's benefits of rest, recreation,and aesthetic pleasure to a wider public, in the larger landscape.

Determined to learn more from Tunnard, firsthand, Halprin sought him out at Harvard's Graduate School of Design. There, aided by a scholarship, Halprin studied architecture and landscape architecture from 1942 to 1943. Tunnard, Gropius, Moholy-Nagy and Marcel Breuer were his influential teachers. William Wurster and his wife, Catherine Bauer, became close friends of Larry and Anna. And, with Tunnard, Halprin helped to produce an issue of *Task* magazine, an activist East Coast journal of environmental planning, with goals comparable to those of Telesis on the West Coast. Over the years, *Task* contained writings by some of Halprin's classmates (who included Philip Johnson, I. M. Pei, Edward L. Barnes, and Paul Rudolph), reports from Eckbo, and a letter from Dan Kiley, then serving on the western front.

In December 1943, a month before receiving a B.L.A. degree from Harvard, Halprin enlisted in the navy. He served as lieutenant junior grade on a destroyer and survived an attack by a kamikaze plane, which severed his ship, during the invasion of Okinawa. After completing his service in April 1945, he settled in the San Francisco Bay Area and began working for Wurster's friend, Thomas Church, while Anna eventually developed the San Francisco Dancers' Workshop. Then, in 1949, Halprin opened his own office, about a year after his collaboration with Church and George Rockrise at the Donnell Garden in Sonoma.

During the next decade, Halprin revealed an extraordinary ability to design elegant gardens in the same sort of urban backyards and live oak and pine-shaded hillsides that Church, too, had transformed. For finely scaled garden detail, Halprin was Church's equal, but his mood and spirit were different. A younger man, more outgoing, more recently arrived on the West Coast, Halprin was more like his own clients. And with a unique zest, he created gardens for living, dancing, growing, being (figures 74 and 75).

The early gardens spoke of the casual and social middle-class way of life developing in the postwar Bay Area. Highly photogenic, they drew attention for their modern style, utilizing both surreal and constructivist formal devices, as well as for the ingenious use of simple construction and exotic plant materials. Halprin extended Church's tradition of using simple construction, which often generated specific form. He frequently employed the same craftsmen Church used, but the detailing was more refined, and often more elegant, than that of Church. Planting was typically more artful and adventurous, too, as Halprin experimented with the German and Scandinavian techniques of contrasting flowering plants with decorative grasses, then adding the broad-leafed evergreens that thrive in the microclimates of the Bay Area.

Halprin and his associate, Jean Walton, also experimented with color, designing parts of a garden completely in grays or reds. Some parts of the garden might be given over to a particular use—a putting green, a

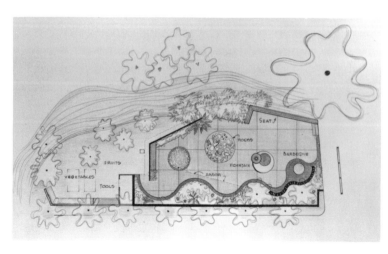

wildflower meadow, an outdoor dining kiosk, a wooden or steel-structured deck. At his own home in Marin county, Halprin made a wooden deck so that his wife, the dancer Anna Halprin, could practice, teach, and perform in a secluded garden. There perhaps for the first time he indicated his vision of the garden (or outdoor space) as a stage—though many of his entry gardens and drives have a ceremonial or processional air. In these early years Halprin's signature, or hallmark, evolved from characteristic forms, detailing, and uses, particularly the stage.

By the mid-1950s the scope of Halprin's practice had expanded. Old Orchard Shopping Center, in Oakbrook, Illinois, was his first design for the semipublic realm. Among structures by architects Loble, Schlossman, and Bennett was Halprin's series of gardens and plazas, drawn from European and Californian prototypes, and elegantly detailed with the help of Richard Vignolo, an early associate. Following Old Orchard's critical and commercial success was a long series of malls and urban revitalization projects, such as Ghirardelli Square, San Francisco (1962–1965), in which shopping and dining, among fountains, outdoor lighting, and planting, were combined with outdoor places for snacking, congregating, performing, and the spontaneous "happenings," that Halprin and his associates thrived on during the 1960s.

In the heady atmosphere of civil rights struggles, Vietnam war protests, urban renewal, and urban racial strife, landscape architecture students around the country dismissed garden design as irrelevant. Halprin, then teaching part-time at the University of California, Berkeley, could empathize with those students, yet he had already responded to their concerns in an eloquent published letter. "The garden in your own immediate neighborhood, preferably at your own doorstep, is the most significant garden in the world," he wrote. And he noted the transitions from one's own garden to a succession of spaces, from self to society and beyond—to "wilderness areas where we can be truly alone with ourselves and where nature can be sensed as the primeval source of life."[11]

Halprin has explored those two poles of human experience—the self and the primeval source of life—more extensively than most other landscape architects of our time. For nearly fifty years he has been applying insights gained from each pole to the areas in between, the public realm of urban parks, plazas, commercial and cultural centers, and other places of congregation, throughout America and abroad: in Italy, Curaçao, and especially in Israel, where he has devoted his creative energies—indeed his whole being—to the building and rebuilding of that much troubled land.[12] He has worked with other highly inventive and probing designers, including Don Carter, Satoru Nishita, Richard Vignolo, Jean Walton, Charles Moore, William Turnbull, Angela Danadjieva, and Sue Yung Li Ikeda. Having also learned from John Cage's music, Anna Halprin's choreography for the dance, Carl Jung's studies of symbols and archetypes, Paul Baum's gestalt psychology, Joseph L. Henderson's anthropological and psychological studies, and many other sources beyond his profession, Halprin has played a major role in shaping the modern landscape, adapting older cities and pristine wilderness areas alike to responsible human use.

Halprin's great range of public (or semipublic) built work, from Ghirardelli Square and Levi Strauss Plaza (ca. 1980), in San Francisco, to the Walter and Elise Haas Promenade, in Jerusalem (1984–1986), can be

76. Walter and Elise Haas Promenade, Jerusalem, 1984–1986. Lawrence Halprin, Landscape Architect. Halprin has worked off and on for years with the aging stone and stark planting of the Holy Land. This public walk is sited high on a hill, with a view out to the old city.

enjoyed and analyzed in isolation from his intentions, explorations, and processes (figure 76). But he believes that processes—the ways in which he energizes people, elicits their untapped creative resources, and gets them to participate in design—are an integral part of his contribution. His "Take Part" process, for instance, developed as a way of bringing citizens together in public workshops in order to participate in the design of their public open spaces—not merely to observe, advise, and consent but to participate with Halprin in shaping the final product. He told his associate, Jim Burns (who became a key player in the "Take Part" process), "The sharing, for me, is significant and is a form of art."[13] And Roger Osbaldeston has observed, "To Halprin, the whole of life is design process."[14]

Rooted in Halprin's own experience, these beliefs were nurtured in the troubled, defiant, and exuberant atmosphere of America in the late 1960s, a time of testing the whole system of values in Western civilization. All forms of authority were questioned. Individualism appeared less valid than collective effort. Goals and products seemed less significant than processes. And repressed emotions and instincts, which Freud had long since shown to be one of the prices paid for Western civilization, somehow had to be released, even if they would invariably uncover disturbing aspects of human nature (or what Halprin refers to as "the shadow side" of life, something not to be ignored in the design process). In the late 1960s, people became fascinated by nonrational and so-called primitive cultures, myth, ritual, symbolism, and the unfathomable—the unconscious mind. Ethnic and racial heritages were rediscovered, and many forms of dichotomy and discrimination, including qualitative judgment, were rejected, in favor of an exploratory, open-ended way of living and being.[15]

Halprin was deeply moved and excited by the new possibilities unfolding during those years. Along with his wife, he discovered a new role for the artist—not the solitary hero but the person who choreographs, or "scores" a wide-ranging set of activities for, and with, the community. Working with others, Halprin conceived and built landscapes that are not complete, he insisted, without the people who bring them to life. Thus, elaborate diagrams, experiments, workshops, and happenings are documented in his *RSVP Cycles* (1969), a book that epitomizes the late 1960s in America as well as, say, John Lennon's lyrics in "Let It Be." Not surprising, the counterculture that rejected conventional behavior, conservative politics, and an undeclared war in Southeast Asia found Halprin's unconventional design processes particularly appealing. And in

77. Lawrence Halprin & Associates, group photo, ca. 1973. While growing rapidly in size through the 1960s, Halprin's office remained an atelier in spirit.

a time and a place that welcomed gurus from the mysterious East, Halprin became a powerful mentor for designers (figure 77).

A high point of this period was Portland's extensive urban renewal, which included the Auditorium Forecourt and Lovejoy Plaza, perhaps Halprin's masterpiece. Lovejoy represents the most finely synthesized combination of Halprin's stage-for-life settings and the abstractions of his beloved, High Sierra wilderness (figure 78, plate 7). Like the Donnell Garden, it also represents a synthesis of talents, with important contributions by Satoru Nishita and the young architect Charles Moore (who, along with his office, Moore/Lyndon/Turnbull/Whitaker, designed the wonderful arbor).[16] In a series of expressionistic, shallow stacks of concrete slabs, the Lovejoy fountain captures the excitement of a mountain stream exploding from rock crevices, crashing in a marvelous, curved coursing, then spreading and flattening to a serene stillness. This one complex gesture, in water and cast stone, characterizes and commands the whole plaza, where visitors become part of the spectacle. They can see, and be seen, from all angles and levels, in singles, couples, groups, and masses. The moment of fusion, when one is aware of being both actor and spectator simultaneously, is exhilarating. And in a space

78. Lovejoy Plaza, Portland, Oregon, aerial view, 1961–1968. Lawrence Halprin & Associates, Landscape Architects. Charles Moore, with Moore/Lyndon/Turnbull/ Whitaker, Architects. A breathtaking expressionist abstraction of a mountain wilderness first energizes, then calms, this memorable plaza, one of the masterpieces of the modern era.

composed of the most common materials of the twentieth century, one experiences a rare dual sensation of explosion and silence.

In the urban context of Portland, the Lovejoy fountain represents the culmination of a journey one may make on foot, in a roughly north-south direction, along tree-lined streets and small linear parks fitted into the city's grid. Along this journey one encounters Pettigrove Park, Halprin's green, tree-shaded retreat, about the size of a city block, which seems like a buffer, a place of quiet pause among high grassy mounds, a few blocks distant from his two bolder plazas, Lovejoy to the south and the Auditorium Forecourt to the north. The popular Forecourt fountain, where Angela Danadjieva made important contributions, is a place mainly for frolic and display of personal energy and daring, although spaces for contemplation can be found on the fringes of the plaza and high up among the "sources," beneath the pines. Here, too, are evocations of mountain streams and waterfalls, but compared with Lovejoy, the Forecourt fountain seems melodramatic, its expression in concrete somewhat raw and thin.

More refined and complex is Freeway Park in Seattle, Washington, a collaborative work of Halprin's office, in which Angela Danadjieva was the principal designer (figure 79).[17] A tour de force of site planning, it

79. Freeway Park, Seattle, Washington, 1970–1976. Lawrence Halprin & Associates, Landscape Architects. Angela Danadjieva, Principal Designer. Edward McCleod & Associates, Associate Landscape Architects. While perhaps overly melodramatic, this internally small park not only allows one to cross the broad freeway comfortably on foot but also offers a series of intriguing spaces. The park's *pièce de résistance* is a waterfall down a dramatic crevice. The plantings are particularly fine.

springs over the interstate highway to reconnect the eastern and western parts of downtown. The plantings are opulent, recalling the ancient forests of the Pacific Northwest. Within the shady, wooded park, an abstracted mountain crevice with its crashing waterfall effectively drowns out the roar of the freeway while producing both spatial constriction and a kind of uneasy intimacy. A place of great beauty, it is tinged with terror—the sublime. Here, the concrete forms are heroic, an appropriate artistic and expressive response to the proximity and scalelessness of the freeway. Elsewhere in the park, as in a number of Halprin's malls, the paving and seating details recall his earlier gardens—a curious reminder of the domestic beginnings of West Coast modern landscape.

The project that has engaged Halprin's deepest emotions and creative energies over some thirty years, the Franklin Delano Roosevelt Memorial in Washington, D.C., embodies many of his ideas of a lifetime (figure 80). Now in the early stages of building after countless delays, the memorial will be not an object in a landscape but the landscape itself, on a site south of the Lincoln Memorial, parallel with the venerable plantation of cherry trees along the tidal basin. Judging from models and Halprin's descriptions, one senses the memorial will provide a poetic, modernist equivalent to the calm enclosures and spaces for ceremonial, channeled movement in a classical landscape.[18] The memorial is designed, or scored, for procession, but its series of outdoor rooms will also invite the reflection, pausing, retracing one's steps, changing one's mind, quickening and slackening one's pace, and reacting to sudden thought or emotion that is natural in the continuous flow of life.

Still evolving, the whole of Halprin's built work resists neat classification. The magic of his best fountains, such as Lovejoy, still powerful in

80. Franklin Delano Roosevelt Memorial, Washington, D.C., from 1974; currently under construction. Lawrence Halprin & Associates, Landscape Architects. Leonard Baskin, Neil Estern, Robert Graham and George Segal, Sculptors. Drawing by Lawrence Halprin. This memorial, a series of interconnected outdoor rooms formed by stone and water walls with memorial carvings and bronze reliefs, overlooks the cherry walk and the tidal basin beyond.

In one of the 4 "garden room" spaces · FDR memorial on Washington's birthday

the more sobering 1990s, defies cerebral analysis as much as the rocky cliffs at Sea Ranch defy the ocean waves. And yet, as Halprin has noted, some sort of critical understanding is needed in the profession he came across by chance some fifty years ago.[19]

Halprin's interest in movement, process, and continual change in social and psychological contexts has a counterpart in the continually evolving processes of nature. His studies of ecological processes—the interactions of soils, topography, vegetation, sunlight, fog, wind, and other fac-

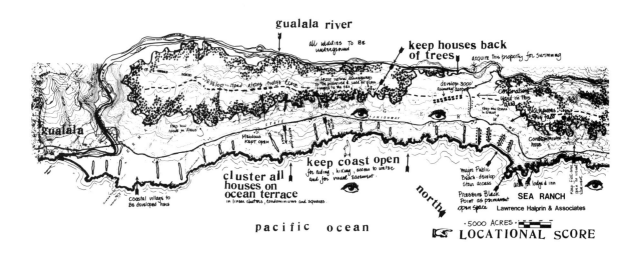

gualala river

all utilities to be underground

keep houses back of trees

acquire this property for swimming

develop road along ridge line

develop 3000' runway/airport

gualala

Meadows kept open

keep coast open
for riding, hiking, access to water and for visual easement.

cluster all houses on ocean terrace
in linear clusters, condominiums and squares.

coastal village to be developed here

north

Major Public Beach - develop stair access

Pressens Black Point as permanent open space

SEA RANCH
Lawrence Halprin & Associates

·5000 ACRES·

pacific ocean

LOCATIONAL SCORE

tors—found their most celebrated application at Sea Ranch, the ten-mile stretch of coast about one hundred miles north of San Francisco, developed as a community of mainly weekend or vacation homes and condominiums from the 1960s onward (figures 81 and 82). But ecological factors can be as significant inside the city as in the larger landscape. In San Francisco, Halprin noted, a shaft of space along Market Street, several miles long, was subject to his firm's ecological inventories and the resulting "ecoscore" for further development and renewal. "Urban living," he concluded, "needs to be based on ecoscoring as a basic biological premise of life from which aesthetics derive."[20]

Halprin's concept of scoring, or choreographing a series of actions to be encouraged or avoided, can be appealing, particularly when a project entails a spectrum of needs and interests—those of multiple users

81. Sea Ranch, California, plan, 1967. Lawrence Halprin & Associates, Landscape Architects. Moore/Lyndon/Turnbull/Whitaker and Joseph Esherick, Architects. Halprin's plans and drawings became more expressive, more popular, and more communicative as his projects grew larger and more public.

82. Sea Ranch. For many years, Ian McHarg referred to this project as a singular illustration, in built form, of his own vision of environmental planning and design. The original plan (unfortunately revised by market constraints) was a remarkable combination of place saving and place making.

as well as a single or multiple client. The open-ended, fluid, inclusive nondogmatic process can be adventurous—but also frustrating in light of changing owners, users, tastes, needs, and legal requirements.

At Sea Ranch, working with an enlightened group including architects Moore/Lyndon/Turnbull/Whitaker and Joseph Esherick, Alfred Boeke (director of planning for the developer, Oceanic Properties), and members of his own firm, Halprin developed a score for clustering homes in the lee of dense cypress windrows; building within clearings of the second-growth redwood/pine forests; keeping meadows open as common space with unobstructed views; arranging rooflines so as to deflect winds; providing houses for a range of incomes; and so on. Sadly, these measures did not entirely hold up under a change of developer-owner, the severe recession of the early 1970s, later market- and profit-driven decisions to subdivide the meadows, architects' and clients' whims, and other developments.[21] Over the years, Sea Ranch has evolved as a magnificent, though flawed and incomplete, expression of how a diverse community might live in harmony with nature.

83. Jacob Riis Plaza, New York City, aerial view, 1965. M. Paul Friedberg & Associates, Landscape Architects. This transformation of the previously drab grounds of a housing project invigorated social reformers and designers alike. The direct appeal to the imaginations of children and their families defined a new 1960s version of the American dream.

Halprin's response to the imperfections of Sea Ranch was not to abandon scores but to make them more visible and comprehensible, more persuasive of long-term rather than short-term goals. One sign of continuity is that Halprin, Moore, and Donlyn Lyndon have been brought back to develop an extension for the lodge at Sea Ranch. But Halprin's own long-term interest in that community is perhaps best revealed in the trees he planted there—more than half a million—evoking memories of his tree-planting years on the kibbutz near Haifa, a joyous greening of bare hills.

Ghirardelli Square, San Francisco (1962–1965), was Halprin's first opportunity to recycle a significant complex of old structures for new uses. Exploring the former chocolate factory and woolen mill with their new owner, William M. Roth, Halprin persuaded him to convert the buildings for commercial and quasi-public use. Later John Matthias and architects Wurster, Bernardi, and Emmons were brought in to work with Halprin and his associate, Don Carter; and their festive square at the base of Russian Hill became America's first urban adaptive use "specialty retail center," the prototype for Boston's Faneuil Hall, New York's South Street Seaport, and Baltimore's Harbor Place. Refurbished, rebuilt, terraced, occupied by shops and restaurants, and often filled with people (initially, with more resident San Franciscans than tourists) coursing through its many levels and gazing out over San Francisco Bay, Ghirardelli Square was a success. In 1982, however, the square's ownership changed hands, and Benjamin Thompson & Associates, of Cambridge, Massachusetts, was retained to help renovate the place for another generation of consumers. Journalist Allen Freeman viewed this work—which includes a new bandstand-staircase, new brick paving, and new graphics—as "fine tuning." Halprin, however, was

84. Jacob Riis Plaza. Friedberg's success at this plaza suggested that designers might be able to revive the city.

disturbed by the square's transformation. "It has changed from a real place to a yuppified cheese and wine place," he remarked.[22] If so, the roots of such change may lie in the social and economic transformations of the last thirty years, nationwide, rather than in any particular design decision.

The fates of two urban landscapes in New York City reinforce this point about pervasive, underlying forces of change. M. Paul Friedberg's much publicized three-acre plaza at the Jacob Riis Houses, on Manhattan's Lower East Side (1965), was built with common, tough, and resilient materials—wood, sand, brick, and concrete—and densely planted with trees around the fringes, to provide both intimate and open places for children to explore and grow (figures 83 and 84). This plaza was "filled with life" in 1966, the year Lady Bird Johnson came to the dedication and shared her optimism for the "good life" to be enjoyed there.[23] By 1985 the award-winning plaza was reported to be underused, inadequately maintained, and vandalized.[24] More recently, the physical condition of the plaza has been improved, but is the plaza ever filled with life? Most likely, until a consensus is reached regarding interrelated social, economic, political, and cultural problems and their solutions, the "good life" may never be known at Riis Plaza.

In contrast, the tiny 50-foot by 100-foot Paley Park, Robert Zion's haven of serenity among honey locusts and a sound-buffering water wall on the Upper East Side (ca. 1965), may survive (figure 85, plate 8).[25] Meanwhile New York's larger artifacts, such as the magnificent Pennsylvania Railroad Station, by McKim, Mead and White (ca. 1900), may always be threatened. When first built, both Penn Station and Paley Park were superlative expressions of the prevailing design aesthetic—

85. Paley Park, New York City, ca. 1965. Zion & Breen, Landscape Architects. The first, most famous, and still most loved pocket park, Paley Park is known to millions of New Yorkers and visitors who have stepped into it, leaving behind the intensity of the modern city. The shaded tables, the moveable chairs, and the great wall of water that all but drowns out the noise of the city constitute a truly urban oasis.

beaux arts monumentalism and the modernist's dream of universal space, respectively. By 1966, when the wrecking ball hit the station, Zion and other modernists had already voiced their vehement opposition to the station's destruction.[26] It was not art, style, function, or public sentiment, however, but soaring property values and development pressures that ultimately determined Penn Station's fate. In any dynamic city of our time, it seems, the forces of creativity and destruction will mutually oppose and reinforce one another—as Mumford had seen.

A sense of place, a feeling for its history, evolution, change, renewal, persistent humanity, and other intrinsic qualities that Mumford found delightful in older cities often transcend purely aesthetic concerns; yet aesthetic quality remains one of the few powerful allies of the urban designer in the struggle against the impersonal forces of a market economy. Halprin and others have often managed to make alliances among the forces of change—ecological, social, commercial, political, and so on. Halprin has even incorporated the fluidity and indeterminacy of change into his design process, a strategy that was particularly successful in the liberal, progressive spirit of certain cities in the 1960s and early 1970s. The ultimate test of that strategy may lie in a combination of social responses to the shaped urban space: Is it loved? Is it maintained? Has its essence been preserved over time? Or, if major change is contemplated, has the original designer/artist/choreographer been invited back to participate in the process of change?

Insofar as Halprin's life and work are one, they cannot be understood apart from tremendous growth and change—in not only biological but also psychological, aesthetic, and professional terms. In 1960, attending a meeting of the International Federation of Landscape Architects (IFLA) in Amsterdam, for instance, Halprin outlined the landscape architect's special contributions to a planning team: the vision of the landscape as the "matrix of life"; the design of meaningful open space; a focus on movement in space, or choreography of human participation in the landscape; an emphasis on improvisation, process, and poetic, sensuous experience; a concern for regionalism and ecology; and design synthesis, encompassing both conservation and the "dynamics of change."[27] At that IFLA meeting and through the early 1960s, Halprin would identify himself as a landscape architect and member of the ASLA.[28] But by the end of the 1960s, he was known as an urban designer, an "eco-architect," or by other titles. In time he would distinguish between "teamwork" and his own process of eliciting "collective creativity." Whatever the venue—in a community workshop, at the office, or on the beach—there would be no predetermined tasks or goals, only endless possibility.

By the end of the 1980s, Halprin had produced films on Salvador Dalí and dance and had published books, some often reprinted, on cities, freeways, urban design, workshops, the creative process of scoring, and his varied life's work. He had had one-man exhibitions of that work in San Francisco and Florence, Italy; and, called to Washington, D.C., by

President Johnson, he had served on the first National Council on the Arts. Today Halprin does not focus on "landscape architecture," so called, but on the creative process.[29] Does the name matter?

Yes and no. It does not matter by what name Halprin moves in the world, scoring, shaping, energizing, and changing places, along with the people in them, so long as one is concerned mainly about certain results: the built work and its relationship to people and the larger environment. These results are all subject to the evolution and change that Halprin has appreciated at least since his reflections on nonhuman design of the earth in "The Shape of Erosion" (1962).[30] Years earlier, his Harvard professors Gropius, Breuer, and Moholy-Nagy had focused on Bauhaus ideals of social change and the creative process, which profoundly influenced Halprin; static form, fixed notions of fine art versus craft, and protective barriers around disciplines were all to dissolve in the more compelling, exciting interaction of different artists working together in the community. "The Bauhaus masters didn't teach drafting," Halprin notes with pride. "They taught *drawing*. They didn't teach how to design a stage—they got you up on stage, acting, and dancing."[31]

As Halprin explains the gestalt, or wholeness, of his life's work, beyond conventional disciplines and professional titles, he finds it necessary to clarify what he means by art: the essence of creativity, the whole process whereby people's lives are enhanced. "I'm interested in art that deals with the essential human condition," he says.[32] And at this point, it does matter that Halprin shuns the title of landscape architect, apparently because that title does not encompass what he has become and aspires to be. One thinks of Olmsted, a man with a vision, setting out to build a profession from fragments of knowledge and skills that others had not yet combined to his satisfaction. One thinks of Mumford, whom Leo Marx has identified as a "synthesizing generalist," unwilling to chose a narrow academic discipline, more interested in the organic wholeness of life, art, politics, economy, philosophy, culture, ecology, and more.[33]

With his great gifts for synthesis, Halprin belongs in such company, but as an artist he will inevitably be appreciated alongside his mentor, Thomas Church, the consummate garden maker. If Church was perhaps too modest in his goals, Halprin has certainly stretched his reach to define for landscape architecture (or environmental design) a much more expansive field. In this sense, Halprin represents the highest ambition for an artist-practitioner who attempts to come to terms with the enormous range of possibilities and difficulties of modern life.

The whole of nature is an endless demonstration of shape and form.
—Henry Moore

It was an enviable commission: to design a sculpture garden for a major art museum and to place within its seventeen acres of gently sloping ground a collection of twelve bronze pieces by Henry Moore. After a limited competition, the Nelson-Atkins Museum of Art in Kansas City, Missouri, awarded this commission to Dan Kiley (figure 86) and Jacquelin Robertson. Planning and design began in 1987, and the garden was open to the public in June 1989.

Early one Sunday morning the following summer, people were wandering among the more familiar sculptures on the stone terrace outside the museum, then spilling out into the new Henry Moore Sculpture Garden. Most of Moore's bronzes had been placed along winding brick walks beneath mature pines and hardwoods on the periphery. The great vista to the south had been preserved, channeled by flanking groves of young ginkgos on new grass terraces that led down to a wider swath of lawn, flanked by linden *allées* (figures 87 and 88). One thought of Jefferson's great lawn at the University of Virginia (Robertson had been dean of the School of Architecture there). But here the grass terraces were more tightly concentrated, and the open space was more dynamic, first compressed by the ginkgos and then released and expanded below. As the day warmed, there were no soaring frisbees or breathless joggers on the lawn, only contemplative walkers, solitary or in pairs and small groups. All seemed appropriate, or "apt," a term Kiley recalls from Olmsted's writings.[1]

86. Dan and Anne Kiley, Charlotte, Vermont, ca. 1967. Living in northern Vermont, Dan Kiley has for decades maintained an international practice of landscape architecture, working with some of the leading architects of our time.

Intent on refining their design, Kiley and Robertson had gone to England, to talk with Moore himself and to study the ways in which Moore's sculptural works have been sited throughout his native land. Thus informed, Kiley and Robertson completed a sculpture garden that accommodates the twelve bronzes with dignity and discretion, while seamlessly merging the garden with the preexisting museum and park—an accomplishment that would seem to owe somewhat less to Robertson's considerable architectural skills than to Kiley's extraordinary experience in landscape architecture, acquired over a sixty-year period that has spanned his apprenticeship with Olmsted's colleagues to his position of eminent modern master today.

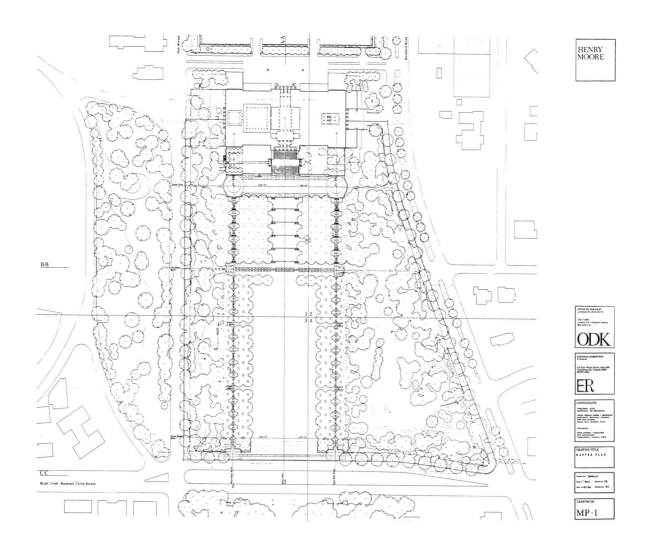

87. Henry Moore Sculpture Garden, Nelson-Atkins Museum of Art, Kansas City, Missouri, 1987–1989: Plan. Dan Kiley, Landscape Architect. Jacquelin Robertson, Architect. Down the great axial sweep of lawn, Kiley has planted two formal flanking bosques and two pairs of paths, straight and winding. The formality gives the great sculptures an architectural reference. The informality of the woodland encourages one to meander, thus prolonging and richly complicating the viewing experience.

88. Henry Moore Sculpture Garden, Nelson-Atkins Museum of Art. The cross-axial path, right, extends between a pair of vine-covered pavilions of trellised metal—each one an entry into the bordering woodland. Rising up the gentle grade in stately measures, the grass terraces (*left*) are planted with bosques of ginkgos and separated by banks of Japanese yews.

Since the close of World War II, Kiley's work has more than complemented some of the finest modern architecture of our time; his work *is* architecture, in its rhythmic modulation of geometric point grids, its direct extension of ground planes, and its often flawless extension of interior space to the larger, continuous space out of doors. Though often apparently effortless, these architectural relationships have been secured with a directness and a certainty rarely achieved in this century at the large scale. In fact, Kiley has often insisted that there is no real difference between architecture and landscape design. His work is a fusion of the two. It is also a kind of sculpture—not merely a setting.

Moore's sculptures, abstract yet often evocative of beings and forces in nature, seem to be at ease in Kiley's landscapes. Both Moore and Kiley express the vitality and organic unity of nature in abstract, concentrated form. A difference of medium and particular shapes, however, may make Moore's pieces more generally accessible—that is, more visible and photogenic—than many of Kiley's landscapes. Although instructed not to, adults may caress the sensuous, often androgynous bronze forms, and children sometimes climb all over them. Some people can see in his works, as Moore himself recognized, human forms as metaphors for land forms, and vice versa.[2] Then all is energy, movement, life: both sculpture and environment.

Kiley's *allées* and grids, abstractions from the orchards and woods of one's daily or seasonal experience, are more difficult to see as a living, breathing being—a sequence of spaces that assumes a life of its own. "Form and space are one and the same thing," observes Moore.[3] His medium, however, offers tangible objective presence, most recognizable as form in a fixed place. Kiley's medium is primarily environmental; he shapes space through which we move, perhaps oblivious to the movement of that space through contractions and expansions, as it seeks its own place in the universe. If this notion of Kiley's seems esoteric, his official statement about the Henry Moore Sculpture Garden is clear and resonant: "This Garden shall stand as a testament of our time and our presence within the cosmos."[4]

Beyond international circles of design professionals (among whom Kiley has long been esteemed as a colleague and peer), he has not had the popular acclaim of Church, Eckbo, Halprin, and Burle Marx. In recent years, awards, publications, and the establishment of the annual Dan Kiley Lecture at Harvard have brought him wider recognition. Kiley has not actively sought that recognition, however, nor has he written much for publication beyond a few brief essays, rich in suggestion, terse in exposition.[5] By 1941 he had decided to live in rural northern New England and concentrate on projects for which architects and clients would trouble to seek him out. After the war he and his wife, Anne, lived in Franconia, New Hampshire. There Kiley designed houses for clients he had met while he and Anne taught skiing. Later the couple moved to Charlotte, Vermont, and reared their eight children in the vicinity of Lake Champlain, Mount Mansfield's ski slopes, and the Burlington airport (essential for maintaining an international practice).

Just before and after World War II, Kiley seemed to be the only landscape architect on the East Coast who understood modern architecture. He earned the respect of his architectural collaborators—Eero

Saarinen, Kevin Roche, I. M. Pei, Harry Weese, Edward L. Barnes, Louis Kahn, Pietro Belluschi, Skidmore, Owings & Merrill, and others. Working with these classically oriented, second-generation modernist architects, mainly on institutional landscapes but also on public and domestic work, Kiley developed his own approach to design, a unique synthesis of modern and classic French design that recalls the spirit of Le Corbusier's work—both modern and classic Greek. Not surprising, architects appreciated Kiley's work sooner than did most landscape architects. As Stuart Dawson recalls, Kiley's work of the 1950s reminded him and his fellow students of Versailles—rather like a black car with running boards, not a state-of-the-art car, two-toned with fins![6]

For years Kiley has appeared an enigma—a designer with a small staff, sometimes a partner or two (notably, Ian Tyndall and Peter Kerr Walker), and an international practice based hundreds of miles from any large metropolitan area. While publishing little, he has served on design juries, boards, and committees and lectured to students around the country. Recent conferences and symposia have also given Kiley some prominent platforms for speaking. But asking Dan Kiley a question about design, education, or office practice can be like trying to catch—or even photograph—a butterfly. You may not get a straightforward answer, for Kiley resists being pinned down. Nevertheless the fluttering and flickering of reflection, insight, wisdom, and jest can be more intriguing than the information requested. "The important thing is not design; it's life itself." "Design is only a description for a process where you go and help somebody or help yourself find a place to live in space." "We are one with the universe. Man *is* nature."[7] Long after the aphorisms and tales have flashed by, the impression of continual movement, of Kiley's irrepressible vitality, remains.

Countering these volatile impressions is Kiley's built work of the past fifty years, ranging from the superb Miller garden and its neighbor, the Hamilton garden, to the grounds of Dulles Airport, the U.S. Air Force Academy, the Third Block of Independence Mall, in Philadelphia, the Hamilton-Cosco Company in Columbus, Indiana (figure 89), the North Carolina National Bank Plaza in Tampa, Florida, and other significant projects around the world. Some whimsical or enchanting feature may engage us—a tiny bubbler and pool in the center of a stone dining table in exurbia or a forest of bald cypresses rising above terraces of water at Fountain Place, in Dallas, but the dominant quality of Kiley's work is structure. Tree-lined drives, groves, and fountains on precise grids, a series of roofless rooms defined by vegetation, wood, concrete, travertine, and gravel: these are elements that Kiley has structured with the confidence of a master craftsman and the sensibility of an artist.

Entering the spaces Kiley has structured, however, and listening to him talk of grading, drainage, particular trees, a love of the land, and human needs, one can be drawn away from the art world's concerns, back to the northern New England farmhouses that have long shaped Kiley's experiences of life. His grandmother Baxter's 200-year-old farmhouse near Nashua, New Hampshire, hugged a rocky ridge overlooking a barnyard, with an upland pasture and pine woods beyond. Kiley's own farmhouse in northern Vermont, once his home and now his office, has a core dating from 1810, with additions built as needed. A row of sugar maples was planted to screen the house from the glaring summer sun, and a double row of poplars lines the unpaved drive. The beauty of the place is derived from intelligent response to human needs, like the beauty of the farmhouses and villages throughout Vermont and New Hampshire—the two best states of the Union, wrote Robert Frost.[8]

89. Hamilton-Cosco Company, Columbus, Indiana, 1962. Harry Weese, Architect. Dan Kiley, Landscape Architect. Kiley accomplishes much by the selection and placement of plants. Here, a simple straight walk leads from a medium-sized parking lot, now delightfully shaded by mature ginkgos. An informal grove of river birch deepens and enlivens the space between walk and building. The birches' rough bark is contrasted with the low, clipped hedges that serve as foreground to the expansive lawn beyond.

When asked about his sources of inspiration, Kiley has spoken of both Le Nôtre and Olmsted, emphasizing Le Nôtre. He has also mentioned Thoreau, Emerson, Goethe, Einstein, Heraclitus, Jung, and the South African writer Laurens van der Post. Kiley seeks connection with a universe in constant motion. He wants to develop the whole man, to realize the greatest potentials of the land and in himself, to stay atuned to the environment, to take a walk in the woods and not trample on the hepaticas, to simplify, to know when to do nothing—when *not* to alter a landscape—and when to relax. From an intuitive sense of what is appropriate, grounded in an understanding of function and structure, like a butterfly hovering about the farmhouse, Kiley moves on to other concerns, such as the poetry of space, which is ineffable. "Poetry means you are released and connected with the Universe in its biggest way," Kiley explains.[9] You feel it, you experience it—or you don't.

Kiley was born in 1912 in Roxbury, Massachusetts, one of those communities near Boston with a layered history of settlement that once included eighteenth-century gentlemen's farms as well as Victorian cottages and streetcar suburbs. The inhabitants have ranged from wealthy to very poor. Kiley's father was a construction manager. For a while the family lived in a triple-decker, a familiar type of Boston-area apartment house, three stories high, of wooden frame with, typically, three flats, each given a front porch, a back porch, and four exposures. Gabled and turreted single-family Victorian houses of two and a half stories mingled with the triple-deckers. Lots were perhaps thirty to fifty feet wide, and backyards and alleys formed tree-shaded mazes that Kiley negotiated as a boy, climbing fences. After the family moved to less densely settled West Roxbury, Kiley spent more time along the southern end of Olmsted's Emerald Necklace of parks, near his high school in Jamaica Plain.

A seasonal change of place, from Boston's inner suburbs during the school year to summers on his grandparents' farm in New Hampshire, gave Kiley the chance to learn about land and space in an unconscious way. His curiosity about birds, for instance, led to an interest in the trees at the Arnold Arboretum, in Jamaica Plain. Memories of the hot smell of juniper and pine out in a rock-strewn New Hampshire field, contrasting with the cool enclosure of a pine woods, are still vivid; Kiley now relates those sensations to a growing awareness of architecture and nature—together, as one.[10]

Grinning, he recalls that he never took home the heavy books from school. He did read Thoreau's *Walden,* which cannot have weighed more than a few ounces; he reread it again and again, and loved it. There he found not only profound reflections on the natural world at macro and micro scale but also echoes of his own disdain for routine labor—cheerless getting and spending—and his inclination to live lightly on this earth.

Thoreau's essay "Walking" (1862) expresses ideas Kiley himself has discovered, perhaps independently: "I wish to speak a word for Nature, for absolute freedom and wildness, as contrasted with a freedom and culture merely civil—to regard man as an inhabitant, or a part and parcel of Nature, rather than a member of society," Thoreau wrote. "I believe there is a subtle magnetism in Nature, which, if we unconsciously yield to it, will direct us aright."[11] In Kiley's attempts to explain the design process, there is a similar yielding to forces beyond one's own will. Developing the clear structure, or bones, of a design, he wants to let the design make its own growth. "You set it in motion," he says, "and it's moving outward. That's an idea that I love: that it's trying to find its place in the universe."[12]

Thoreau's walking was both a physical journey beyond the town of Concord, Massachusetts, and a mental journey without bounds through space and time. The solitary walk freed Thoreau's mind of mundane preoccupations so that he might discover something untamed, unknown, still wild and thus alive, in himself and his environment. For Kiley, the act of shaping spaces on the land—no matter how crisp and geometric the final form—has been a similar quest for the untamed and alive. When Kiley speaks of spatial continuity and interlocking spatial structure, he explains, "I am still seeking the same thing you find when you take a walk in nature. You walk through very tight woods, then you come out into an open field. You move again into a sugar bush area, with trees wider apart. Trees are always changing. The spaces are always moving, and the scene's always changing and moving from in to out and all around. It's infinite. The whole thrust of that spatial movement is an infinite, exciting thing to work with. That's the medium you're working with in modern landscape design."[13]

Kiley's own path was not so solitary as Thoreau's, but it was singular. In 1930, when Kiley graduated from high school, jobs were scarce. He could not find work in what intrigued him—interior design. Eventually a postgraduate course in horticulture led him toward landscape architecture. Because of the depression, major Boston-area firms, including the Olmsted Brothers and Arthur Shurcliff's office, were phasing out much of their private residential practice to take on whatever public and institutional work could be found. (Landscape architect John Nolen, in Cambridge, Massachusetts, had focused on city and regional planning long before the depression set in.) Kiley wrote to these and other firms and was delighted when Warren Manning, of Cambridge, replied. Manning, whose father maintained a nursery in nearby Billerica, had been the horticultural expert for the Olmsteds on such projects as Biltmore, the Vanderbilt estate in North Carolina (1888–1895), and the World's Columbian Exposition of 1893, in Chicago. When, in late 1931, Manning offered Kiley an apprenticeship without pay, Kiley gladly accepted. After a year, he was earning fifty cents an hour. Within a few more years, Kiley was Manning's chief designer in the field.

Manning was not a designer but an expert horticulturist and a philosopher of the land. "He was a lovely, wonderful man," Kiley recalls.[14] During his six years with Manning, Kiley learned a great deal about plants and worked on ecological studies long before *ecology* became a household word. He toured the Boston Harbor Islands with Manning and studied ways to stop their erosion and make them beautiful. He also contributed to a few Works Progress Administration projects and worked on a town planning study for Hampton Beach, New Hampshire, making sure that new buildings would be appropriately sited.

When not serving as Manning's chauffeur, driving a Model A convertible, Kiley had some opportunity to learn from Manning's associates, including Charles Gillette, A. D. Taylor, and especially Arthur Sylvester, whose fine drawings Kiley found inspiring. Much of Kiley's time, however, was spent in the field, installing gardens under Manning's general instructions rather than with precise planting plans. On some projects, Kiley would dig up and transplant specimens from the nearby woods, or a truck would arrive from the nursery and Kiley would design as he planted. Later, a more experienced associate would visit the site to attend to any problems that might arise.

This sort of apprenticeship—rare today—gave Kiley a unique understanding of what is essential in landscape architecture before he worked with some of the finest modern architects of his time and, in turn, learned from them. Beginning before the age of twenty, before any "higher" education could mold his thoughts, and before any avant-garde ideas wafted through the office or its magazine racks, Kiley spent six years solving functional problems without reference to any rigid system. Like Olmsted, Manning worked in both naturalistic and more rectilinear, or architectural, modes of landscape design, but his observations and writings were less focused on subtleties of design than on land use, especially at a national scale.[15] Sylvester, who had graduated from Harvard and received the Charles Eliot Traveling Fellowship, taught Kiley some techniques of beaux arts rendering, but Kiley's first true mentor, Manning, a founding member of the ASLA, advised Kiley to stay away from both Harvard and the ASLA. What he offered was insight from a lifetime of experience in solving problems of the land, independently and unself-consciously. If ever Kiley met a truly Emersonian spirit, intuitive, self-reliant, and wary of all imitation, it was Manning.

Harvard's department of landscape architecture nurtured a different spirit—not entirely Olmstedian but reverential toward certain ideas about nature and historical precedent that were meant to continue Olmsted's legacy. The best products of that department included graduates devoted to landscape conservation and the national parks. The worst, as Elbert Peets implied, could not think for themselves; their imaginations had been stifled by too rigid an interpretation of Olmstedian and beaux arts principles of design.[16] Kiley went to Harvard, nonetheless, as a special student, from 1936 to 1938, while continuing to work for Manning some thirty hours a week.

Harvard's department of landscape architecture had been instituted by Frederick Law Olmsted, Jr., in 1900–1901. The elder Olmsted, anxious to have his son complete his own mission of civilizing Americans through great works of planning and design, had urged his son to become "much more the master of all the branches of your profession than anyone else has had opportunity of being before."[17] A dutiful son, Olmsted, Jr., assumed this awesome mission and to some extent succeeded. Along with other distinguished educators, including Henry Vincent Hubbard and Walter Chambers, the younger Olmsted institutionalized the teaching of landscape architecture by conveying a body of knowledge drawn from horticulture, engineering, construction, history, and principles of design. The younger Olmsted's strengths, as Shary Page Berg observes, were his abilities to organize and to systematize.[18] However, once the design process had been reduced to a system of preconceived solutions to hypothetical problems, it had no life.

Trained to solve functional, spatial problems on the land, Kiley fitted into the Harvard system no better than his classmate Garrett Eckbo, whose independence of mind had been fostered by more liberal teaching at Berkeley and by a year of designing gardens for clients in Southern California, before arriving at Harvard in 1936. Another classmate, James Rose, who had come from Matamoras, Pennsylvania, a small town along the Delaware River, and studied at Cornell University, was very bright and unwilling to follow rules or apply formulas in the design studios.

The three students were at first encouraged by the arrival of Walter Gropius early in 1937; under his direction, Harvard's department of architecture quickly became a place of ferment, of new ideas about art, society, and technology. An atmosphere of excitement, exploration, something unknown and "wild" in Thoreau's sense, emerged in the loftier reaches of Harvard's Robinson Hall, while the landscape architecture professors, below, tried to ignore it. New technologies had no impact on landscape design, Professor Bremer Pond insisted; a tree was still a tree. Indeed, the naturalistic landscape of trees, shrubs, and lawn appeared equally suitable for a classical building or a modern one. Familiar, seemingly undemanding, it could provide the invisible setting that architects often preferred.

Gropius brought with him the Bauhaus ideal of collaboration among different design disciplines. And it was in his collaborative studio that Eckbo first adapted Miesian space to landscape design, an experiment in spatial design from which Kiley learned a great deal. Ironically, Gropius had no particular interest in design on the land or in shaping the spaces between buildings for meaningful, memorable experience. (In fact his predecessor at Harvard, Prix de Rome winner Jean-Jacques Haffner, had shown considerably more curiosity about modern garden design in his *Compositions de jardins,* of 1931.) What Gropius sought was a fairly neutral space for modern buildings. For inspiration, then, Kiley, Eckbo, and Rose turned to the writings of Christopher Tunnard, Lewis Mumford, Le Corbusier, and others.

To begin to appreciate how conservative the profession of landscape architecture in America was in the mid-1930s, one might peruse the shelter magazines and professional journals. Fletcher Steele's article of 1930, "New Pioneering in Garden Design," with its references to French modernist designs by Gabriel Guevrekian, Pierre Le Grain, Le Corbusier, and others, was an early effort to open a dialogue on modern design, but his colleagues in the ASLA showed scant interest.[19] Norman Newton cautioned that the fundamental issue was not modernity but quality; rather than ask, "Is it modern?" Newton would ask, "Is it good and beautiful?"[20] It was from the younger generation, then, that James Marston Fitch sought some fresh ideas on landscape design for *Architectural Record;* he asked Harvard students Kiley, Eckbo, and Rose for the series of articles that appeared in the *Record* in 1939 and 1940. By then Eckbo and Rose had already published some experimental work in *Pencil Points* and *Magazine of Art.*[21] They also did most of the writing for the *Record* articles; Kiley collaborated mainly on the ideas.

Those ideas, on landscape design in urban, rural, and primeval environments, are significant. If republished in a slim volume, the articles would still be enlightening to planners and designers, for Eckbo, Rose, and Kiley were looking far beyond the surface and superficial appreciation of these environments. They considered the interrelation of factors such as dwelling, human labor, mechanization, productivity, economy, recreation, and environmental equilibrium. In honeycombs and beavers' dams, parkways and puppet shows, they found evidence of organisms seeking "the natural environment most favorable to the complete development of their species."[22]

The implications of deriving new forms of landscape design from these students' investigations have yet to be fully appreciated. They saw, for instance, beauty as well as utility in the rice terraces of China, the wheat fields of North Dakota, and the vineyards along the Rhine. The farmer, the "first landscape designer," used whatever knowledge and techniques were available to meet his needs for production at minimal expense. Untroubled by theories of design and beauty, the farmer shaped and altered his land according to current and anticipated needs. The results, noted the students, dramatically expressed human achievements and aspirations in designs that could rival the gardens of the Villa D'Este or the Alhambra.[23] The students were not yet world travelers; they simply believed this to be true.

The three students' rebellion in Harvard's landscape architecture studios has become a legend. Working nearly full time, however, Kiley could not afford the luxury of agonizing over studio projects. Lack of time made him austere, direct. He would look at a problem, get out the "double-elephant boards" (large stretchers), lay out a quick sketch before he had developed a design, and start laying down colors—base color, ochre, and gray washes—then develop the design quickly, in a few days rather than weeks, with perhaps a sketch or two scribbled on a scrap of paper. On the side he experimented with Japanese brushes and rice paper, signing his name "Ki-Lee." He also took Harvard's introductory course in music, which, along with meeting Eckbo and Rose, was his most important experience at Harvard.[24]

Kiley left Harvard when, in 1938, Manning died and his firm was dissolved. Sylvester became head of the National Park Service in Concord, New Hampshire, and hired Kiley as a draftsman. As opportunities arose, Kiley was—like the Zen swordsmen he admires—poised, ready. He worked for the City Planning Board in Concord, collaborated with Louis Kahn on some housing projects in Washington, D.C., then enlisted in the army. Selected for the Office of Strategic Services, Kiley went on to direct its Presentations Branch after his boss, Eero Saarinen, stepped down. After the war, Captain Kiley was sent abroad to lay out the courtroom for the Nuremburg trials. There he gained international recognition—and discovered Europe.

Seeing the work of Le Nôtre for the first time—at Sceaux, Chantilly, Versailles, Vaux-le-Vicomte—was astonishing for Kiley. Black and white lantern slides at Harvard had never conveyed the power of these gardens—the control of large spaces through strong, clear spatial structure—and the beauty, which is both sensuous and abstract. Uninspired landscape history courses and the antihistoricist stance of modern architects had virtually killed any interest Kiley might have had in works of the past.[25] Nothing had prepared him, then, for the experience of walking along popular- or sycamore-shaded paths of fine, yielding gravel and gazing upon serene canals and shafts of space extended to infinity. Historians have noted that Le Nôtre improved the grounds of the Tuileries and Chantilly by simplifying and unifying their designs. But once Kiley had experienced the actual space, the scale, and the sensuous details of Le Nôtre's great work, the whole French design tradition and other works of the past became both accessible and exciting to him. Form was no longer a preoccupation, something to aim for; it became the by-product of efforts to solve a problem of spatial design in a simple, elegant manner.

90. Oakland Museum, Oakland, California,
1969: Aerial view. Kevin Roche & John
Dinkeloo, Associates, Architects. Office
of Dan Kiley, Landscape Designer. Geraldine Knight Scott, Landscape Architectural
Associate. The great terraced roof garden is richly overplanted in Mediterranean textures and colors, providing
framed views to Lake Merritt, Oakland,
Berkeley, and the hills beyond.

Today it is not difficult to trace some of the classic French qualities in Kiley's work. For St. Louis, Missouri, he conceived of masses of trees that would give scale and a powerful sense of movement to the space beneath the great arch of the Jefferson National Expansion Memorial (in a winning competition scheme with Saarinen, in 1947). In Columbus, Indiana, until recent alterations, one could drive up to the outdoor teller machines of the Irwin Bank and Trust Company, of 1970, through Kiley's grove of little leaf lindens, evocative of the horse chestnuts in the Tuileries. Whether the resulting landscape is considered modern or classic does not trouble Kiley. What interests him are two concerns of the modern designer: appropriateness and the continuity, or dynamic movement, of space.

At the Oakland Museum (1962–1969), architect Kevin Roche determined the basic structure of the gardens: a series of roof gardens, stepping down from north to south and incorporating some fine existing Blue Atlas cedars (figure 90). Kiley's appropriate response was to focus on the selection of plants and their maintenance. Working with a horticultural expert from the Bay Area, landscape architect Geraldine Knight Scott, Kiley selected a rich mixture of drought-tolerant flowering vines, shrubs, groundcovers, water lilies for a pool, sturdy weeping Bradford pears, and fast-growing eucalyptus. A complete plant-feeding and watering system, the first of its kind for a major institutional roof garden, was also installed. Although some replanting and refurbishing have since been required, the gardens remain memorable: a multilayered series of viewing platforms that provide rich, textured contrasts to the ponderous reinforced-concrete structure, without upstaging the museum's fine collection of outdoor sculpture.

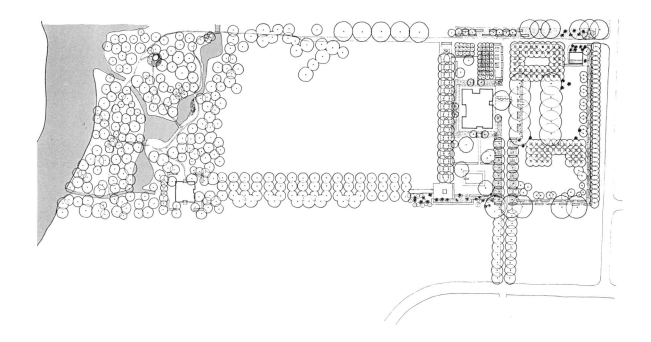

91. Miller Garden, Columbus, Indiana, 1955: Plan. Eero Saarinen and Kevin Roche, Architects. Dan Kiley, Landscape Architect. Kiley's interlocking and spiraling point grids and cross-axial *allées* produce a dynamic form more like a built-up city, such as Rome, or a replanted forest, than the axial classicism of Palladio or Le Nôtre. It is perhaps the openness, and the availability of the diagonal glance or movement, that gives these grids their life. Here, Kiley has escaped the intellectualism of the architecture, while respecting its more open, Miesian origins.

Appropriateness is the main justification for preserving and enhancing the great vista from the garden front of the Nelson-Atkins Museum of Art down through the Henry Moore Sculpture Garden in Kansas City, for the central portico of that symmetrical neoclassical building was originally designed to command a view. (In addition, the people of Kansas City were very fond of the view and the great open space.)

Equally appropriate is Kiley's expansion of the spatial order of Saarinen and Roche's Miller House, by creating roomlike enclosures off the central spine of the horse chestnut *allée* that slides right by the house itself, rather than approaching the house straight on (figure 91). The exterior spatial structure, formed by trees and hedges, reflects that of the interior, where four independent clusters of spaces unfold outward from a large, asymmetrically planned central space. Appropriate, too, is the change in mood at the Miller residence, from the cool, precise, rectilinear spaces of house and garden on a raised terrace to the romantic atmosphere created by a clump of willows on a lawn in the floodplain below. Moods change with the seasons as well. In late summer, the drowsy, warm humid atmosphere, the ungathered apples in the orchard, and the maternal heaviness of Moore's sculpture all contribute

to a pervasive serenity—ripe, full, satisfying, taking the chill off modernist perfection (figure 92). Kiley would be pleased, for at Vaux-le-Vicomte, he has always found the impeccable maintenance a bit cold, sterile; he prefers to walk where the leaves have been left to blend with the gravel.

The Miller garden, Kiley's masterpiece, was designed for a client rare in modern times, a real patron. Irwin Miller, the driving force behind the program to secure for Columbus, Indiana, fine public and institutional buildings by eminent contemporary architects, is not only interested in the new and experimental;[26] he also appreciates the need for careful maintenance, without which Kiley's work could never achieve its promise. The ingenuity of Kiley's plan for the Miller garden does not shock or even amuse the eye. Rather, it leads one gently from space to space through a witty and ambiguous game of discovery. Among the surprises is the pair of great weeping beeches that pushes up against the glass walls of the pavilion, on the west, shading the living areas from the afternoon sun (figure 93). Another is the *allée* of honey locusts that runs along the western edge of the terrace, between the house and the floodplain below. First seen cross-axially, this *allée* allows glimpses, between tree trunks, of the distant floodplain and willows. Only later, walking the length of the *allée,* does one glimpse the sculptural treasures by Moore and Lipschitz, at either end. The peripheral arborvitae hedges are interrupted and stepped, implying entry while visually denying it. The spaces one moves through are clearly defined yet fluid, ever expanding outward from the house to the street and the river. In no other work has Kiley been able to attempt and achieve so much.

94. North Carolina National Bank, Tampa, Florida, 1988: Plan. Harry Wolf, Architect. Dan Kiley, Landscape Architect. This complex garden of point and linear grids explores the richness of layers of plantings, both vertically and horizontally, with combinations of leaf, flower, and their shadow in a tropical climate. The qualities of water, from quiet and bubbling to exuberant and all encompassing, are explored with great rigor.

95. North Carolina National Bank, Tampa, Florida. A shaded water channel leads to a sunny pool and a clearing within the grove of crape myrtles.

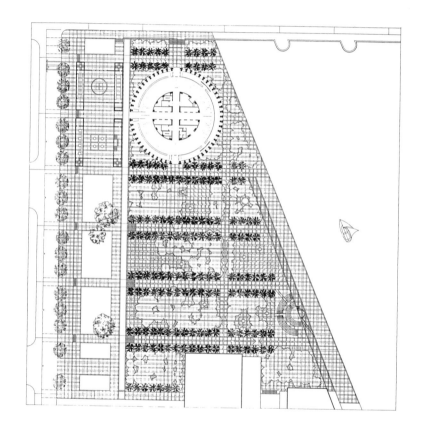

The sheer beauty of Kiley's continuous spaces, once recognized, can be mesmerizing, dazzling, particularly at the recently completed North Carolina National Bank Plaza, in Tampa, Florida (figures 94 and 95). There Kiley and architect Harry Wolf have created a series of grand and intimate spaces, ranging from the civic to the contemplative. Water is used as a mirror, as a precious resource, and as in a surreal dream, submerging the visitor in a kaleidoscope of light and reflection. Pavings of stone, cast stone, and gravel, along with panels of grass and runnels of water, are woven into intricate geometric patterns. These are overlaid by the random patterns of shade cast by the informally planted groves of some 800 crape myrtles. Here, as in many of Kiley's finest landscapes, the resulting forms transcend the particular functions that generated them. In this case, the functions were essentially urbane, civilizing: providing a setting for the cylindrical bank tower; allowing gracious public access from street to bank and gardens; and inviting the uses of strolling, sitting, and congregating in a small amphitheater.

In conversation, Kiley tends to emphasize functional, practical issues—not form for its own sake. He told students at Berkeley in 1965, "You should stick to the fundamentals of the need in order to get the most organic and the strongest kind of result."[27] Only after distilling a complex program to an essence, by simplifying, forgetting form in the interest of solving functional problems, would Kiley make the "discreet leap" toward a formal solution that may transcend all mundane conditions and requirements (figure 96).

This insistence on the direct response to need (including a range of desires and emotions) lies behind much of Kiley's ambivalence toward discussions of art and design. He hates vague and esoteric abstractions. He

Kiley's influence on the development of landscape architecture has gradually expanded as some of his thoughts and projects have begun to appear more frequently in the design magazines. His office, meanwhile, remains small and informal. "I like it that way," he says. "It gives me a nicer, richer life, to be able to do things I'm in touch with. Directly. And I'm also in touch from afar."[30]

Chapter 7

**The Modernization
of the Schools**

"Common sense is actually nothing more than a deposit of prejudices laid down in the mind prior to the age of eighteen. Every new idea one encounters in later years must combat this accretion of 'self-evident' concepts."[1] This paraphrase from Einstein might have come from a notebook of Stanley White or Hideo Sasaki, two educators in landscape architecture whose impact on generations of students was broad and, for the most receptive, exceedingly deep (figures 97 and 98). White was a professor of landscape architecture at the University of Illinois from 1922 to 1959. Among his students was Hideo Sasaki, a graduate of Illinois and Harvard, who taught at the Harvard Graduate School of Design for two decades while maintaining a demanding collaborative practice. Both men were extraordinary teachers, ever curious about new ideas, new methods, and the expansion of the landscape architect's role. Above all, both men got students to think in fresh, creative ways. Yet two educators in the same field could hardly be more different.

Sasaki's thinking, like his manner of teaching and practicing, is exceptionally clear, organized, rational, penetrating. Though reserved and rather shy, Sasaki would approach a problem with an intellectual zest that students soon sensed. Then, carried along by the swift flow of his logical exposition, they would watch, amazed, as the complexities of the issue at hand were carefully disentangled, analyzed, and brought back to a new synthesis, a framework for design. This was a highly conscious exercise on Sasaki's part; he knew the incoming students were, for the most part, unprepared for his way of thinking. He once explained, "We roll up our sleeves and go to work on the signal problem of forcing students to think in terms of abstract ideas and intellectual values. This is necessary because, as we discover, the student has never been made to look an idea in the eye and give it a real challenge. So we

97. Portrait of Stanley H. White, ca. 1965.
Professor of Landscape Architecture,
University of Illinois, 1922–1959.

98. Hideo Sasaki, with pointer, and T. Bonnell,
a student. Sasaki taught at the Graduate
School of Design, Harvard University,
nearly continuously from 1950 through
1970, serving as chairman of the department of landscape architecture from
1958 to 1968.

start with the meanings of words, and lay bare the nature of criticism. . . . For most students there is a sense of seeing things for the first time in a true light."[2]

White considered Sasaki an extraordinary thinker and organizer—"the mastermind," he fondly conceded. In turn, Sasaki appreciated White's many-faceted contributions. In 1950 he encouraged White to organize the landscape architect's study of nature on a broad base of natural sciences. Four years later, White outlined such a study at Harvard's summer school in his course, "Plants as Factors in Design." In the 1960s, as chairman of Harvard's landscape architect department, Sasaki persuaded White to return as a visiting lecturer and critic for several academic years. In so doing, Sasaki exposed students to a mind decidedly unlike his own.

Magic, mystery, high-wire acts, and reaching for the impalpable were White's forte. Intrigued by the unknown regions of the mind from which creativity arises, White encouraged students to take chances and trust their intuition. Design, or any other creative act, entailed two critical stages, he would explain: "First the idea; then the proof. The proof is, of course, straight logic. But what is the idea? Something between magic and philosophy—the wonderful stuff which may be large-part intuition, some hocus-pocus, with tremendous bravery, an act inscrutable against ordinary standards. It is the mental humor, the ghost of thought, like the cool breath off the ocean which says a breeze is coming before the wind blows."[3]

Both approaches to a problem of landscape design, the rational and the intuitive, have timeless validity. But what is most significant for the development of American landscape architecture is that White and Sasaki flourished in academia when each was superbly fitted to make his unique contribution. White's teaching career spanned the last years of the "country place era" (Norman Newton's phrase) and the rise of modernism in America. Sasaki began to teach and practice just after World War II, at the beginning of a boom in land development and urban renewal. He continued to teach and practice until the student uprisings of the late 1960s and the rise of the environmental movement. Had either educator emerged at a different time, the development of the profession might have been quite different.

White, with his flexible mind and broad grasp of the humanistic and scientific bases of landscape architecture, had no prejudices for or against any particular form of landscape design. While not driven to rebel against the beliefs or practices of his elders (as did Eckbo, Kiley, and Rose in the late 1930s), White remained free of dogmatic or prescriptive theories. "You can't design anything you cannot *conceive* of," he would tell students, thus obliquely emphasizing ideas rather than precepts.

White was an ideal teacher to bridge the perceived gaps between traditional and modern design. Inquisitive and patient, he would entertain just about any new idea, rejecting nothing from history and tradition (figure 99). The design process that fascinated him was timeless. He would make a fist—that was the site, the piece of ground. Then he would embrace the fist in the palm of his other hand—that was the "right" solution or plan for the site. What mattered was design that intensified the character of the site and form that suited the land like a neatly fitted garment.

Sasaki, too, entertained a wide range of formal solutions to a design
problem. He could appreciate the increasingly sophisticated gardens of
postwar California, although their zigzags and sweeping lines did not
appeal to him personally.[4] The search for modern formal expression interested him less than the clear structuring and shaping of the physical
environment as a whole, particularly the urban environment, where
sensitively designed, humane landscapes were all too rare. His main
concern was the integrated environment, superb examples of which already existed in Japan.[5]

In 1957, reviewing several books on Japanese architecture and gardens,
Sasaki noted that much of the influence of the current "rash of Japanifi-
cation" was likely to be superficial. Yet Japan's traditional buildings and
gardens indeed offered lessons for the modern Western designer. "The
development of design ideas, in the United States at least, has now
reached a point which was reached in Japan some four to five centuries
ago," he wrote. "The ideas of modular expression, the 'flow' of space,
the integration of indoors and outdoors, the use of inherent character-

istics of materials, etc., have been commonly accepted only recently in the United States."[6]

Americans' curiosity about Japan and its culture after World War II had very little to do with Sasaki's rise to prominence as an educator and practitioner. The fact that this California-born Japanese-American flourished among the institutions and corporations of the Northeast has more to do with his outstanding personal qualities than with his ancestry. Disciplined, highly intelligent, trained in business management as well as in landscape architecture and the fine arts, Sasaki understood the workings of complex organizations and the people who achieved positions of power within them. He also appreciated the contributions of natural scientists and others to landscape architecture. Collaboration and teamwork were methods used not only by his Bauhaus-trained and -influenced colleagues but also by his clients, among them, the most successful American corporations and eminent institutions of the day. In short, Sasaki arrived on the academic scene and in the boardroom at a time when a disciplined, skillful manager/critic of broad and deep cultivation was much needed and appreciated.

In some ways, Stanley White and Hideo Sasaki were worlds apart. They grew up at opposite ends of a continent, in different subcultures and generations, and, as professionals, they moved in different though overlapping circles. But two powerful interests drew them together: their commitment to reviving the larger scale and social purposes of Frederick Law Olmsted's work in landscape design and their concern for the cultural and spiritual aspects of the landscape. Both White and Sasaki referred to Oswald Spengler's notion of landscape as a totality of physical manifestations of culture on the earth. White passionately believed, along with Spengler, that without landscape, "life's soul and thought are inconceivable."[7] And Sasaki measured the cultural achievement of a civilization largely by the visual quality of its environment. In 1957, addressing a panel on urban design at the University of Illinois, Sasaki spoke on "Quality in Landscape, a Spiritual Necessity."[8] In 1959, White concluded a panel on ecology and design with the idea that "The spiritual is part of the contribution of the landscape architect."[9] Poetry and ecology were, for him, inseparable concerns.

Stanley White was born in Brooklyn, New York, in 1891—the year his family moved up the East River to leafy, suburban Mount Vernon. In time, the Whites' large wooden frame house, with its gables, octagonal turret, wrap-around porch, and stable in the rear would shelter six children in all. Stanley's younger brother, the writer Elwyn Brooks (E. B.) White, wrote of the house as a castle, a fortress. The family itself was a kind of fortress, close knit, mutually supportive, cooperative and resourceful. The elder Mr. White had risen from "bundle boy" (or wrapper of packages) to president within a piano manufacturing company. A sober, upright, optimistic businessman, he dabbled in songwriting, loved the outdoors, and encouraged his children to be self-reliant. Mrs. White, daughter of William Hart, the Hudson River school painter, was devoted to her children and rarely entertained guests outside the family circle. Their parlor was filled with musical instruments (Stanley took to the violin), and everyone played, sang, or composed, but no one excelled. There were, after all, many distractions in and about the "castle," leading each child into several paths of self-discovery rather than a single lifelong preoccupation.[10]

When Stanley was in his teens, the family made annual sojourns in August to a rented camp on Great Pond, one of the Belgrade Lakes, in Maine. A homemade boat, constructed by Stanley and his older brother Albert and shipped to the camp, provided transportation and adventures for the family as a whole. Years later, E. B. White left a verbal sketch of his family in that boat—a Monet-like scene of women in bows, ribbons, and parasols and men at the tiller. With the realism of a George Caleb Bingham (or Grandfather Hart?), Stanley also told of their early unsupervised wanderings: "As children we used to scale roof-tops, shoot rats in the manure pit, build boats, keep pigeons, dam streams, make our own sleds and skis, swing on birch trees, operate peep-shows, trap cats and chickens, explore swamps and tidewaters, climb mountains and engage in all sorts of impossible and extravagant undertakings. Our escapades made us resourceful, courageous and knowing, [and] steeped us in the meanings of commonplace delights of the local scene."[11] Even getting in and out of trouble, independently, "tasting life at first hand," White considered enormously important to one's spiritual and practical development.

Stanley and Albert White entered Cornell in the same year, 1908, and graduated together in 1912. The two brothers also founded a fraternity together, studied agriculture at the university, and eventually married two sisters. Albert never settled into a satisfying career, however. Stanley went on to Harvard, received the M.L.A. degree in 1915, worked briefly in the offices of Fletcher Steele, the Olmsted Brothers, A. D. Taylor, and Jacob L. Crane, and taught landscape architecture on a part-time basis at the Lowthorpe School in Groton, Massachusetts, from 1918 to 1922. From 1920 to 1922 he tried running his own landscape architectural practice, but it "fizzled," as he recalled.[12] In 1936–

1937, he worked on the Resettlement Administration's greenbelt town of Greendale, Wisconsin. By then, however, he had found his calling, in education. He told a gathering of the National Conference of Instruction in Landscape Architecture (NCILA) in 1957, after some forty years of teaching, "Everything I had done was, as far as the University's pay to me was concerned, simply a by-product of my fooling around with this amazing problem, this fascinating problem of how to teach."[13]

E. B. White considered Stanley a born teacher who "imparted information as casually as a tree drops its leaves in the fall."[14] The mysteries of centrifugal force, gravity and momentum, paddling a canoe, handling a jackknife, reading the newspaper, and playing the harmonic circle on the piano Stanley made comprehensible to his younger brother. He performed similar feats for generations of students at the University of Illinois, with some memorable clowning and wacky charm. Anyone who studied with him—and who also happened to come across *Charlotte's Web, Stuart Little,* or other writings by E. B. White in the *New Yorker*—could make the connection between the two brothers and their eccentric, elusive, faintly skeptical yet warmly affirmative views of the world. "All that I hope to say in books, all that I ever hope to say, is that I love the world," wrote E. B. White.[15] Stanley said as much in his own bemused, not-quite-distilled notes and memoranda.

White thrived at the University of Illinois, where the landscape architecture department had grown from a course given in the College of Agriculture in 1868 to a full professional curriculum by 1907–1908 and, by 1912, to an independent division within the Department of Horticulture. By the time White arrived, in 1922, city planning was one of the division's strengths. Charles Mulford Robinson, author of *Modern Civic Art, or The City Made Beautiful* (1903), had been a visiting professor from 1913 until his death in 1917. Harland Bartholomew, the eminent planner, spent one month a year teaching there from 1920 to about 1952. Irving L. Peterson and Karl B. Lohmann each taught at Illinois for thirty years or more and participated in national and local planning organizations. Even after 1931, when the landscape architecture program was transferred to the new College of Fine and Applied Arts, city planning remained a strong component of that department.[16]

While his colleagues reinforced the social purposes of landscape architecture, White explored other paths. He was the prime mover in creating the "Landscape Exchange Problems," first offered in 1924–25 as an informal, national competition, whereby landscape architecture students undertook a series of common design problems under common restrictions. Ferruccio Vitale was chairman of the ASLA committee that set up the exchanges, and White did most of the initial, routine work. By distributing a series of design problems to schools and universities around the country and by holding a national competition for the winners of each departmental competition, the Landscape Exchanges provided a number of benefits, including communication among the institutions, standards of excellence, a focus on project scale design, recognition of individual achievement, and (indirectly) a recognition of the quality of instruction at the different schools. White was aware that the exchanges could lead to dull standardization, but he valued their tendency to communicate and stimulate. In retrospect, a list of the authors and jurors of these Exchange Problems reads like a who's who in the field: in the 1920s, Ferruccio Vitale, Bryant Fleming, A. D. Taylor, O. C. Simonds, and Percival Gallagher; in the 1950s, Hideo Sasaki, Theodore Osmundson, Lawrence Halprin, J. O. Simonds, Sidney Shurcliff, and others.[17]

White taught landscape architecture as a high art, firmly grounded in the natural sciences, yet potentially mastered only by persons of broad cultivation in the humanities and a generalist's impartial view of the larger context. His lectures and notes were filled with references to painting, music, literature, philosophy, and quotations from far-ranging thinkers, such as Voltaire, Spengler, Thoreau, Ruskin, Mumford, Giedion, D'Arcy Thompson, and A. N. Whitehead. At times it seemed as if White lived in the world of ideas. Then one day he would dash into the classroom, wearing a black academic gown, a violin cradled in his arms, and roller skates on his feet. In a construction class, he would place a piece of wood or concrete on a chair and jump up and down on it until it broke, to explain principles of stress. One moment, he would do something zany to get students' attention. The next moment he would pitch them into the cosmos with a dissertation on geological time, asserting that the "modern" is merely whatever came out of the ice age: "The effects of great age of erosion forms or of high forests, the primordial stability of ancient systems, the relentless patience of earth's maturity and its consequent resistance to change, the very inertia of nature, reduce all momentary outbursts of the culture to most trivial insignificance. Earth history assumes a majestic role and inevitably dominates the play with a tragic seriousness."[18]

By 1953, when White wrote this, most students must have known that nature was continually changing; that to speak of nature's inertia was to raise issues of relativity and scale. "Where is the moon?" White repeatedly asked one class for an entire semester—until the moment when, in the middle of the final exam, he snapped up the window shade and beamed as he pointed, "There!" That's how he taught. He also elicited from students the highest aspirations, some combination of the public service, the integrity of design, and the generalist's impartial view main-

Plate 1

Garden for Mr. and Mrs. J. Irwin Miller, Columbus, Indiana, 1955. *Allée* of honey locust trees and sculpture by Henry Moore. Dan Kiley, Landscape Architect. Eero Saarinen and Kevin Roche, Architects.

Plate 2

Weyerhaeuser World Headquarters, Federal Way, between Seattle and Tacoma, Washington, 1963–1972. Skidmore, Owings & Merrill, Architects. Sasaki, Walker and Associates, Landscape Architects.

Plate 3

Odette Monteiro garden, Rio de Janeiro, 1948; current residence of Luis César Fernandez. Roberto Burle Marx, Landscape Architect.

Plate 4

Las Arboledas, Mexico City, 1958–1961. Red wall. Luis Barragán, Architect and Landscape Architect.

Plate 5

California Scenario, Costa Mesa, California, 1980–1986. Isamu Noguchi, Landscape Architect and Sculptor.

Plate 6

Garden for Mr. and Mrs. Dewey Donnell, Sonoma, California, 1948. Thomas Church, Landscape Architect.

Plate 7

Lovejoy Plaza, Portland, Oregon, 1961–1968. Lawrence Halprin & Associates, Landscape Architects.

Plate 8

Paley Park, New York City, ca. 1965. Zion & Breen, Landscape Architects.

Plate 9

Garden of Planes, Bloedel Reserve, Bainbridge Island, Washington, 1981–1982. Richard Haag, Landscape Architect.

Plate 10

Deere and Company Headquarters, Moline, Illinois, 1963. Eero Saarinen and Associates, Architects. Sasaki, Walker and Associates, Landscape Architects. Henry Moore, Sculptor.

Plate 11

Foothill College, Los Altos Hills, California, 1960. Sasaki, Walker and Associates, Landscape Architects. Ernest J. Kump and Associates; and Masten and Hurd, Architects.

Plate 12

Tanner Fountain, Harvard University. Peter Walker with the SWA Group, Landscape Architects.

tained by the Olmsteds. White's ideal landscape architect would be a poet-philosopher who could penetrate the complexities of a given problem, rationalize it, and draw out of its multiple demands a design solution appropriate to the land, its vegetation, and natural processes, as well as to functional and cultural needs.

By the time ecology became an important concern among educators in the profession in the early 1950s, White happily took up Sasaki's suggestion of organizing the landscape architect's study of the natural sciences. The twenty-eight-page document he produced, "An Introduction to the Science of the Natural Environment" (1954), listed enough scientific readings and pursuits for a generalist's lifetime—and it was prefaced by a song and a passage from Shakespeare's *As You Like It*.[19] White never lost sight of the whole person. He would not specialize to the point of losing some essential part of the whole. His upbringing, his inclinations, and the state of the landscape architectural profession during his lifetime all reinforced this focus on the well-rounded, articulate generalist, trained to think and to lead. Some proof of his teaching will, ultimately, lie in his students—among them, Hideo Sasaki, Richard Haag, Charles Harris, Stuart Dawson, Lawrence Walquist, Robert O'Donnell, Philip Lewis, Lawrence Zuelke, Peter Walker—and in their students.

Hideo Sasaki was born in 1919 in Reedley, California, just southeast of Fresno, in the San Joaquin Valley. The son of a farmer, he grew up in a farming community and naturally acquired an interest in plants and the natural sciences. He was also inclined toward fine art and foreign languages; and mathematics, although less interesting to him, posed no difficulty. After receiving an associate of arts degree from Reedley Junior

College in 1939, he went on to the University of California at Los Angeles (UCLA), with no specific career goals other than to get away from farming.[20]

While Sasaki was studying business administration and minoring in art at UCLA, a fellow student told him about the field of city planning, which appeared to combine many of Sasaki's interests. Sasaki then transferred to the University of California, Berkeley, the only campus in the University of California system where a program of city planning was offered—in the landscape architecture department. There, in 1940–41, Sasaki found landscape architecture more appealing than planning. Things and ideas were more intriguing to him than the politics of planning. Then the politics of war intervened, and the internment of Japanese-Americans abruptly ended his studies in California.

To escape the confines of internment, Sasaki volunteered to work in the sugar beet fields of Colorado. Later he worked in Chicago, where the extensive park system (much of it by the Olmsted firm and Jens Jensen) and the forest preserves made a deep impression; Sasaki found in those large landscapes a scale, a breadth, and a simplicity that moved him. He was naturally prepared, then, for the larger scale of physical design, and its social and cultural implications, which he would soon encounter at the University of Illinois.

Sasaki spent two years at the University of Illinois, from 1944 to 1946. Because wartime enrollment was down, he had few fellow students; the class of 1946 had only two graduates. There were at least six faculty members, however—Irving L. Peterson, Otto G. Schaffer, Harland Bartholomew, Karl B. Lohmann, Florence Bell Robinson, and Stanley White—all of whom had been teaching in the department since the

1920s.[21] Beaux arts methods of design were competently taught, unchallenged by modernist design ideas. And the continuity of this seasoned team of educators, carrying forth the ideals of a brave young profession in spite of nearly empty classrooms and the uncertainties of wartime, must have been reassuring to students.

An independent-minded student, however, Sasaki spent countless hours in the library doing research for a paper entitled, "The Inferiority Complex of Landscape Architects." Never published, the paper dealt with the relationships of landscape architecture to the larger and better-known professions of architecture and engineering. This topic, not quite so bluntly identified, would reappear from time to time in *Landscape Architecture* and other professional magazines. Changing one's title to "site planner" and deemphasizing the role of horticulture (to avoid the epithet of "bush planter") were among the tactics adopted in practice. Teaching, however, called for a more comprehensive strategy, and few educators were as articulate on these matters as Sasaki—and Stanley White.

In 1946 Sasaki received his B.F.A. in landscape architecture with highest honors from the University of Illinois. After receiving the M.L.A. degree from Harvard in 1948 and spending that summer in the site planning division of SOM in New York, Sasaki returned to Illinois in 1948 as a young instructor. There, for two years, he was a colleague of White, with whom he shared not only social, cultural, and spiritual concerns but also a more pragmatic interest in the landscape architect's professional role and status.

"Landscape architecture may have its back against the wall," White observed in 1952. The main threats seemed to be the public's ignorance of the profession and competition for leadership from other professionals. White believed that landscape architecture arose out of protest against what architects, engineers, and horticulturists were doing with the land and that the tensions within the inherently critical profession would not soon disappear. His strategy for reinforcing the landscape architect's position would involve several moves—among them, to recognize the base of natural science that sets landscape architects apart from architects and engineers, to inform the public about what landscape architects do, to improve the methods—and the business—of professional practice, and to train more competent professionals and thereby "save for posterity the most valid approach to the most fundamental resource of creation, the landscape."[22]

Sasaki adopted about three-quarters of this strategy. Among his finest contributions to the profession was to play a major role in raising the teaching and practice of landscape architecture from near obscurity (during wartime) to prominence within academic and professional circles. By demonstrating the landscape architect's role in collaborative planning and design, Sasaki did for middle- and large-scale projects what Thomas Church did for the West Coast house and garden: he made the landscape architect an essential player, sometimes a leader. What Sasaki did not do, personally, was to inform the general public. Although he encouraged and financially assisted a group of Harvard students to mount an exhibition of the elder Olmsted's career—an exhibition that traveled to schools around the country and resulted in a book—Sasaki did not himself write for a broad audience.[23] He produced no television shows, "happenings," or festive public events. Nor, for all his mimeographed output, did Stanley White publish much. Why not?

A number of reasons could be offered. There was the landscape architect's traditional reluctance to call attention to oneself. In this gentleman's profession, publishing outside one's field may have seemed like public relations or advertising. Before academics had to publish or perish, White was perhaps too engrossed in teaching to address any audience, let alone the public, in print. Sasaki has quietly remarked, "I would like what I've done in my life to be judged on the basis of what I did, not so much what I've said."[24] Perhaps both men were preoccupied with doing. Then, too, the tools of communication were simpler in those days, while the amount of information and ideas to be communicated and analyzed was less. Perhaps in school, as in innumerable facets of life, people were more accustomed than we are today to personal human contact, which could be perfunctory, or tedious, or terrifying, but also inspirational (figure 100).

White admired the great teachers of the past—and emulated them. "They started the student on his own power by the sheer magic of revealing the excitement of what they were teaching," he observed. "How did they instil this precious thing called love? And how did they manage it without sacrificing the learned disciplines they knew how to implant? . . . They made both the ideas and the student seem important and were able to play one against the other. . . . There are times when the teacher waits for days to secure the right situation for development of a particular idea. These are golden moments—and they are not on the calendar—but they are carried in memory by the student as long as he lives."[25]

Sasaki's effect on students was more cerebral yet no less personal and inspiring. In 1950 he looked beyond the teaching methods at hand—

100. Hideo Sasaki with Stuart O. Dawson, a student and, later, a colleague at Sasaki, Dawson, DeMay and Associates.

logical sequences of coordinated courses versus case studies—and identified the essential activity common to both. This was critical thinking, whereby one understands and solves any given problem. A design problem, "essentially a process of relating all the operational factors into a comprehensive whole, including the factors of cost and effect," in Sasaki's view, would be solved in three stages: research, analysis, and synthesis. Methods of the first two stages could be taught, he noted. Synthesis would depend on the designer's own genius, something to be guided and cultivated.[26]

Sasaki's genius as an educator lay partly in organization—his method of building up a diverse, advanced curriculum and managing teams of instructors, eliciting the finest efforts of his students, colleagues, and clients. He revealed a discriminating eye for aesthetic quality, as well as the humane instincts of a good manager. Above all, Sasaki provided a powerful vision of landscape architecture as a truly collaborative activity, led by the intellect and sustained by goodwill among members of a team.

Together with Walter Gropius, G. Holmes Perkins, Reginald Isaacs, and others, Sasaki ran collaborative design studios at Harvard, where problems were undertaken jointly by students of architecture, planning, and landscape architecture. He recalls that Gropius never gave up his notion of the architect as master builder, superior to all other design professionals. Nevertheless, in an atmosphere of intellectual inquiry and free discussion, Sasaki and his colleagues and students succeeded in demonstrating the landscape architect's essential contributions to the increasingly complex continuum of planning and design. Both in the studio and in practice, Sasaki realized his dream of the integrated team.

White and Sasaki brilliantly epitomize two eras in landscape architectural education. By the eve of World War II, White had taught for several decades of the earlier era, a time when a single educator could, if pressed, teach a course in any of the subjects considered essential to the field: construction, plant materials, design, and history. Specific problem areas, such as city planning or garden design or roadway engineering, would be familiar to White and most of his colleagues. Together a resident faculty would be expected to offer basic instruction in all the core fields. Also, for most educators teaching was a full-time occupation. White worked on actual projects only intermittently, usually during summer vacations. Bartholomew, taking one month a year from his planning practice to teach, was an exception.

But after the doldrums of World War II, with national recovery, rebuilding, and vast new development underway, the teaching of landscape architecture was transformed. No longer could a single educator teach nearly all there was to learn. From the 1950s onward, the core of knowledge considered essential expanded so rapidly, especially in the sciences, that specialists had to be brought in from other disciplines and from practice, to offer more varied courses or segments, in greater depth. This recruiting of specialists Sasaki considered a "breakthrough" in the teaching process. At schools intent on guiding the cutting edge of the profession, the professor of landscape architecture would assume the roles of manager, coordinator, and critic—the very roles that Sasaki assumed in his firm. Once this pattern of coordinating visiting experts was established, it was natural for the lines between teaching and practice to become blurred.

For Harvard, this was a radical change. Among the university's eminent teacher-practitioners of landscape architecture, Henry Vincent Hubbard, who taught there from 1906 to 1941, had perhaps set the tone. "When he left his classes at the end of the day," wrote colleague Bremer Pond, "he was able to put aside completely all thought of Robinson Hall. . . . Any activity or professional work was never allowed to interfere with his teaching schedule, nor was their existence intimated in any way to his students, although this latter habit was probably due to his extreme reserve as well as to his dislike of talking about what he himself had done."[27]

No less reserved, Sasaki found it expedient, stimulating, and financially imperative to integrate his teaching and practice, particularly while he chaired Harvard's department of landscape architecture, from 1958 to 1968. Coping with the department's miniscule budget for salaries, honoraria, and scholarships, Sasaki could maintain only a limited core faculty, including Norman T. Newton and the young Charles W. Harris, as well as Sasaki's former students (figures 101 and 102). He offered many small honoraria and scholarships, and he relied on the intrinsic interest of the design problems, the school's prestige, altruism, and idealism to

101. Norman T. Newton, Charles Eliot Professor of Landscape Architecture, Harvard Graduate School of Design, 1965.

102. Charles W. Harris, Professor of Landscape Architecture, Harvard Graduate School of Design, 1963.

attract visiting jurors and critics. Sasaki's firm offered summer and part-time jobs to help support students. In turn, graduates would remain in the firm for a few years or more, serving also as instructors or visiting critics for little or no pay—in effect, "giving back" something to the institution that had nourished them. All in all, it was a unique symbiosis between practice and teaching.

Sasaki also maintained a diverse, state-of-the-art curriculum by the continual influx of specialists and generalists. While Kevin Lynch, his friend and colleague at MIT, was still working on *The Image of the City* (1960), he gave guest lectures in Sasaki's classes, as Sasaki did in his. In one academic year, 1963–64, Sasaki brought in Lynch and planner Donald Appleyard from MIT; Edmund N. Bacon, executive director of the Philadelphia Planning Commission; Macklin L. Hancock, founder of Project Planning Associates in Toronto; Victor Olgyay, an architect from Princeton studying climatic influences on architecture; Louis J. Bakanowsky, an architect and sculptor on the Harvard faculty; Philip Lewis, a University of Wisconsin professor then heading the state's Recreation Resources and Design Division; Stanley White, focusing on small house design and expressive qualities of land forms; Don Olson, Kenneth DeMay, and others from Sasaki's firm; and specialists in aerial photo analysis, soil science, forestry, biology, sociology, oceanography, hydraulics, lighting, civil engineering, city planning, and so on.

For Sasaki's students, graduate school entailed two or three years of immersion, absorbing new kinds of information and seeing their connections, learning to think analytically, and working toward a synthesis in design. (Students who had earned B.L.A. degrees and ASLA certificates of merit could enroll for a single-year master's program.) In 1963, student Joseph Volpe wrote a long, enthusiastic letter to Garrett Eckbo, reporting on Harvard's generally "excellent" program in landscape architecture. Although planting design was weak, in Volpe's view—and architectonic ideas tended to dominate—he appreciated the balance of views offered by the many visitors, including Stanley White, Burle Marx, Robert Zion, and Dan Kiley. Volpe, now an award-winning practitioner and professor of landscape architecture at the University of Massachusetts, concluded, "Hideo is the best design professor I have ever had."[28]

Many other students have said as much, and they have spread Sasaki's influence nationwide, including Harry Porter, professor of landscape architecture and formerly dean of the School of Architecture, University of Virginia; William J. Johnson, formerly professor of landscape architecture and formerly dean of the School of Natural Resources, University of Michigan, now a partner of Peter Walker William Johnson and Partners, San Francisco; Stuart Dawson, principal at Sasaki Associates and frequently visiting critic at Harvard and other schools; Gary Karner, professor of landscape architecture at California Polytechnic State University, San Luis Obispo, and consulting principal, The SWA Group; Peter Walker, formerly adjunct professor and chairman, department of landscape architecture at Harvard, now a partner of Peter Walker William Johnson and Partners, San Francisco; and Richard Haag, principal of Richard Haag Associates and professor, founder and chairman, Department of Landscape Architecture, University of Washington, in Seattle.

Among the eminent designers who have studied under White and Sasaki, Richard Haag honors both men when, after thirty years of teaching and practice, he asserts that "practice is merely an extension (albeit

103. Stanley H. White and Richard Haag. An exceptionally gifted student of both Stanley White and Hideo Sasaki, Haag moved on to begin a new program of landscape architecture at the University of Washington, in Seattle, in 1958, as well as to establish his own practice of landscape architecture.

104. Richard Haag, at Gas Works Park (1970–1978), Seattle, Washington, 1990. Richard Haag Associates, Landscape Architects. Here, on the shores of Lake Union, Haag incorporated the obsolete industrial structures into his plan for the new park and also initiated experiments in bioremediation, whereby the polluted soil would be slowly reclaimed through natural processes.

important) of teaching; the best way to teach is by demonstration" (figure 103).[29] What Haag demonstrates, through works ranging from a poetic series of gardens on Bainbridge Island, in Puget Sound, to the recycling of a defunct gas plant in Seattle, is imagination, energy, a defiance of conventional "wisdom," and a willingness to work patiently within the time frame of earth's processes. He may have puzzled a few students with his thoughts about design, yin-yang relationships, and the collective unconscious.[30] But he has also passed on to them something of what he was exposed to under his two mentors: White's romantic, poetic sensibilities and his interest in natural processes, and Sasaki's clear thought, depth of culture, and broad vision (figures 104–106, plate 9).

Harvard professor of landscape architecture Charles Harris has summed up the deeply personal impact of both White's and Sasaki's teaching: "Each of these men implanted in our minds and hearts a sense of the field of landscape architecture, its role and possibilities for public service that made it worthy of a life-long dedication."[31] Harris's memories of these men and their times suggest a golden age. "We were all young and idealistic," Sasaki recalls. "We thought the world had no problems that could not be solved. We were not worried about the future or about fame or fortune. We were all very much concerned

about ideas, and thinking up new ways. Those periods happen from time to time. A coalescing of different forces and ideas."[32]

Times changed. Society changed. Students changed. The civil rights movement and an undeclared war in Southeast Asia posed questions of public and private morality, environmental degradation, and basic human rights. Authority was questioned. Multiple allegiances came into conflict. Students shut down some universities, including Harvard. In Sasaki's view, the universities were the "one precious thing they should not have bashed. That's where I parted company with [the students]."[33] Literally. In 1968, Sasaki felt it was time to step down as chairman at Harvard. After 1970 he was no longer on the Harvard faculty. And another era in the teaching of landscape architecture began, without the active participation of White and Sasaki.

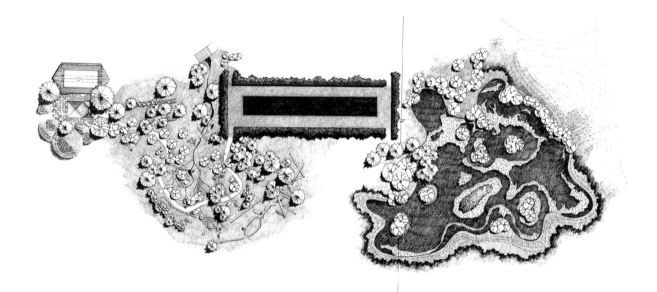

Living in Denver after his retirement from the University of Illinois in 1959, White could contemplate the Continental Divide and reflect, "But we should thank God for earthquakes which rescue us, however monstrously, from Permian deserts and steaming Paleozoic jungles, and give us mountain scenery in which to pitch our tents."[34] White died in 1979.

Living in Lafayette, California, a few miles east of San Francisco Bay, on a high ridge with a view of Mount Diablo, Sasaki continues to consult on projects of landscape architecture and to serve on design review boards and juries. Though often asked, he rarely lectures. Occasional contact with students and young instructors, however, leaves him optimistic. He admires the talented, enthusiastic young instructors, charged with the energy and idealism essential to their art. "Teaching," he smiles, "you have to tell students anything can be done."[35]

105. A series of gardens, The Bloedel Reserve, Bainbridge Island, Washington, plan: 1985. Richard Haag, Landscape Architect. In this series of gardens, one moves from geometrically ordered spaces to areas that appear wild, and again, from geometry to the wild. For Haag, a journey through these gardens reminds one of the immutable bond between human beings and the natural world.

106. Reflection Garden, The Bloedel Reserve, 1978–1985.

Chapter 8

**The Corporate Office,
a New Organism for
Practice: First Wave**

Recently Hideo Sasaki reflected on the early years of his multidisciplinary design firm, then known as Sasaki, Walker and Associates: "I've always felt that practice—the way we practice—is the same as teaching," he observed. "It's teaching a different group, perhaps a more mature group" (figure 107).[1]

This attitude, which was also typical of the early years of Wallace-McHarg Associates and Johnson, Johnson and Roy, is not typical among landscape architects today. Why, then, did Sasaki and so many of his former colleagues and students look back on the late 1950s and 1960s as a time of greater idealism, optimism, and lack of concern for earning a living, getting ahead, positioning oneself, or making one's mark? Why was the team so important and its work (let alone individual achievement) so little publicized?

At that time, excitement over new ideas, methods, and areas of investigation at the Harvard Graduate School of Design, as elsewhere, was sustained through the intense growth, change, ferment, even tragedy in the world outside. The idealistic dream of John F. Kennedy was short-lived, but the confidence it inspired lived on for many years in Sasaki's department and practice. Through guest appearances and collaborative projects, Sasaki ensured that the more hopeful yet pragmatic aspects of the "world outside" would continually inform academia, and vice versa. These exchanges not only stimulated intellectual inquiry; they focused on the urgent tasks awaiting students after graduation, at a time when the material resources and human will to create were abundant.

Sasaki opened his first office near Boston in 1953. Dan Kiley was then one of the few landscape architects to work with the leading modern architects of the East Coast, such as SOM and Saarinen. Soon Sasaki,

107. Portrait of Hideo Sasaki, ca. 1970. Serving as senior critic and chief spokesman for Sasaki, Walker and Associates (now, Sasaki Associates, Inc.), Sasaki presided over a large group practice—eventually more than 300 members—of landscape architects, planners, architects, engineers, and communication specialists.

too, was attracting these architects. He impressed them with his fine sensibility for design, informed by both a solid background in beaux arts methods of site planning and practical experience in site planning for distinctly modern buildings. Given his sure instincts for office organization and management and his continuing ties to Harvard (which, for a while, offered the only graduate program of landscape architecture in the country), Sasaki took on increasingly more large-scale, complex planning and design projects throughout the country and abroad. In time his office became the postwar training ground for a certain type of office that would, by the late 1970s, become dominant in the field: the corporate, multidisciplinary landscape architectural firm. A closer look at how this firm evolved can help to identify the roots of many leading practices of our time (figure 108).

Sasaki spent the summer of 1948 working in the site planning division of SOM's New York office. For three years (1948–1950 and 1952–1953), while teaching at the University of Illinois, in Champaign-Urbana, Sasaki also worked for Perkins and Will, a Chicago firm then known for the design of the innovative Crow Island School (Winnetka, Illinois, 1939) with Eliel Saarinen. After the war, with experience in the design of more schools as well as apartment buildings, office buildings, hospitals, and mass-produced housing, Perkins and Will became a multidisciplinary firm with a strong focus on community design.

108. Group portrait of members of Hideo Sasaki's office, Watertown, Massachusetts, ca. 1965: from left, Hideo Sasaki, Stuart O. Dawson, Richard Dober, John Frey, Larry Walquist, Don Olson, Marvin Adelman, Don Sakuma.

While working at Perkins and Will, Sasaki met one of his future partners, landscape architect Paul Novak. He also met architects who openly challenged the men who, by the quantity of their production, were the real planners and designers of the environment: builders and developers. Philip Will, who later served as president of the AIA, denounced the behavioral conformity and waste of land in typical, narrow-market-oriented housing subdivisions. He believed teams of responsible architects, builders, land planners, and engineers must collaborate on a larger scale, with great vision. "All we need to do," he noted in 1960, "is open up our vistas and learn to work together. . . . For in truth, we are the architects and builders and planners of towns and cities, and what we do now will come back, either to haunt or to fulfill us."[2]

By the time these words appeared in print, Sasaki was already heading an office that assumed a similar mission, particularly for the urban environment. In 1954 he and Novak had formed a partnership, and the two had worked on urban design projects such as the Michael Reese Hospital, on the South Side of Chicago, a collaborative effort with Reginald Isaacs (then chairman of Harvard's planning department) and Chester

Nagel, of The Architects Collaborative (TAC). Soon afterward, Isaacs, Sasaki, and Nagel was formed as an ad hoc joint venture to study the urban environs of the Harvard Medical School, in Boston. Later Sasaki joined his former student, Richard Strong, in a similar venture: Sasaki, Strong & Associates, in Toronto.

Juggling the demands of practice and teaching during the 1950s, Sasaki wrote only a few short, pithy articles for professional and departmental magazines. In 1955 he warned that the city as a function and a cultural expression was endangered. After millions of urban Americans had fled to the suburbs, taking with them their wealth and leadership, some eroded inner-city areas needed radical rebuilding. Others, slowly deteriorating, needed rehabilitation, or "community conservation," which Isaacs had pioneered in Chicago. Alluding to studies that he and Isaacs had prepared for ACTION, a national nonprofit, nonpolitical citizens' group, Sasaki asked, "Can a better environment be created?" Despite the complexity and diversity of the city, he believed residents should be able to grasp the whole. Landscape architects could contribute parks, green spaces, better street patterns, and siting of buildings, and, with others, they could aim to transcend function and economics. The good environment should have a "visually satisfying expression, which in some respects is the measure of cultural achievement of a civilization."[3]

Such was Sasaki's broad concept of landscape architecture at a time when the profession sorely needed vision and leadership. Two years later, in 1957, after Novak had returned to Chicago, Sasaki made one of his former students, Peter Walker, a partner. And as Sasaki, Walker and Associates assumed a greater role in urban renewal, mixed-use developments, and campus planning and design, there appeared to be no limits to their potential for shaping the physical environment. Grady Clay, then editor of *Landscape Architecture,* was urging landscape architects to get into positions of power—on budget committees, planning boards, and advisory boards to mayors, company presidents, and others. "You should be in the forefront of the city planning movement," he exhorted, "leading, not following the pack."[4] Before long Sasaki's office was one that assumed such leadership—less overt than Clay intended, perhaps—through the exemplary work of a subtly directed team.

This team became multidisciplinary as it grew from a core of versatile landscape architects whose complementary strengths amounted to the range of skills traditionally expected of a single, well-rounded professional—notably, planning, design, construction, horticulture, and presentation. In a time of increasing specialization among other professionals (as in law, medicine, the sciences, and the humanities), these skills of a landscape architect also became specialties, or parts of a whole, to be refined, coordinated, and managed.

By 1960, Sasaki had hired a young architect, Kenneth DeMay, to assist in a range of landscape architectural projects. Throughout that decade, in fact, landscape design was recognized as the primary service of Sasaki's office. But in time, as opportunities arose, Sasaki added architecture and civil engineering to the capabilities of the office, and other professionals were brought in with particular environmental, artistic, and technical skills. Here, Sasaki was building on his positive experiences at SOM and Perkins and Will. By then other multidisciplinary firms had also developed from a base of architectural practice, such as Hellmuth, Obata and Kassabaum (HOK), in St. Louis; RTKL, in Baltimore; and Gropius's firm, TAC, in Cambridge, Massachusetts. However, like Macklin Hancock, his former student in Toronto, Sasaki was integrating the several disciplines on a new basis—land planning, site design, and the context of the larger environment.[5]

The ideological roots of Sasaki, Walker and Associates can be traced to the Bauhaus. Gropius, founder of that school in Weimar in 1919, once identified its great value in freeing students of art and design from the "subjective recipes" of one master. The Bauhaus had been set up to demonstrate "how a multitude of individuals, willing to work concertedly but without losing their identity, could evolve a kinship of expression in their response to the challenges of the day."[6] In fact, Gropius was so committed to the ideal of teamwork that, when he surveyed the disorder of modern cities and suburbs, he would not hold modern architects or modernism responsible; rather, he cited the lack of genuine collaboration, based on mutual respect, commitment to a common effort, and individual leadership and responsibility within the group. For coherence of design, he insisted that the final decisions be left to a single member of the team, the designer in charge.

In their early years, both TAC and SOM had maintained the ideal of anonymity within the firm, pointing to the splendid Gothic cathedrals whose designers remained unknown. Gropius believed that relative anonymity, along with a free flow of ideas and criticism, would tend to inhibit "pretentious individualism." Sasaki, too, sought anonymity—to a point. Any publicity routinely went to the firm, not to the designer. But within the firm, he wanted the designer in charge to be recognized.

The Chicago office of SOM provided a model of organization that worked well for Sasaki: the project team, led by a design partner and a management partner. But Sasaki also learned from Eero Saarinen, who ran his office somewhat like a studio, gathering about him capable assistants so that he, the master, could serve as teacher and critic. This became Sasaki's main role in his office: chief design critic. Thus, an amalgam of models from SOM and Saarinen allowed Sasaki's office to expand rapidly, without burdening the chief critic and designers with all the responsibility for management.

Whether with colleagues, clients, or students, Sasaki taught through subtle critique. After five o'clock on a Friday afternoon at the office, for instance, sherry would be served, a tradition carried over from Friday afternoon reviews at Harvard. A project manager would present the issues, problems, and solutions, and Sasaki would encourage critiques. While others spoke, Sasaki would listen intently. Occasionally, he would mention a detail, previously overlooked, that had some bearing on the project's solution. Duane Niederman, who worked part-time at Sasaki's in the late 1950s while studying for a planning degree at Harvard, recalls those Friday afternoons and the calming effect that Sasaki had over the whole office. Whenever Sasaki returned from the school, slight tensions and uncertainties seemed to dissolve.[7]

Sasaki could also put clients at ease. Instead of selling the firm's strengths, he would talk freely about ideas and opportunities to solve a problem, treating clients much like his own colleagues. On an unprecedented type of project, Sasaki would call in colleagues to review the possibilities for design. For Sea Pines Plantation, for instance, developer Charles Fraser's 4,000-acre new community on Hilton Head Island, South Carolina, Sasaki wanted to adapt the Radburn idea—clustered houses, culs-de-sac, greenways, and common open space—on a greater

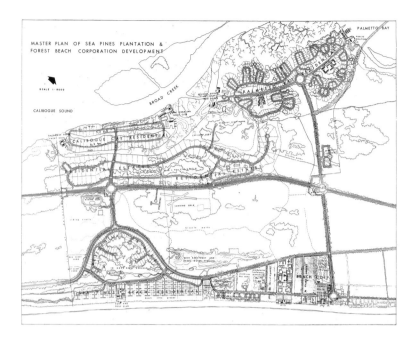

109. Sea Pines Plantation, Hilton Head Island, South Carolina, detail of master plan, ca. 1962. Charles Fraser, Developer. Sasaki, Walker and Associates, Landscape Architects and Planners. The plan includes the development of culs-de-sac and greenways at the water's edge of the site, to increase the residents' access to the beach.

scale, with a more complex program and distinctly modern architecture. Intrigued, several of Sasaki's best students came back from their own teaching and practices to review the project (figure 109).

The sharpest criticism of the Sea Pines project came from Lewis Clarke, a British architect who had studied landscape architecture under the versatile environmentalist Brian Hackett, then under Sasaki, before he began teaching at North Carolina State University. Despite the firm's efforts to cluster the homes and shops and to preserve dunes, Clarke was vehemently opposed to any development at all on that site, one of the last remaining virgin beaches on the East Coast. Ironically, Clarke was among the highly talented individuals whom Sasaki had sought for his firm, along with Charles W. Harris, Don Olson, William J. Johnson, and Mai Arbegast. Arbegast, however, remained in Berkeley, California, to teach and to practice within a small office. Johnson was drawn back to his native Michigan, where he became a leader in both academia and a large corporate landscape architectural practice (figures 110–112).[8] "I always took the view that I wanted the best," Sasaki recalls, admitting that strong-willed individuals could be difficult to hold in a firm and work with on a team.[9]

110. William J. Johnson, Dean, School of Natural Resources, University of Michigan, at Ann Arbor, 1975–1983.

In 1958, when Sasaki agreed to become chairman of Harvard's department of landscape architecture, the fluid, informal association of designers in his office became more structured. Stuart Dawson recalls that Sasaki had a natural tendency to delegate responsibilities, like a good museum director or college president.[10] A core staff, the project manager (and/or project designer) and his associates, would be assisted by a supporting staff of other designers, draftspersons, and assistants, whose roles would keep changing. Richard Dober, a planner, became executive director of the office. Other associates, many drawn from Harvard's faculty and graduate students, worked part-time. Sasaki's goal, both in the office and at the school, was to balance "the best experience and the bright, enthusiastic young people."

In 1960 Dober noted three tasks of office management: (1) to hold a group of talented, broadly informed professionals who share common philosophies; (2) to allow for individuals' growth through theoretical and practical experience; and (3) to respond to clients' unpredictable, short-term demands as well as their more manageable long-term needs. The project manager–project designer system was one pragmatic response to these needs. Another was research, or what Dober called "venture capital in ideas." Project research, aimed at solving immediate problems, could be done fairly quickly in the office library. Design research, involving more time and a refinement of methods, might lead to the discovery of new relationships among aspects of a design problem. The expected returns could be fresh insight, a stockpile of ideas, and greater depth of understanding.[11]

Sasaki's office enjoyed the proximity of congenial colleagues, bright students, and job opportunities in the Boston area. From the beginning, however, the office was sustained by work outside New England. Sasaki

111. University of Michigan, Studies for Expansion of the Central Campus, ca. 1965: Plan. Johnson, Johnson & Roy, Landscape Architects.

112. University of Michigan, at Ann Arbor, aerial view of Central Campus, ca. 1965. Sketch by William J. Johnson.

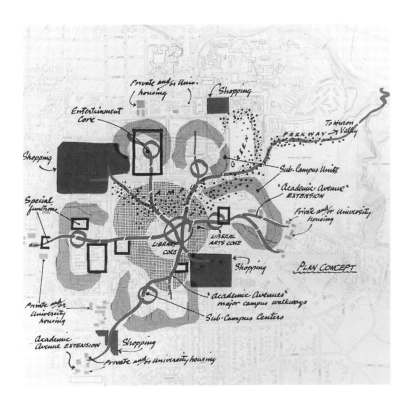

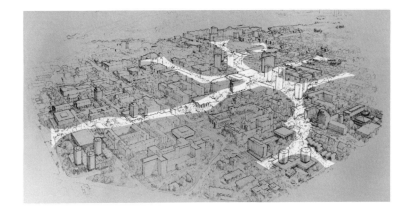

flew around the country and abroad to meet with clients and visit sites. Commercial air travel (a relatively new phenomenon) enlarged the scope of the firm, and worldwide exposure enhanced the firm's prestige. Still, until the 1960s, the firm remained small by today's standards—about twelve full-time professionals in 1959—so that Sasaki could be engaged in each project and elicit the special talents of each member of the staff. In the late 1950s, for instance, the drawings of William J. Johnson, George Connolly, and Steve Oles became an integral part of the firm's design process.

In those early years, Sasaki, Walker and Associates developed a flexible, pragmatic approach to design that could accommodate both modern and traditional buildings, an approach particularly useful for campus expansion and urban design. Sasaki himself was interested in a broad range of design expression; he cared less about precise details of form and style than about asking the right questions, identifying key issues, and coordinating the best talents to be found. Within his office, designers were generally aware of the ideological schism between modernism and history, yet they believed that the great historical periods and national traditions of landscape architecture could be integrated with modernism. The clients, particularly those architects of the second generation of modernists, were also generally receptive to landscape imagery drawn from the great historic periods of Europe, Japan, and China. Historical accuracy was less relevant to their collective efforts than an accommodating, often rather romantic, setting for the building—the dominant object.

The first designers whom Sasaki guided, challenged, and inspired included landscape architects Stuart Dawson and Peter Walker, and Masao Kinoshita, an architect, urban designer, and sculptor.[12] Subjected to in-house critiques from their colleagues as well as from Sasaki, these designers were able to develop some personal expression, while helping to establish standards, through their conversations, photographs, drawings, and plans. Beginning in 1960, when the regional office in San Francisco was formed, the work of the firm was informed by a larger body of national and international experience. And by the end of that decade, the firm had developed some mildly eclectic forms of modernism, combining eighteenth-century English and second-hand Japanese forms. Grading, road design, circulation systems, and the proper setting of buildings were the main concerns. Occasionally a piece of sculpture or a series of artworks would be incorporated into the design.

However artfully conceived and executed, the firm's landscape designs were not generally perceived as works of art—not by the client, the architect (or architect/client), the users, the public, or the members of the firm. The landscape architecture at the John Deere Headquarters (1961–1964), for instance, Dawson's early masterwork and one of the finest efforts of Sasaki's collaborative practice, was conceived as a great view, to be seen from the several floors of offices in Eero Saarinen's splendid building (figures 113 and 114, plate 10). As in an English landscape garden, Henry Moore's bronze sculpture is sited on an island in a naturalistic man-made lake, framed by willows. This lake and sculpture, along with a more distant lake and the surrounding woodlands of native sugar maples, red maples, hawthorn, and white ash, all lead the eye from the foreground base of the building to the distant fields and forests. Here the vista became an expression of corporate power—serene, understated, and enduring.

113. Deere and Company Headquarters, Moline, Illinois, 1963: Plan. Eero Saarinen and Associates, Architects. Sasaki, Walker and Associates, Landscape Architects. Stuart Dawson, Principal Designer. Henry Moore, Sculptor. This great viewing garden complements the building, providing for it a heightened, dramatic setting. Both grand and elegantly refined, the garden provides a foreground and a visual and symbolic connection to the countryside beyond.

114. Deere and Company Headquarters.

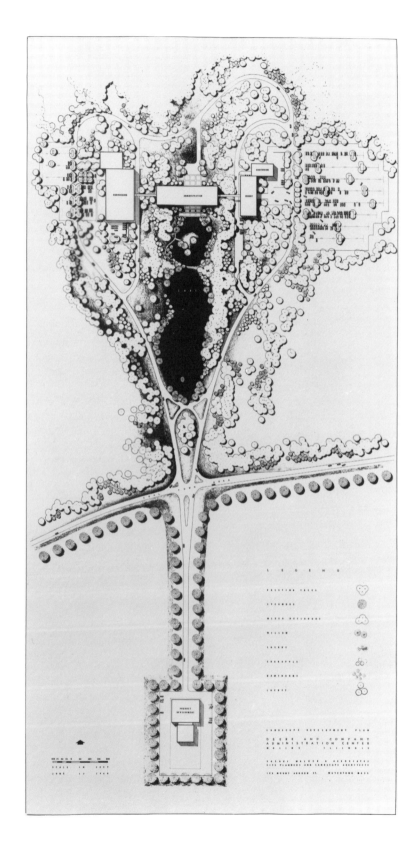

In the Olmstedian pastoral tradition, Sasaki directed the design of landscapes that did not call attention to themselves but rather served as quiet, dignified settings for modern buildings and sculpture. Functional needs, such as heat exchange for a building's air-conditioning system, could be served by a naturalistic lake—as at Deere—but qualitative issues and spiritual needs were also considered. Aesthetic values have always been very important to Sasaki. "They may not be necessary for survival," he has said, "but they are necessary for a full life."[13]

The final design of the Deere headquarters building, as Jory Johnson has noted, came directly out of Saarinen's previous visit to Japan.[14] And in developing the ideas for both the building and its "Japanese" garden, Saarinen had the critical assistance of Masao Kinoshita.[15] Calm and elegant yet robust, the Cor-ten steel building wears well, both materially and aesthetically. It also expresses the technology and the industrial character of Deere's tractors and other farm equipment. Younger critics today may be disappointed, however, by the lack of formal or symbolic connection between the building and its larger landscape. A postmodern preoccupation with context, metaphor, and iconography may discourage them from trying to see the Deere headquarters in its own time—a time when modernism encouraged dreams of pure form, form with a life of its own, and universal space.

Sasaki was not personally drawn toward overtly symbolic expression. His eye and mind were engaged in the creation of a harmonious, integrated environment in which building and landscape were complementary yet distinct, each element fulfilling its own functions and expressing its own purposes. A few years before the Deere commission came into the office, Sasaki observed:

115. Constitution Plaza, Hartford, Connecticut, ca. 1965: Aerial view. Charles DuBose, Coordinating Architect. Sasaki, Walker and Associates, Landscape Architects. Masao Kinoshita and Stuart O. Dawson, Principal Designers. One of the first comprehensive downtown renewal projects with pedestrian promenades and garden courts, Constitution Plaza ultimately extended over a dozen city blocks. This great modern urban garden was built entirely on the roof of a multilevel parking structure.

The materials and methods with which [the landscape architect] must work and the functions he must resolve may lead to a design expression which may often be almost in direct contrast to that of his sister art, architecture, which he has traditionally aped too frequently. . . . Where the materials of post, beams, and panels [of the Japanese structure] have given rise to such geometric (rectangular) forms in architecture, the rocks, plants, earth, and water have given rise to almost completely biomorphic forms. The two design expressions have reached an equally high peak of development, and the two in combination have created an integrated environment almost incomparable in their appropriateness.[16]

Often mentioned in office critiques and Friday afternoon reviews, this contrast between geometric and biomorphic forms was to become a standard design principle of Sasaki, Walker and Associates. At Constitution Plaza, in Hartford, Connecticut (from 1959), for instance, Dawson's courtyards of massed rhododendrons and irregularly placed

flowering trees provide strong contrast to Kinoshita's geometric organization of pedestrian walkways and groves (figure 115). The heart of the plaza—in reality, a roof garden over a multilevel parking garage—contains elements of a traditional European town center, including Kinoshita's monumental fountain, clock tower, lighting, and paving. From there one enters the willow court, by Dawson, an unexpected green sanctuary of willows rising from raised grassy mounds (where bedded-out summer annuals are an unfortunate recent addition). These mounds resemble islands in a sea of hexagonally patterned asphalt, now faded to light gray. Nearly surrounded by office towers and first-floor shops, this sheltered willow court remains visually open to the plaza's urban center, with views of the clock tower, groves, and benches, all lightly framed by a trellis.

While Constitution Plaza was rising in Connecticut, Walker and his colleagues were guided by similar principles at the new Foothill College, in Los Altos, California (figure 116, plate 11). Working closely with architects Ernest J. Kump and Masten and Hurd on the master plan, the landscape architects introduced the concept of gently contoured mounds to recall the surrounding foothills and to contrast with the rectilinear layout of academic buildings. The site is a hilltop—an acropolis of learning—linked by a massive wooden bridge to an adjacent knoll that accommodates the pool and sports complex. Parking is contained on low-lying grounds, originally planted as orchards. By broad staircases, one ascends the unirrigated, summer-dry, golden brown hills to enter the green oasis of open courtyards, laced by two systems of pedestrian circulation: one rectilinear, aligned with the bases of the buildings and sheltered by their generous eaves; the other curvilinear, meandering among rolling lawns and mounds. The heart of the campus is a paved, rectilinear plaza, framed by regular groves of trees. Slightly sunken, the plaza can serve as an informal amphitheater while enhancing the eminence of its presiding structure, the library.

In small urban places, such as the roof garden of Place Bonaventure, in Montreal (1967), and Greenacre Park, in New York City (1972), the landscape spaces are entirely architectural in character—like outdoor rooms. There Kinoshita achieved contrast in smaller details of form and texture. At focal points, rectilinear blocks of hewn, dressed stone and ashlar masonry are juxtaposed with rough-cut stone and boulders, while water falls in cascades, spilling, foaming, and muffling urban sounds.

The contrasts between rectilinear (or geometric) and biomorphic forms are heightened at Golden Gateway Center, San Francisco (from 1960). Whereas Sidney Walton Park is sited on grade, Alcoa Plaza lies on structure—the first plaza-on-structure for Sasaki, Walker and Associates/San Francisco (figures 117 and 118). The park is a rolling grass plane, biomorphic in both vertical and horizontal dimensions. A fountain occupies a central spot where paths converge; and in the fountain rises François Stahly's sculpture, fractionating the water into droplets, just as a nearby ring of poplars fractionates light among its quivering leaves. The plaza, in contrast, provides a series of outdoor rooms at the base of the Alcoa Building, by Edward C. Bassett, of SOM. The architectural character of its site—the roof of a parking garage—is expressed in the roomlike spaces, articulated by fencing, paving, and seat-height planters. Each room contains a piece of sculpture. Opposite one entrance to the building is a monumental fountain by John Woodard, and at each corner of the plaza is a belvedere, offering marvelous views of city, bay, and bridges.

Two corporate headquarters, one in the Midwest and one in the Pacific Northwest, both by SOM and Sasaki, Walker and Associates, reveal a considerable range of expression. In each case, the building and the landscape are complementary, but only in the second does the building seem to merge with, and become, landscape.

The Upjohn Corporation's world headquarters, in Kalamazoo, Michigan, begun in the late 1950s, was the result of a close collaboration between Bruce Graham, of SOM, and Walker (figure 119). As at Deere and Company, the 100-acre parklike setting of the Upjohn Building was handled in broad, sweeping contours and drifts of willows (on lower ground), along with birches, sugar maples, and pines farther up from the water's edge. Seemingly natural, this formerly agricultural land was completely reshaped, graded, and replanted. From a distance, it resembles a mature English landscape garden. But adjacent to the building, on slightly raised terraces, are regular groves of trees that separate the seemingly natural from the clearly man-made. Like orchards in the agricultural landscape, these groves encompass spaces that demand greater maintenance, and, once in their midst, as in a classic French garden, one moves easily into the architectural domain of courtyards and intensive human use.

Despite the hints of English, French, and even Japanese garden elements, the landscape and courtyards of Upjohn are among the clearest expressions of the serenity and timelessness that modernism seemed to promise. The allusions to traditional Japanese gardens in Upjohn's terraces and courtyards are so attenuated and abstract that the play of pure form, texture, reflections, and dappled light and shade becomes visually interesting in its own right. Each courtyard was designed to be

117. Alcoa Plaza, Golden Gateway Center, San Francisco, 1961. Skidmore, Owings & Merrill; Wurster, Bernardi & Emmons, Architects. Edward C. Bassett, Principal Designer. Sasaki, Walker and Associates, Landscape Architects. Peter Walker, Principal Designer. John Woodard, Sculptor (fountain). A formal rooftop urban park with a sculpture garden (with works by Henry Moore, Marino Marini, Charles Perry, and J. P. Stern), Alcoa Plaza is composed of two large and four small outdoor rooms, along with corner belvederes that provide views of the city and the bay.

118. Sidney Walton Square, Golden Gateway Center, from 1960. Wurster, Bernardi & Emmons; DeMars and Reay; Anshen and Allen; Skidmore, Owings & Merrill, Architects. François Stahly, Sculptor (fountain). Sasaki, Walker and Associates, Landscape Architects. Peter Walker, Principal Designer. This little park in the center of the high-rise redevelopment project provides a contrast of light and shadow over its stylized hills and valleys. The public is encouraged to use the lawns informally for relaxation and play.

119. Upjohn Company Headquarters, Kalamazoo, Michigan, 1961. Skidmore, Owings & Merrill, Architects. Bruce Graham, Principal Designer, Sasaki, Walker and Associates, Landscape Architects. Peter Walker, Principal Designer. This corporate villa raised on a stone plinth overlooks a naturalistic countryside of formed lakes and hills. The parterres and site boundaries are planted with formal orchards and woods, respectively. The entrances show Japanese influence. Although eclectic, the composition extends the formal beginnings established at CIGNA (See figures 37 and 38).

seen slightly differently from each of the distinguished glass-walled offices of the corporation (figure 120). These courtyards range in expression from biomorphic, with rectilinear accents, to rectilinear, with biomorphic accents. Transitions are accomplished with a gradual change of materials, from bands of stone, gravel, and sand that extend the architectural space of the building, to specimen trees, curvilinear paths, and other elements that suggest the world of nature, stylized and refined.

Viewed across their man-made lakes, both the Upjohn and the Weyerhaeuser buildings appear long and low, making calm statements of corporate presence in their respective rural landscapes. Weyerhaeuser, however, is more deeply engaged in its rugged, frontier setting (figure 121). Viewed from the highway, the building, by Edward C. Bassett, and the landscape, by Walker, seem to merge so that barriers and boundaries disappear. The steel-framed, concrete-clad structure consists of glass-walled terraces that step back from the base to the fifth floor. Just so, running perpendicular to the building, are the stepped-back terraces for parking, which allow access to the building at grade, from several levels. And as the parked automobiles nearly disappear from view beneath the canopies of mature sycamore *allées,* one is more conscious of a few natural elements that seem to dominate: water, sky, and forests of Douglas fir.

From inside the building at Weyerhaeuser, the open office landscape flows easily through mullionless walls of glass to the greater environment beyond. Thus, the building's interior and exterior landscapes visually participate in the layered planting that stretches across the building from hill to hill and across parking terraces, from offices to forest. The

120. Upjohn Company Headquarters, courtyard. In a series of courtyards, a play of
architectural and biomorphic forms produces a variety of asymmetrical views
from the surrounding offices.

121. Weyerhaeuser World Headquarters,
Federal Way, between Seattle and Tacoma, Washington, 1963–1972. Skidmore, Owings & Merrill, Architects, San
Francisco. Edward C. Bassett, Principal
Designer. Sasaki, Walker and Associates,
Landscape Architects. Peter Walker, Principal Designer. The rough Northwest
landscape is stretched with ivy across the
faces of the building. Fronted by a small
lake, the building appears like a bridge between two hills covered by coniferous
forests. The expression of roughness in
the landscape was inspired by Olmsted's
original vista of Mt. Rainier at the University of Washington, Seattle.

scale is massive, the few designed features restrained. Only in a few elements would one detect Sasaki, Walker and Associates' predilection for rectilinear and biomorphic contrasts. Compare the occasional sculptural object that marks a place of arrival—a great unhewn boulder, ivy clinging to its faces—with the simple, square-cut stone markers that indicate directions with a word or two. In this case, a few fragments of nature are more ostensibly revered than objects clearly formed by art.

"Our practice has always been rather reserved in design approach, rather pragmatic," Sasaki reflects. "Rarely have we tried to achieve fine art in design."[17] And he explains the distinction between fine art and design with an example from the Upjohn commission. In the courtyards, the landscape architect would select and arrange materials such as stone, whereas the sculptor would put his personal imprint on a material. In both cases, visual quality is critical, but the scope for personal expression would vary. In Sasaki's view, the landscape architect would allow visual interest to emanate mainly from the nature of the materials, their placement, and the realization of the purposes intended (figure 122).

The first wave of corporate offices was imbued with something of this attitude toward art and design. The fact that some of the built work of Sasaki, Walker and Associates transcended function and visual interest, communicating shared values and emotions, is a testament to Sasaki's respect for artistic expression. In his balanced view of landscape architecture, art, design, social purpose, ecology, and economics could all be rationally integrated. The continuum between planning and design could be seamless, for planning *was* design.

122. Crocker Plaza, San Francisco, ca. 1971. Welton Becket & Associates, Architects. Sasaki, Walker and Associates, Landscape Architects. Peter Walker, Principal Designer. The subterranean opening serves as entry to both the building and the subway. The landscape of this small square, or entry court, steps down along the staircase.

Looking back over his long-term involvements with schools, review boards, and commissions—seven years on the design review board of Arizona State University, at Tempe; nine years on the U.S. Commission of Fine Arts; nineteen years with the architectural review panel of the U.S. Department of Housing and Community Development—Sasaki is most proud of his thirty-year association with the University of Colorado, at Boulder. In 1961 he developed a twenty-year master plan for the postwar expansion of that campus, a setting not only ennobled by the 14,000-foot peaks of the Rocky Mountains on the western horizon but also made special by personal memories (figures 123 –125). Sasaki's wife, Kisa, is an alumna of the university, and he first visited the campus during their courtship.

Just after World War I, architects Day and Klauder, of Philadelphia, had established the prevailing idiom of the Boulder campus: variations on traditional Italian hilltown building, with irregular massing, walls of local stone, clay tile roofs, three-sided courts, and picturesque skylines. In 1961, when the enrollment of some 10,000 was expected to double in ten years, Sasaki's firm was engaged as master planners and design consultants. Pietro Belluschi served as senior architectural design consultant, and several nationally and locally prominent architects were brought in, including Harry Weese, William C. Muchow Associates, Hobart D. Wagener & Associates, and Fisher and Davis.[18]

What Sasaki and his colleagues Dawson, DeMay, Dober, and, later, Jack Robinson achieved on the Boulder campus was exemplary: a planned expansion of the campus that brought new, larger-scaled modern structures into harmonious relation with older, smaller Italianate buildings. By extending and repeating the existing courtyards and malls, the traditional patterns of pedestrian movement and linked open spaces were preserved. Traditional materials, too, including the local Lyons stone and clay tiles, were incorporated into bold, modern structures of reinforced concrete.

As a design consultant on the complex Engineering Sciences Center (1963–1966) from the outset, Sasaki identified and clarified the key issues. "In such a large program," he noted, "one should probably not try to contain such diverse parts in one or two envelopes. Let diversity be articulated, in response not only to the program but also to the region and the environment."[19] Here, as elsewhere on campus, Sasaki's main ideas regarding overall concept, architectural design, and the linking of spaces and functions were implemented. William C. Muchow, architect in charge, recalled the project as a true collaboration in which everyone brought something valuable to the final product. And having served for decades on the design review board of the campus along with Sasaki, he commented, "I think the Colorado University campus is what it is today because of Hideo's involvement."[20]

The campus also benefited from Sasaki's planting design and critiques over the years. While he appreciated the beauty of aspens and cottonwoods growing along streams and on the wilder fringes of the campus, he viewed the central campus as a cultivated landscape where introduced red oaks, maples, and hawthorns could flourish on lawns irrigated by Boulder's ample water supply—a glacier. Native spruces, pines, and junipers were also planted for contrasting color, texture, or long life. And beauty rather than ecology determined some of Sasaki's choices. "I love maples because of the color and the size of their leaves," he confesses.[21]

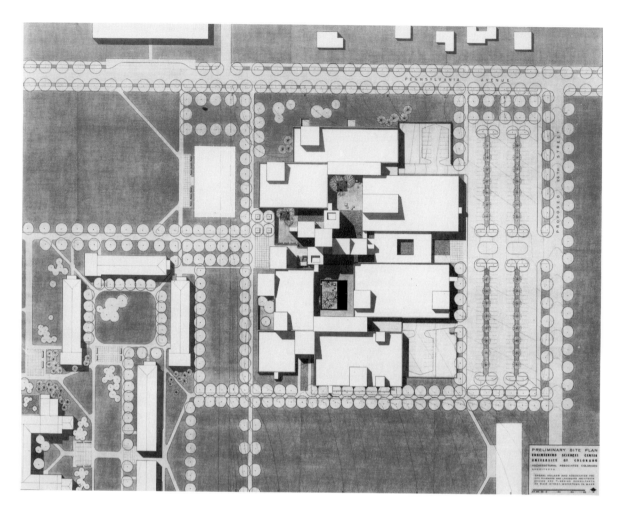

123. University of Colorado, at Boulder, Preliminary Site Plan for the Engineering Sciences Center, from 1963. Architectural Associates Colorado, Architects. Sasaki, Walker and Associates, Landscape Architects, Planners and Architectural Design Consultants. Hideo Sasaki, Principal Planner. Kenneth DeMay, Architectural Design Consultant. Pietro Belluschi, Senior Architectural Design Consultant. The plan extends the existing campus traditions of architecture and site planning, while responding with great sensitivity to the unrivaled natural setting of the Rocky Mountains.

124. University of Colorado, at Boulder, campus buildings erected before World War II. Day & Klauder, Architects. In their time, these structures were praised for their fresh interpretation of Italian hilltown architecture, independent of symmetry and the classical orders, and for the resulting silhouette of roofs against mountains and sky.

125. University of Colorado, at Boulder. Engineering Sciences Center, amid panoramic view of the campus. William C. Muchow Associates; Hobart D. Wagener & Associates; Fisher & Davis; Architectural Associates of Colorado, Architects. William C. Muchow, Partner in Charge. Sasaki, Walker and Associates, Design Consultants, Site Planners and Landscape Architects; Kenneth DeMay, Principal Designer. Pietro Belluschi, Senior Architectural Design Consultant. Campus spaces are focused by the heavy stone objects of the buildings set on rolling plains at the base of the eastern slope of the Rocky Mountains.

As university presidents and administrators came and departed, Sasaki's direct influence in shaping the Boulder campus varied. The fact that he remained on the design review board, however, and was continually called in for advice—by local architects, buildings and grounds staff, and others—illuminates one of his strengths as a practitioner. Sasaki's role at Boulder and elsewhere was to serve as design consultant on the total environment, including architectural design. Contributing as an equal on a team, he could focus on the problems at hand rather than on personalities or professional turf.[22]

Sasaki's multidisciplinary, corporate practice evolved—not consciously according to a plan, he recalls, but quite naturally, in the process of identifying and solving problems of increasing complexity. If a certain capability was found lacking in-house, it was soon added. In time, architects who had originally been hired to help out on a landscape architectural project assumed commissions to design buildings. That was the pattern of growth. "In those days," Sasaki recalls, "we were so idealistic and so intense in our interest in our work that it didn't matter what the problem was; we just wanted to solve it! On weekends and evenings, people would come over with their children. Or we all went together to look at different projects. I even had Bill Johnson teach a drawing class in the evenings, and Kisa took lessons. It wasn't a school—just something we were all interested in. It was more a way of life than a job."[23]

However varied, first-wave practice appears to have had at least this common ground: collaboration among specialists on large-scale projects and offices that allowed some individual initiative and expression within the team. Projects might be subject to review by a single critic, yet the sense of adventure, seeking solutions to untried problems, continually experimenting and discovering, kept spirits high within the offices. What now seems remarkable about this first wave, after twenty-five years of further evolution, is the number of built projects of high quality, the depth of commitment to collective goals and ideals, and the strength of conviction that a finer, sounder environment could indeed be planned and designed.

Chapter 9

**The Environment:
Science Overshadows Art**

The setting was one of California's finest ecotones: the meeting of land and ocean at Monterey Bay, where dunes, rocks, low-growing plants, and wind-sculpted Monterey pines gave way to mixed woodlands of pines and coast live oak. The place was a conference center, Asilomar. The time, July 1957; the topic, the future of landscape architecture; the participants, some sixty-five educators, practitioners, and students. Inevitably the discussions drifted into the tempestuous waters of ethics, morality, and the relative importance of sociology, technology, science, and art.

"Why don't we spend more time studying geology and botany, a little bit about zoology, more about the science of weather . . . and more about people in relation to their environment—in other words, more about human ecology?" asked Harlow Whittemore, of the University of Michigan.[1] However, given the nation's current preoccupation with technology and scientific research, the social arts faced stiff competition, noted Francis Dean, a partner of Eckbo, Royston, and Williams who was teaching part-time at the University of Southern California. Where did landscape fit into society? Dean wondered. Lewis Clarke believed that, with their broad vision, landscape architects could be leaders in architectural and planning efforts. Robert Royston put in a good word for utopian ideas, strong convictions, and potential links with the behavioral sciences. Wary of abstractions, Garrett Eckbo urged a return to the primitive way of looking at the world, through the senses.

"We are in an art field and we should not make any bones about it," Lawrence Halprin reminded the group. "What we are after is a sense of poetry in the landscape, a magnificent lift which will enrich the lives of the people who are moving about in the landscape that we're doing

126. Portrait of Ian McHarg, 1988. Through his writings and practice, his teaching at the University of Pennsylvania for three decades, his public television series, and his lecturing around the United States and abroad, McHarg has become the most well-known landscape architect and planner since Frederick Law Olmsted.

for them. Anything less than that is cheating them, and it is cheating ourselves."[2] As the topic shifted to gardens, one voice played against the others like a gruff bass, challenging the landscape architect's preoccupation with suburban private gardens, while "the poor miserable characters who live in an environment [with] no light, let alone anything else, never saw the services of a landscape architect."[3] Having spoken, Ian McHarg fell silent.

At that 1957 meeting of the National Conference on Instruction in Landscape Architecture (NCILA), McHarg had already acknowledged the considerable accomplishment of modern landscape architecture, which, he felt, was summed up by California gardens and the works of Roberto Burle Marx. McHarg also believed that the profession was rightly engaged in creating works of art, but he added, "We've got to give just as much consideration to the social function as to the art."[4] On that summer day, then, with no mention of the natural sciences, no reference to ecology or environmentalism, McHarg did not present precisely the image by which he is known today. And if any living American landscape architect is internationally known today by professionals and the general public, Ian McHarg is known (figure 126)—that bold spokesman for environmental values, prolific writer for a broad audience, "steward of the biosphere," and scourge of the squalid cities that have inexorably spread over the earth.

In fact, McHarg does not detest cities. A recent academic year spent in the San Francisco Bay Area, 1986–1987, confirmed McHarg's lifelong interest in and enjoyment of humane cities. He found Berkeley appealing as a dense, low-rise city in a forest.[5] And he was enchanted by his neighborhood in the Pacific Heights district of San Francisco, with its views of the Golden Gate Bridge, the Marin Headlands, the ocean, and the bay; its ambience of nearby shops and parks; and its grid of streets, powerful enough to absorb a fantastic, eclectic array of architectural and landscape elements. McHarg's main reservation was that living in Pacific Heights was "obscenely expensive," and its amenities beyond the reach of most urban residents of the Bay Area.[6]

One of McHarg's first articles, "The Humane City: Must the Man of Distinction Always Move to the Suburbs?" (1958), stressed the importance of both cities and art. An admirer and avid reader of Lewis Mumford, McHarg shares Mumford's belief in the city as the place where the best aspects of a civilization are, or should be, concentrated. One of many postwar ironies, however, is that just as the suburban relocations of large corporations gave landscape architects some great opportunities, the corporations' departure from the cities led to further urban blight and the vicious cycle of middle-class flight from ever-worsening urban environments. "Why allow our derelict and ugly cities to become our memorials?" McHarg asked. And he proposed a new role for landscape architects: not the horticulturist or adviser to wealthy suburban home owners but the artist, "expressing the essence of nature in art and, in so doing, . . . making the city humane."[7]

In pursuing new solutions to the problems of human settlement, McHarg came across two powerful allies: the media and the natural sciences, particularly ecology. The fact that he did not invent the notion of an ecological approach to design (nor was he the first to employ it) in no way diminishes his stature. He is one of this century's most brilliant and influential figures, a powerful force within his profession and beyond, in part because of the way he has used the media to bring environmental values into the forefront of political, legal, social, and even artistic activity in our time. If, in the process, art became overshadowed by science, the consequences are still emerging while the recent past is not yet clearly understood.

To appreciate McHarg's environmental contribution and that of several distinguished colleagues, such as Brian Hackett, Philip Lewis, G. Angus Hills, and Carl Steinitz, some recollection of America in the years immediately following World War II is useful. At that time, science was beginning to assume an increasing importance in landscape architecture, as in countless other facets of Americans' life and work. The haunting demonstration of what political and military applications of science could achieve, in the bombings of Hiroshima and Nagasaki, lingered in the minds and on the consciences of many people—Nobel Prize–winning physicists, schoolchildren, political leaders, ordinary citizens, educators, and others. In 1946, after observing the development of the atomic bomb through four years of war, James B. Conant, president of Harvard, gave a series of lectures at Yale in which he recommended measures to broaden and deepen Americans' understanding of science. Matters of public policy, he noted, would increasingly be influenced by highly technical, scientific considerations. Thus, in a new age of machines and experts, American democracy itself depended on the assimilation of science into our "secular cultural pattern."[8]

In 1950, Hideo Sasaki persuaded Stanley White to organize the landscape architect's study of nature on the broad basis of natural sciences.[9] In 1951, when the NCILA met at Harvard, one of the topics discussed was the ecological approach to analysis and design.[10] Although ecological considerations had been assimilated into the landscape design process decades earlier, notably in the work of Charles Eliot, Warren Manning, Jens Jensen, and Frank Waugh, a reawakened interest in natural science, systems, and rational methods in the 1950s made the idea of an ecological approach seem timely and appropriate. In 1953, an informal survey of some two dozen landscape architecture programs in the United States showed that plant ecology and geology were emphasized at schools such as Ohio State University and the Agricultural and Mechanical College of Texas (Texas A&M). Also, some form of coordinated mapping system, including a "pale overlay" of an aerial photograph over a topographical map, was recognized as a valuable tool.[11] That year, Robert F. White, professor of landscape architecture at Texas A&M, urged that more scientific data must inform the design process. "Even on casual observance," he wrote, "the amount and scope of information we do not have but which we need for the good of our professional lifeblood appears staggering."[12]

In the midst of national recovery and industrial expansion, these words carried a warning—but none of the poignant urgency that later appeared in *Silent Spring* (1962), in which Rachel Carson revealed the threat of pesticides and other synthetic chemicals to all life on earth. Ecological awareness in the early 1950s in America was still nourished on literature of another tone, perhaps epitomized in Aldo Leopold's *A Sand County Almanac* (1949), in which minutely observed fact, reflections on the need for environmental law and ethics, and calm, clearheaded warnings are mingled with mystery, poetry, and gentle humor. Even if few landscape architects had read Leopold's wonderful book in the 1950s, the profession would soon inherit Leopold's concerns for ecological balance and stewardship of natural resources.

One early postwar application of an ecological approach to planning was carried out in the early 1950s at Harvard in a collaborative studio taught by Sasaki and members of the faculty in architecture and planning. Sasaki had the students analyze a particular site in terms of soil conditions, runoff patterns, vegetation patterns, and other factors, which led to the recommendation of certain areas for development and others for preservation. "Up to that time," Sasaki recalls, "planners always used to make a quantitative program. But for the first time, we rationalized *where* [development] should be, not what and how much, but *where*. And Holmes Perkins [then chairman of Harvard's planning department] said, 'That's the first time landscape architects have really contributed in a meaningful way toward this planning process.'"[13]

Someday, when the history of ecological approaches to design is written, these studies will be seen in perspective. Here, a glance at the methods developed by a few prominent individuals must suffice. In the mid-1960s, under the direction of Charles Harris at Harvard, graduate students Raymond Belknap, John Furtado, and Grant Jones undertook a thesis project in which they identified fifteen individuals from around the country, each with a different method of landscape analysis. Later, Belknap and Furtado investigated three outstanding methods—those of G. Angus Hills, Philip Lewis, and Ian McHarg. Their findings, published by the Conservation Foundation in 1967, represent not a definitive assessment but a well-placed slice through the mass of research and analysis being done at the time.[14]

Angus Hills's contributions to land use planning stem from his early work as a soil surveyer, followed by studies of land forms, vegetative succession, and forest ecology. In 1944 he began research on Canada's renewable natural resources for the Ontario Department of Lands and Forests. Through the 1950s, he developed methods of classifying and evaluating land for agriculture and forestry. Then in 1961 his report,

The Ecological Basis for Land-Use Planning, showed how his methods could be applied to other resources, such as fish, wildlife, and outdoor land-oriented recreation. By 1966, he was able to rank sites according to their capability (or "true" potential), their suitability (or immediate potential), and their feasibility (or likely potential).

Like Brian Hackett in England and C. S. Christian in Australia, Hills began his analysis with the concept of "natural units," or land forms. These were then subdivided into increasingly smaller units of "physiographic site classes" and site types. The analogy with breaking down matter into atoms, and further, into protons, neutrons, and electrons, and so forth, is clear. By the mid-1960s, Hills appeared to be establishing a systematic, scientific basis for evaluating sites. In contrast, the methods of Lewis and McHarg appeared to evince more "intuitive input," including the shared values of local residents and the highly personal values of professionals. Not surprising, both Lewis and McHarg were trained in landscape architecture.

A graduate of the University of Illinois (B.F.L.A., 1950), Lewis earned his M.L.A. at Harvard in 1953 and won the Charles Eliot Traveling Fellowship for 1953–54. Thereafter, for the state of Wisconsin's Department of Resource Development, he began to inventory and analyze recreational opportunities. Noting patterns of naturally occurring resources within small study areas, Lewis coined the term *environmental corridor,* which became a device for mapping entire regions. He used overlay mapping systems, and he emphasized communication. Not only did he make people aware of environmental values; he also drew local citizens and interest groups into the process of collecting data, thereby paving the way for wide support of his planning proposals. Further, by developing a numerical ranking system for qualities and features of the landscape, Lewis made his data accessible to the computer, a tool that Carl Steinitz, of Harvard, and Donald Belcher, of Cornell, were using in their regional planning studies by the mid-1960s.[15]

To assign numerical ranking to values, such as visual quality and physical well-being, is, of course, debatable. Some might question the very notion of quantifying any qualitative factor. Most research is motivated, in part, by intuitive preferences and personal values and goals. Yet attempts to rationalize the process of land use decision making by rigorous scientific methods continued. As Belknap and Furtado concluded, "Scientific justification and its eventual future use may come later. Meanwhile, the emotional appeal and the intuitive approach may be the best that we have."[16]

Underlying Belknap's and Furtado's admirable study and permeating many of the subsequent debates over environmental process versus design was an aversion to anything arbitrary. Before long, subjectivity, personal preference, and intuition became suspect. Part of the problem may lie in the public's assumption that science and rigorous scientific methods are somehow pure and value free; that therefore a scientist's recommendations are above dispute. Power and influence, it seemed, awaited the landscape architect who could develop scientific methods of analysis that would ultimately lead to defensible processes of design.

Such processes have become routine for large-scale planning and design in a democratic society increasingly flooded by information and raw data. But in the mid-1960s, when computers were still bulky, relatively rare, and costly, those who used this new technology to develop meth-

127. Peter Rogers (left) and Carl Steinitz, exchanging insights while modeling the processes of "urbanization and landscape change," 1967. These soon became the subject of a studio at Harvard, taught by Steinitz and Rogers, as well as of their book, *A Systems Analysis Model of Urbanization and Change: An Experiment in Interdisciplinary Education* (MIT Press, 1970).

odologies for defensible processes were pioneers, including Dr. Ervin Zube, then a partner in a research consulting firm as well as professor and head of landscape architecture and regional planning at the University of Massachusetts; and Dr. Robert H. Twiss, Jr., then a resource planner with the U.S. Forest Experiment Station in Berkeley and professor at the University of California, Berkeley. Zube, Twiss, Steinitz, and others, including top students drawn from the natural sciences and the arts, not only made their reputations on research rather than practice; they took the highly pragmatic field of landscape architecture, elevated its intellectual content, and raised the status of full-time teaching and research. As one student in landscape architecture at Harvard noted with approval in 1968, "The Department does not run a prep school for practical professional office work."[17]

Since the mid-1960s, Carl Steinitz, an architect-planner who earned his Ph.D. under Kevin Lynch's direction at MIT, has pursued the social and visual issues implicit in Lynch's *The Image of the City* (1960). To Lynch's efforts to include the public's perceptions in the planning process, however, he added a greater interest in the kinds of analysis that computers made possible with ever-increasing sophistication. In 1968, with Peter Rogers at Harvard, Steinitz offered a graduate seminar that used state-of-the-art computer technology in modeling the processes of urbanization and major changes in the landscape (figure 127). Steinitz also joined Charles Harris in creating Harvard's "omnibus" studio, focused on a large-scale project that required several guest lecturers and skills: aerial photo analysis, computer graphics, overlay mapping and analysis of public perceptions, along with plants, design, and construction. As a result, some students found role models for the cool, highly analytical, yet compassionate landscape architect determined to lead by the power of defensible processes (figures 128 and 129).[18]

Among the landscape architects who ultimately wielded such power, McHarg has been the most colorful, surely the most visible, and among the most inspiring—and yet his own considerable gifts for design have not been used to produce an impressive body of built work. For years, McHarg used Halprin's work at Sea Ranch as a singular example of eco-logical design (with contributions from a student of McHarg). Now McHarg regrets that his adopted home, Philadelphia, contains no proj-ect of his own design. Moreover, he regrets that, among his finest graduate students, superbly trained in the arts and sciences, few have been able to work to their full capacities—in spite of certain gains in environmental legislation and in the public's awareness of environ-mental issues.

Ever since McHarg declared war against "man, the planetary disease," sometime in the early 1960s, he has led the charge, using wit, anger, irony, symbolism, unassailable fact, personal memory, and poetic ex-pression to enlighten his audience. Could any one person have done more, one wonders; or is there something in late twentieth-century American society, some particular strain of the planetary disease-pro-ducing virus that has grown stronger against each successive attack?

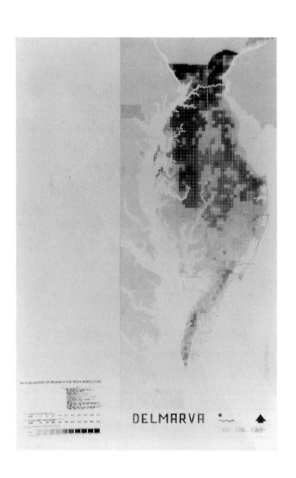

McHarg was born in Scotland in 1920. The nearest city to his childhood home was not, so he recalls, humane. Glasgow, which owed its growth and density to nineteenth-century industrial expansion, was covered with smoke and grime in a cold, windy, damp climate that intensified the city's gloom while it made the fields, wildflowers, streams, and woods to the west all the more delightful by contrast. Surviving the depression, McHarg studied for two and a half years at the Glasgow College of Art, then discovered landscape architecture. Practice in that field did not live up to his lofty expectations. He served in World War II as an officer in the Second Independent Parachute Brigade Group in Italy. War was hell. Two weeks' leave in an Italian hilltown near the coast brought quiet and well-being.[19]

After the war McHarg studied at Harvard (1946–1950), earning master's degrees in both landscape architecture and city planning. During his first year, classes were collaborative among the departments of landscape architecture, architecture (under Gropius and others from the Bauhaus), and planning (under Holmes Perkins, with Sir William Holford and eventually others from the British garden cities and new towns movement). Still considering himself an artist, McHarg did some tempera paintings and drawings at Harvard; but perhaps more significant was his collaboration with students Robert L. Geddes, William Conklin, and Marvin Sevely on a thesis—an urban renewal study of downtown Providence, Rhode Island, in 1950 (figures 130 and 131). This was the first collaborative thesis in the history of the Harvard Graduate School of Design, featuring a four-lane one-way highway that looped around the central business district (CBD); a cylindrical office tower sheathed in glass and diagonally gridded stainless steel; and a new urban park, designed as a recreational amenity and as a buffer to help

130. Proposal for urban renewal of downtown Providence, Rhode Island, 1950. Model: Looking south. Joint thesis project for degrees of master of city planning from the Harvard Graduate School of Design, by Ian McHarg, Robert L. Geddes, William J. Conklin, and Marvin Sevely. The *Rhode Islander Magazine*, June 11, 1950, noted the four students' belief that "cities are the fruit of civilization. They are at once the product and the genesis of culture."

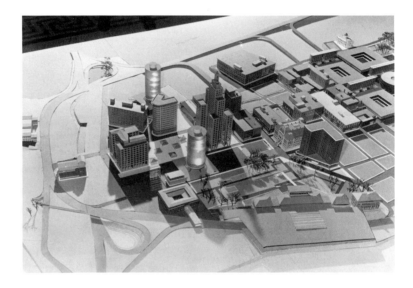

preserve new property values.[20] Recently McHarg speculated, "If I had stayed in the United States [after graduation], I suppose I would have become a director of a small redevelopment authority."[21]

Instead, he returned to Scotland with his wife, Pauline, and their young son; fell ill with pulmonary tuberculosis; went from a depressing sanitorium outside Edinburgh to an invigorating one in Switzerland; climbed in the Swiss Alps for six months; and returned to the United States by 1954, to revive the landscape architecture program at the University of Pennsylvania. Ever since, McHarg has been a seeker of health and well-being. He did not invent the expression "man, a planetary disease" (Loren Eiseley's phrase), but his provocative exploitation of the meta-

131. Ian McHarg, as a student, addresses a jury reviewing his joint thesis project, 1950. Walter Gropius is seated in the first row, third from left.

phor, in speeches and articles and on television, may have obscured the literal meaning that illness and health hold for McHarg personally.

Le Corbusier's interest in space, sun, and verdure has never seemed convincing to McHarg. Nor has Gropius's emphasis on the social mission of modern architecture rung true for McHarg. Like Mumford, McHarg regrets the apparent preoccupation of these and other modernists with technology or the expression of technology. McHarg's sympathy lies with architects such as Louis Kahn, whose poetic vision of space and light, form and design, was matched by a concern for the simplest human actions and needs—a quiet, private space in which to sip a cup of tea, for instance. Kahn anticipated the ecological approach

132. View of Manhattan Island, n.d. This haunting view of New York City, featured in
McHarg's *Design with Nature* (1969), suggests the perils of unlimited and uncontrolled urbanization.

to design, McHarg believes, for Kahn's notion of "existence-will" encouraged designers to fathom what a material (or a site) wanted to be
in order to let that essence come into being. From Kahn, too, McHarg
derived his concept of form—not something imposed but a particular
phase of the evolutionary process.[22]

Mies van der Rohe impressed McHarg not with skyscrapers or the Illinois Institute of Technology but with an unbuilt one-acre scheme of
1938, in which a "princely" group of three houses form private courtyards. In the late 1950s, McHarg collaborated with Philip Johnson on a
denser court-house scheme of about twenty houses per acre in Philadelphia; this, too, remained unbuilt—because it was deemed not dense
enough for its urban site.[23] Undeterred, McHarg continued for the
next several years to focus on what he considered to be an essential
concern of the landscape architect: making the city humane, not only
for those who lived there by choice or by default but also for those
who had fled—the polite, urbane, highly civilized person (and his
family), without whom the city could not be expected to survive
(figure 132).

Around 1960, McHarg's focus of attention shifted from the survival of
the city to the survival of the planet. This shift—nothing less than the
evolution of a new worldview—can be traced in the contrast between
McHarg's work of the 1950s and the work that followed. In 1950, to
understand urban renewal procedures for his collaborative thesis, Mc-
Harg spent about a day a week at the Federal Reserve Bank of Boston,
learning about the planning of CBDs in Boston and Providence.[24] A few
years later, in Britain, McHarg drew up elaborate tables of rents, square
footages, densities, and capital and maintenance costs to substantiate his

argument that open space was indeed affordable for publicly subsidized housing.[25] Working within the prevailing system of "economic determinism," then, McHarg used economic means to serve his own ends—the making of more humane cities.

In 1960, McHarg began to explore another attitude toward planning, later termed *ecological determinism*. As Anne Spirn has observed, the arrival of ecologist Richard Muhlenberg at the University of Pennsylvania, in 1960, had a profound effect on McHarg's thinking.[26] By that time, however, the scale of McHarg's concerns was already shifting from the city to the larger environment. Instead of an intense interest in the physical and spiritual well-being of urban people, McHarg began to exhibit a revulsion for the abstraction of contemporary Western Man and his cancerous sprawl of human settlements oozing from inhumane cities.

McHarg's own account of his conversion to ecology involves a close friend, Louis Kahn, and an unnamed scientist. About 1960, Kahn and McHarg were engaged to locate a 250-acre site for a "Temple of Science" (the research branch of a large corporation). Before a site had been determined, however, Kahn had designed the building. Chagrined, McHarg resolved to retain the upper hand in future jobs, whenever possible, by hiring the architect himself. Through the "Temple of Science" project, McHarg also happened to meet a scientist who had been charged with designing a space capsule for one man and his minimum requirements. These turned out to consist mainly of light, algae, and bacteria—which, along with a human being, would form a mutually sustaining system in ecological balance. Enlightened, McHarg found his mission: to explain how the world works.[27]

In 1960–1961, in his televised interviews with eminent scientists, religious leaders, and intellectuals, McHarg laid the foundations of the environmental message he would deliver for the next quarter century. The Judeo-Christian biblical injunction for Man to subdue and have dominion over the earth and all its creatures was one of the notions McHarg had set out to demolish for the viewers of his public television series, "The House We Live In." Another notion he discredited was the Man-centered view of the world, inherited from ancient Greece and Rome and Renaissance humanists throughout Europe. Each Sunday afternoon, McHarg would ask one of his guests to address these and other concerns, hoping to elicit from them some basis for determining a new set of principles, or ethics, that must guide Atomic Man, the first Man capable of destroying all of life on earth.

In passing, McHarg revealed some of his own feelings, motivations, and dreams. "Much of my own boyhood physical environment is lost," he told Margaret Mead, "that is why I am so involved in Man and Environment." And he explained to her the need for developing a new philosophy, some abstract conception that modern man could grasp—because simple, vital connections to the environment, such as knowing the sources of one's food, light, and shade, were increasingly being lost.[28] To Paul Tillich's remarks on St. Francis of Assisi, McHarg added his impression that Renaissance gardens represented a form of arrogance, the attempt to impose human patterns on the landscape. "And they were bad nature, so surely they could not survive save for maintenance," McHarg continued. "I think they were also bad art and I think they were very imperfect views of Paradise."[29]

McHarg's preference for the picturesque English garden and its Oriental counterparts is well known. "I think of art in terms of man and environment," he told Alan Watts. The art expressed in the Japanese garden especially moved McHarg, for he considered gardens predominantly places of contemplation—not places for barbecues and social gathering but metaphysical symbols. Watts, author of *The Way of Zen,* informed McHarg that the Zen garden was not symbolic but rather evocative of a state of mind. And he suggested that the Western way of thinking about things, classifying and therefore separating things, was not the route to the mirrorlike wisdom—a simple acceptance of the concrete world as it is—represented by Zen.[30]

In his professional life, McHarg chose not the way of Zen but the well-engineered highway of Western science. To physiologist Hans Selye, McHarg confessed, "My heart yearns for devices which would indeed allow the physiologist to measure the inhibiting powers of certain environmental factors . . . atmospheric pollution, carbon dioxide cloud, excessive transmission of infra-red as opposed to ultra-violet light," and so on.[31] Knowing intuitively what ought to be done for the health of all living creatures on the planet was not sufficient. McHarg wanted the scientific proof of cause and effect; for science, like the media, has become so powerful in our time that it cannot be ignored.

The impact of McHarg's *Design with Nature* (1969) could be seen not only in the shifts within the design and planning professions but also in the popular media. McHarg now regrets that *Time* and *Life* selected his most outrageous verbal attacks for quotation out of context; however, while environmentalists were seen as threats to the growth of the gross national product and while tempers and emotions were already running high over other matters of patriotism, life, and death, perhaps a few reported bursts of rage were necessary for McHarg to command national attention.[32] At any rate, by 1969 the mood of the entire country had changed dramatically in a single decade. The Civil Rights movement and the unpopularity of the Vietnam War had given many Americans, especially college students, some acquaintance with the very idea of resisting social, political, and economic pressures. And while television brought nightly reports of environmental degradation, by military means and business as usual, more environmental awareness was aroused by articles, books, conferences and events such as the first Earth Day, April 22, 1970. In 1969, the National Environmental Policy Act was passed, mandating environmental impact statements for a wide range of projects, and in the decade that followed, more environmental legislation was slowly put in place.

In practice, McHarg has typically offered scientific arguments for a particular land-use plan, backed by economic justification—often bottom-line profits. Yet the starting point of analysis is the natural environment—not human need or greed (figure 133). As his former partner, architect-planner Dr. David A. Wallace, has explained, McHarg's planning begins with a "presumption for nature," a belief that natural processes should strongly influence the pattern of development.[33] Here, a glimpse at the early work of Wallace-McHarg Associates (which became Wallace, McHarg, Roberts and Todd in the mid-1960s) should indicate the range and scale of actual projects that were subjected to McHarg's planning process.

In 1962, a group of landowners in the horse and dairy country northwest of Baltimore formed their own nonprofit planning council in an

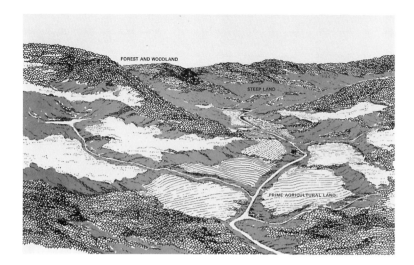

FOREST AND WOODLAND

STEEP LAND

PRIME AGRICULTURAL LAND

133. "Land Features," from the Metropolitan Open Space from Natural Process study, Wallace, McHarg, Roberts and Todd, Landscape Architects and Planners. Ian McHarg, Principal Investigator; in Ian McHarg, *Design with Nature*. In this book—containing autobiography, philosophy, and case studies drawn from his professional practice in the 1960s—McHarg outlined particular processes whereby various aspects of site analysis and suitability were mapped, then overlaid, to suggest patterns of development as well as of preservation.

attempt to guide the future development of their cherished hills and valleys. For assistance, this council approached Wallace, then known as a leading planner of Baltimore's first major urban renewal project, Charles Center, along with James W. Rouse and others, from the mid-1950s.[34] Wallace, an effective public speaker, writer, and urban designer, in turn sought an ecological perspective from McHarg. The Wallace-McHarg partnership was then formed, and the results of their study, "Plan for the Valleys," published and widely distributed in 1963, was reprinted and later summarized in journals and books.[35] The firm's recommendations (along valley floor: no development; on wooded valley walls of gentle slope: limited development; on open plateau: concentrated development) were to be enforced by existing and new legislation at county and state levels. Further, the firm's land-use analysis was backed up by anticipated land values, totaling $7 million more than would have been produced by the specter of uncontrolled growth.

A study of this scale and sophistication called for an interdisciplinary team. William H. Roberts, a design consultant on this project, later became a partner of McHarg and Wallace and an associate professor in the department of landscape architecture and regional planning (of which McHarg was chairman for three decades) at the University of Pennsylvania's Graduate School of Fine Arts. Other colleagues from this school who consulted on the "Plan for the Valleys" were Dr. William G. Grigsby, for economics, and Ann Louise Strong, for governmental and legal matters.[36] Soon Wallace, McHarg, Roberts and Todd contained a brain trust of complementary specialists who could tackle such complex projects as the Richmond Parkway Study, in New York; a comprehensive landscape plan for Washington, D.C.; and ecological planning for the Sea Pines Company's new community on Amelia Island, Florida.[37]

At The Woodlands, an 18,000-acre new town north of Houston, Wallace, McHarg, Roberts and Todd served on a team of planning consultants from 1970 to 1974. By then the firm had developed a method of gathering and processing environmental data that, in effect, gave the firm unprecedented power. As McHarg noted, "Anyone who employed the data and the method would reach the same conclusions." Moreover, the firm's land and site planning principles would be upheld because "any engineer, architect, landscape architect, developer and the client himself were bound by the data and the method."[38] A second innovation was the utilization of a $50 million grant from the Department of Housing and Urban Development in recognition of the firm's environmental impact analysis—the sort of analysis that might never have been encouraged by a federal program without the efforts of McHarg and a few others in communicating environmental values. A third innovation was to proceed from analysis of environmental data to guidelines for site planning and design strategies, particularly the astute handling of stormwater drainage on the flood-prone site. Today, however indistinguishable from other suburbs at first glance, The Woodlands remains a demonstration of landscape design informed by natural processes and implemented, over time, by teams of planners and designers.[39]

As did Olmsted, McHarg believes in institutionalizing his values, skills, and understanding through the educational process. "I regard myself as a teacher," McHarg declared in the early 1970s. "It's absolutely the most important thing I do."[40] As chairman of the department of landscape architecture and regional planning at the University of Pennsylvania from 1954 to 1986, McHarg was able to recruit and retain for the profession hundreds of idealistic young architects and natural scientists, as well as students with bachelor's degrees in landscape architecture. Some students were more inclined toward art and design. Others leaned toward resource inventory, analysis, and regional planning. These were students McHarg hoped to train as spokesmen for "the natural science parameter in the planning process."[41] At very least, McHarg wanted all students to have a grounding in college-level mathematics and natural sciences, for they were to become applied ecologists, bridging the gap between the natural sciences and the design professions. "The cause I ask them to espouse will bring them neither power nor money, but they are devoted to it," he once remarked.[42]

Brushing aside claims that he had downplayed design, McHarg recently defined his ideal, the informed designer: "somebody who is aware of the environment and the social purposes of his plan [figure 134] and who, on the basis of these understandings, then gives form which is meaningful form, and which does contribute to health and well-being."[43] Over the years, McHarg has sent some of the best of these informed designers—among them, architects Dennis Wilkinson, John Ross, and John Evans—to Halprin's office, where they thrived and then moved on. Now McHarg longs to demonstrate personally what such an informed designer could achieve in built form. Meanwhile, his current projects include an autobiography and a resource inventory of some

11,200 sample areas throughout the United States, intended to assess and predict environmental quality nationwide.[44]

With their broad scope of social and environmental concern, McHarg and his colleagues have often been viewed as inheritors of the Olmsted legacy. A few ironies are rarely mentioned, however. As codesigner of Central Park, New York, Olmsted agonized over his inability to command the respect and obedience of the park foremen and laborers. He could not get them to follow his precise directions for grading, planting, maintenance, and public instruction in the use of the park. Yet, as he confessed to Calvert Vaux in 1865, he was not sure that he could claim to be an artist. Only years later did he confidently assume the status as an artist. His claims were made with the restraint and lack of drama to be expected by a man of his milieu and background. Still, insofar as his parks were perceived as artistic in essence (and barring further Tammany Hall–style corruption), Olmsted could expect his directions for the design of parks to be followed.[45]

The fact that McHarg looked to science rather than art to sustain his directives says as much about evolving American society and culture as about McHarg—or Olmsted. In the late nineteenth century, renowned artists in America were viewed as ennoblers of the culture and the physical environment. Moreover, their stature within their own spheres often amounted to a degree of power and influence in the larger society. Witness the influence of Burnham, Olmsted, and their collaborators stemming from the Chicago exposition in 1893. But twentieth-century developments, including the demise of the beaux arts system and the City Beautiful movement, the incomplete acceptance of Bauhaus ideals in America, the split between fine art and landscape design,

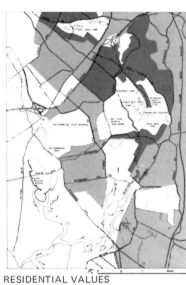

SCENIC VALUES

RECREATION VALUES

RESIDENTIAL VALUES

FOREST VALUES

WILDLIFE VALUES

INSTITUTIONAL VALUES

134. From the Richmond Parkway Study, New York City, in *Design with Nature:* a series of maps (to be used as overlays), indicating areas of ecological, economic, social, and cultural value. Wallace, McHarg, Roberts and Todd, Landscape Architects and Planners. Ian McHarg, Partner in Charge. Narendra Juneja, Project Supervisor. At regional scale, McHarg showed how ecological information could be used to inform designers of the inherent constraints and opportunities of portions of a region. The ultimate goal was to design landscapes in which people might dwell compatibly within nature.

wars, changes in social, moral, and environmental standards, and the phenomenal rise of science, technology, and the media profoundly altered popular notions of artists and scientists in this country.

Rather than ask whether McHarg or any other idealistic landscape architect of our time should have emphasized science over art—a question that fueled the debates noted in the following chapter—one might consider the current options of artists and landscape architects. Knowing what we do know about the physical environment, informed by McHarg and his colleagues, where do we go from here?

Chapter 10

**The Corporate Office,
Second Wave**

Every professional organization gains some self-awareness through the process of making annual awards, which serve as a mirror, reflecting the profession's preferred image as well its main concerns and directions. Seen in perspective, year after year, the awards also give some insight into the evolution of certain offices, and of office practice generally. Although coverage of the ASLA's annual awards in *Landscape Architecture* has been uneven (with only a brief text and small illustrations placed in the back, among the advertisements, in the 1960s), some changes in the nature and scale of work are clear. In 1978, for instance, a new category of award, Research and Analysis, was created, to reflect the profession's growing involvement in projects with no traditional site planning or design component. "Fifteen years ago," it was noted, "many of these projects—such as an environmental impact assessment of 14,000 miles of utility rights-of-way—would have overwhelmed all but a tiny handful of firms."[1]

During those intervening fifteen years, what factors induced firms to seek out such large-scale projects, more oriented toward policy and procedure than physical product and craft? What processes of growth, development, and control were involved? And what were the results, measured in social, economic, environmental, and cultural terms? Our final chapter, an inquiry into these concerns, traces the shifting balances of skills, goals, and priorities among some of the larger corporate offices. By 1978, for instance, many firms that had been established for a decade or more had changed through expansions, internal diversification, splits, and mergers, much like other American businesses. To consider the implications of these events, it helps to compare the two waves of office development.

The early 1960s saw the maturing of the first wave of multidisciplinary offices, led by Sasaki, Walker and Associates (from 1957) and soon followed by Wallace-McHarg Associates and Johnson, Johnson and Roy. As we have seen, this wave was characterized by high idealism, a sense of vast opportunities and needs, a personal resistance to profit motives (however great the need to demonstrate profitability), and unshaken beliefs in collaboration—part of the Olmstedian and Bauhaus legacies. In philosophical foundations and broad goals, these first-wave firms resembled some of the older, prominent landscape architectural offices, such as Royston, Hanamoto, Mayes and Beck in San Francisco and Collins, Simonds and Simonds (later, Environmental Planning & Design) in Pittsburgh. What distinguished the first-wave firms were the internal structures that developed among professionals with unlike though complementary skills and the implicit long-range goal—leadership by an elite team of equals, whose work would command the highest respect among those who have power and influence, as in Olmsted's day.

The second wave, begun in the late 1960s, included firms and spinoffs from the first wave; the incorporation of older, established partnerships, such as Eckbo, Dean, Austin and Williams (which became EDAW, Inc.); and architectural firms with sizable landscape divisions, such as Hellmuth, Obata and Kassabaum (HOK). This wave was characterized by the inclusion of even more disciplines, drawn from the natural and social sciences as well as the arts; rapid growth of personnel and internal structures; professional specialization; use of corporate status; and the accumulation of capital for corporate investment and (sometimes) shared benefits. Responding to unprecedented opportunities for landscape architects, these offices were soon capable of handling both large-scale development—whole new communities and new towns, campuses, corporate and military facilities—and large-scale planning,

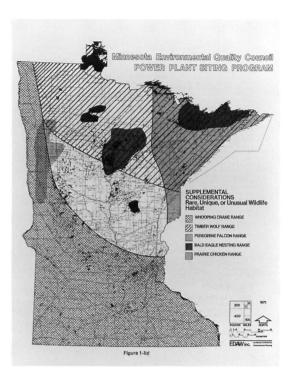

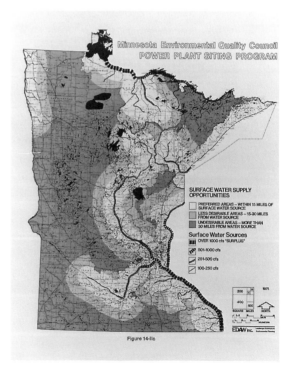

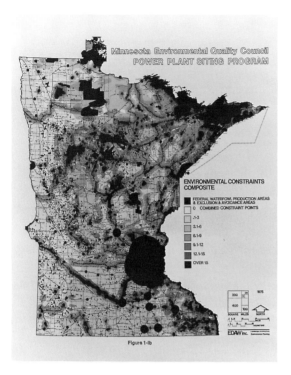

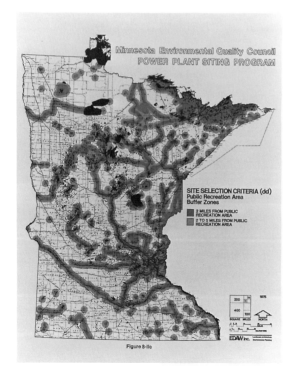

135. Siting study for Minnesota Power Plant, 1975: "Environmental Constraints Composite." EDAW, Inc., Planners and Landscape Architects. In the early 1970s, the corporate offices expanded the new tools for site analysis and applied them to a wide range of uses, including site selection, site utilization, environmental assessment, and constraint mechanisms. These studies, carried out for both public and private clients, ranged in scale from regional to site specific.

such as resource inventory and analysis, and environmental impact reports (figures 135–138).

One curious aspect of the second wave of corporate offices is its assimilation into the mainstream of planning and design enterprises in America without creating a stir, despite its significant impact on the quality of the environment. The relative invisibility of these second-wave offices can be traced, in part, to a deep-seated ambivalence among landscape architects: on the one hand, the wish to avoid criticism, preferring to be left alone in their patient search for solutions to a particular problem; on the other hand, the longing for recognition, not only for one's own achievements but for those of a cherished profession.

Long before the annual ASLA awards were prominently featured in *Landscape Architecture,* the profession was looking elsewhere for its self-image and direction. In 1969 the ASLA commissioned a study of the profession, to be directed by the Olmsted scholar Dr. Albert Fein. Fein was responsible to an ASLA committee, consisting of Garrett Eckbo, Charles Harris, William Johnson, Philip Lewis, Ian McHarg, and Edward Stone II and chaired by former ASLA president Theodore Osmundson. Consultants and contributors included planner-architect Edmund Bacon, ecologist Frederick E. Smith, and historians J. B. Jackson and James M. Fitch. The Gallup Organization conducted an extensive poll, and funds for the three-year study were provided by the Ford Foundation and contributions from interested individuals and organizations. The results, Fein's report of 1972, help to explain why the second wave of office development attracted some of the most gifted and enterprising young people in landscape architecture.[2]

136. The California Housing, Tustin, California, ca. 1975. Backen, Arrigoni & Ross, Architects. POD, Landscape Architects. Roger MacErlane, Principal Designer. This is a dense housing complex built around a swim club, using the guidelines set forth by Serge Chermayeff and Christopher Alexander, in their book, *Community and Privacy* (1963).

According to this report, one problem still haunting landscape architects was self-definition. Some wanted to see the profession's boundaries expanded, while others—joined by architects, engineers, planners, and other competing professionals—preferred that current boundaries be maintained. Among those landscape architects who were eager for expansion, most aspired to greater involvement in familiar project types. Relatively few desired expansion into whole new areas, such as regional resource planning; among those who did, educators were most numerous, followed by students. In sheer numbers and in its forward orientation, then, academia (with its relatively youthful faculty and students) constituted the profession's cutting edge.[3]

This study reflects the surge of public interest in environmental issues during 1969–1971, when it occurred to some that landscape architecture might be *the* profession to lead the struggle to save the planet. And yet the findings of Caroline Shillaber, librarian of Harvard's Graduate School of Design, were sobering: reference librarians at many large universities barely knew of the existence of landscape architecture; in current encyclopedias, articles on the profession were decades out of date; and although research in the field was on the threshold of expanding, only a handful of schools around the country had substantial libraries of works on landscape architecture and planning—notably,

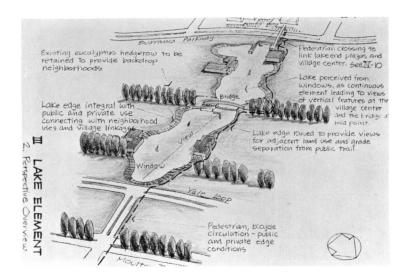

137. Woodbridge, Irvine, California, 1973: Landscape study, macro-scale. The Irvine Company, Developers. The SWA Group, Landscape Architects and Site Planners. Richard Law, Principal Designer. This new community plan, containing 9,000 dwelling units and attendant facilities around a man-made lake, drew on the remarkable group of subdevelopers, architects, engineers, and landscape architects that served the Irvine Company, in Southern California, in the late 1960s. Roads, utilities, homes, apartments, parks of all scales, greenways, town centers, schools, and commercial and civic spaces were built through planning, building, and marketing at incredible speed. One quadrant was completed from raw land in less than two years. At one point, sales were accomplished by lottery.

138. Woodbridge, aerial view.

Harvard, the University of California, Berkeley, Cornell, and the universities of Michigan, Illinois, and Pennsylvania.[4]

If landscape architecture was still a well-kept secret around 1970, where did landscape architects come from? About 20 percent of practicing landscape architects, faculty, and students came from rural or farming communities, roughly 30 percent came from small towns (under 50,000 people), and only half came from cities and suburbs. In contrast, somewhat fewer engineers and considerably fewer architects and urban planners had rural or small-town backgrounds. All of the design professionals were overwhelmingly Caucasian, middle- or upper-middle class, and male. Landscape architects tended to be slightly younger than other design professionals overall, suggesting a gain for the profession in recent years, but they should expect to earn substantially less income than architects, planners, and engineers. Moreover, while practicing landscape architects were likely to work on interdisciplinary teams, few could expect to become managers. The pollsters concluded, "Landscape architects are unlikely to function in a situation in which their professional authority can be exercised without question."[5]

These demographic facts help to explain the fervor of a few leading landscape architects, who were eager to expand the influence of their noble profession. The means varied, of course. Sasaki aimed to engage the intellects and expand the visions of those who came to Harvard— many of them, from small towns and rural communities, via the land grant colleges. McHarg was determined to take liberal arts majors and sophisticated architects (many from abroad) and train them to be applied ecologists and informed designers. Using computerized data, Philip Lewis, Charles Harris, and Carl Steinitz got students to incorporate public perceptions and preferences into the large-scale planning process. By the late 1960s, several worthwhile methodologies were becoming available—while values and goals were not yet polarized.

Fein's study of 1969–1971 revealed a strong consensus among practitioners, educators, and students that two concerns should remain central to the profession: ecological needs and aesthetics. Public welfare and enjoyment followed closely behind. This balance of interests was matched by some traditional goals of the majority. Nearly eight out of ten students aspired to practice in a landscape architectural firm rather than in a planning or architecture firm or in government service. Moreover, the great majority of landscape architects were not much interested in transportation or regional resource planning—fields in which only landscape architecture faculty were, in significant numbers, deeply concerned.[6]

These findings suggest that an exceptionally bright, ambitious young person who entered the little-known, not-very-remunerative but apparently rising field of landscape architecture around 1969–70 ought to have had some sense of the uphill climb ahead; that he or she was probably inner directed and idealistic; that artistic concerns were as likely to be paramount as environmental ones; and that securing a position in a major firm would seem to be critical for realizing one's personal goals—working with the best architects, planners, and clients on significant projects and expanding boundaries where the strength of the profession already lay.

Ironically, American architects had been talking about expanding *their* professional boundaries for at least a decade. "The total environment is the real problem and, in a sense, the new frontier of architecture," Eero Saarinen wrote in 1959. At that time, toward the end of a career distinguished by highly expressive individual buildings, Saarinen wanted to direct attention beyond the object. "A way must be found for uniting the whole," he noted, "because the total environment is more important than the single building."[7] Echoes of these ideas were heard among leading architects throughout the 1960s. And although the word *environment* did not denote a fragile, much abused planet until the late 1960s, the architectural journals gave good coverage of environmental design issues.

In January 1960, *Progressive Architecture* published its annual design awards, along with comments from the jury, which included William Caudill, Louis Kahn, Ralph Rapson, José Luis Sert, and Lyndon Welch. This jury, and several previous ones, had recognized more quality in planning, urban design, and the spaces between buildings than in the buildings themselves. In 1963, an AIA commission, consisting of Robert F. Hastings, S. C. Hollister, and G. Holmes Perkins, concluded that architects should provide leadership in environmental design, and it recommended changes in professional education that would broaden an architect's scope of knowledge and authority.[8] In response, in 1964, the ASLA issued a formal protest. Calling for further collaboration among design professionals, the ASLA insisted that "history and precedence have delegated the stewardship of the landscape" to the profession of landscape architecture.[9]

This was only superficially a struggle for turf, for both architects and landscape architects were evaluating future directions and long-held values. Not yet troubled by postmodern controversies, both professions could expand their scope of operations and question some results of modernist planning and design—such as single-purpose zoning and the death of the street—without discarding all modernist ideals. For architects, this expansion of professional concerns appears to have occurred without much dissent in public. The AIA awards jury for 1964, for instance, was equally concerned about the urban environment as a whole and "simple, direct expressions of the structure, materials and purpose" of a building.[10] Four years later, while the nation was being torn apart and polarized by the accelerating war in Vietnam, five middle-aged men on the AIA Honor Awards jury—Max O. Urban, Joseph Amisano, Sigmund F. Blum, John W. Morse, and Walter A. Netsch—urged architects to extend themselves for socially significant projects, to look beyond the contented client and aesthetics of the moment, and to deal with problems of the inner city. They also agreed that future juries should include a younger member of the profession.[11]

In landscape architecture, disagreement about professional roles and ideals may have struck more deeply than did the postmodern controversies in architecture. Architects had no reason to question the objectivity of a structure placed somewhere between the earth and the sky. Nor need they be troubled if a building looked as if it had been consciously constructed or designed. Some landscape architects, however, began to disparage the vast amount of unfortunate alterations that had been made on the earth itself, to the point of overlooking exemplary work. Landscape architecture, a profession that had lacked clear criteria for aesthetic judgments ever since the demise of the beaux arts system, began to lose standards for any judgment at all. Design itself—especially modernist design, with its apparent freedom, universality, and rootlessness—became suspect. And Olmsted, once proud to have established landscape architecture as an "Art of Design," became the standard bearer of "natural" or apparently nondesigned landscapes.

These developments led to the loss of synthesis among three traditional concerns of the landscape architect: people, the environment, and the intuitive, creative act. As the competition from other design professionals mounted, as faculty members more discreetly competed for grants and students, and as cyclical downturns in the building industry and recurrent energy crises brought on hard times, so the profession's crisis of identity deepened. And passion for one particular concern of landscape architecture eclipsed the others.

Consider what this meant for the second-wave multidisciplinary firms. Bright young students, and older students who had come to landscape architecture from other fields, were eager to start practicing, on "relevant," meaningful projects. Opportunities for planning vast regions, protecting watersheds and coastlines, and creating whole new communities from scratch existed in the South and the West and in countries such as Venezuela or Kuwait. In the Northeast and Midwest, where most of the established graduate schools were located, there were development opportunities in housing and campus planning and infinite scope for urban renewal, conservation, and regional planning. Such projects required the diverse talents and skills to be found within the second-wave firms. These, then, became the magnets for aspiring graduates imbued with the values, and perhaps the passions, of their mentors.

In the transition from first-wave to second-wave offices, however, some aspects of practice had changed. Passion was less useful to the management of a corporation than a clear head and a degree of worldliness. Strong egos and conflicting principles tended to become submerged. In place of one or two strong leaders within the firm, power and authority became diffused, and responsibilities kept shifting. In place of strong, demanding clients, second-wave offices tended to serve teams or consortiums of clients, including community groups, nonprofit organizations, and bureaucracies.

Before considering the individual cases of a few corporate firms, some common factors in their evolution should be noted. First, their size and financial strength, coming out of the recession of the early 1970s, allowed them to decentralize into a series of branch offices. Earlier, small branch offices had been set up in order to supervise construction on a major project, to stabilize a market area, or to complete a specific planning effort. But after the recovery, beginning around 1975, these offices multiplied and flourished, first as regional marketing centers, later for project management, and later still as repositories for ambitious partners or principals.

These offices were initially intended to offer a sensitive response to the technical and political problems of the region. The effort to maintain high-quality standards throughout the systems, however, soon required some standardization and controls. Promotional materials and accounting procedures were easily standardized through regular meetings of branch and central office managers. Design was less easily guided by these management techniques, however, as it includes elements of research, development, and risk. Corporations then resorted to a degree of artistic direction and control of style. In essence, this entailed a shift of emphasis, from the quest for unique product to the more easily standardized area of process, as found in the planning and environmental thinking of the day.

As these corporate formats and procedures became more precise and replicatable, a number of large architectural firms, such as HOK and

SOM, organized their own planning and landscape design offices within their architectural and engineering management systems. This meant that less work was done in concert between the large corporate architects and the large corporate landscape architects. At the same time, the expanding bureaucracies in public and semipublic agencies, such as planning and development agencies, insurance companies, and savings and loan banks, required longer, more proscribed reviews. This put even more emphasis on process rather than unique product.

By the late 1970s, corporate offices had begun to take on larger percentages of planning work, in contrast to projects intended to be built. At The SWA Group, this approached 60 percent of revenues and, at EDAW, Inc., it reached 90 percent. This series of events meant that managers, planners, and processors rather than designers gained political direction of the firms. By the early 1980s, when staffs often numbered a hundred or more, Garrett Eckbo, Hideo Sasaki, Peter Walker, William Johnson, and Ian McHarg had already left the large firms they had founded. Lawrence Halprin, too, had left his large, unwieldy studio practice. Like the younger people who resisted submersion, these men formed smaller firms, became consultants, and/or returned to academic life.[12]

For an understanding of some differences between first- and second-wave practice, a few specific cases are illuminating. When *Design with Nature* first appeared in 1969, for instance, no one would mistake the book for a second-wave office brochure, despite the lengthy documentation of recent projects by Wallace, McHarg, Roberts and Todd (WMRT). Ian McHarg's discussion of how the planet might be saved through ecologically sensitive planning was permeated with his own life story, his convictions, his passions, even his deepest fears. One little-known fact is that the first, handsome, and expensive edition was entirely designed and largely funded by McHarg himself.[13] This book was the gift of one first-wave leader to his profession. At that time, the environmental processes for which McHarg is known today were not yet clearly articulated. Michael Laurie, one of McHarg's former students and a professor at the University of California, Berkeley, noted that neither the book nor McHarg's lectures (which were often dramatic, electrifying performances) actually provided a method—nor should they. McHarg, he observed, offered "certain values and an approach specific to a particular time and place. It is up to us to listen and learn."[14]

For WMRT, which evolved into WRT after McHarg's departure, the development from broad values and pioneering approaches to proven methods was apparent by 1974, when *Progressive Architecture* (*PA*) profiled the firm.[15] A chronological survey of the firm's projects began with the "Plan for the Valleys" (1962) and the planning and design of Baltimore's Inner Harbor (from 1964). WMRT's clients and collaborators of the early 1960s included Pietro Belluschi, I. M. Pei, Louis Kahn, Kenzo Tange, and Edward Durrell Stone. By 1966, working with Whittlesey, Conklin & Rossant, and Alan M. Voorhees, WMRT was using computers to assemble and analyze study area properties for a development guidelines project in Lower Manhattan. In 1969–1970, for a study of Baltimore's regional core, WMRT evolved a "Probability Growth Model," flexible enough to be used in New Orleans, Los Angeles, and Buffalo.

The Los Angeles office of WMRT was formed in order to complete a 1970–1972 general development plan for a consortium of clients: the City of Los Angeles and the Committee for Central City Planning, composed of twenty-two of the city's largest employers. Other consultants, citizens' groups, and private institutions were also involved in this effort to transform Los Angeles by means of mass transit, an industrial park, an urban park and lake, and the social and physical rehabilitation of Skid Row. Throughout this *PA* profile, recent award-winning projects were featured along with reiterations of McHarg's values. The survival of the city, for instance, was recognized as a key to preserving the countryside. In place of McHarg's passionate, at times inflammatory language, however, is the tone of patience and confidence. William H. Roberts and Thomas A. Todd speak of being centralists, committed to recentralizing the city and to regional land-use planning. In this profile, McHarg was conspicuous by his silence.

The story of the Sasaki firm's second wave is complicated by the expansion to a second, regional office only two years after Sasaki, Walker and Associates was formed in Watertown, Massachusetts. The commission for Foothill College, in Los Altos, California, called for something more than an outpost, some 3,000 miles from Massachusetts. Thus, from December 1959, Peter Walker headed the San Francisco office of this East Coast multidisciplinary firm during its transition from first- to second-wave practice.

Part of the reason Sasaki, Walker and Associates/San Francisco (SWA) moved so quickly into its second wave is that the West Coast, propelled into rapid urbanization by wartime production and postwar expansion, was still relatively unfettered by constraints that regulated East Coast development. California and the West had no centuries-old political, financial, cultural, and social institutions to serve as impediments, although in Northern California some understanding of the blended Yankee-Mediterranean-Hispanic culture was useful. In any event, people came to California in the 1960s expecting—even yearning for—changes in life-style. And until the late 1960s, California offered an irresistible combination of factors for development: fewer regulatory constraints, more pent-up demand from a growing population, a recognizable market for change, and more unaltered (and breathtakingly beautiful) hinterland and coastline than anywhere else in the country—with the possible exception of Florida, the other mecca for growth and development in the postwar decades.

In San Francisco, Walker tried to combine the best of the two waves of practice: the idealism of the first, with the financial and professional benefits of the second. Given the accelerated pace of professional development possible in the early 1960s, the speed with which SWA grasped opportunities on the West Coast was not exceptional. But West Coast development had less urban context to consider. Builders and developers had fewer preconceptions. And even academic clients, such as Foothill College's president, Calvin Flint, had an entrepreneurial streak. Walker learned to use each meeting with clients somewhat as Sasaki would, not only with leading architects and developers of vision but also with commercial builders and town administrators. Big ideas and ways to solve problems would be discussed, and by subtle means, the client would be educated to see every project as an opportunity to do fine work—better yet, something wonderful!

By 1969, Walker and his earliest associates—George Omi, Gene Rosenberg, Edmond Kagi, Gary Karner, Richard Law, and Kalvin Platt—had been joined by twenty-eight younger professionals and ten staff members, forming a heterogeneous, loosely structured group. Under one roof in Sausalito, SWA brought together landscape architects and planners (some of whom, like Platt, also had degrees in architecture), a civil engineer, an accountant with an M.B.A., and painter-photographer Gerry Campbell. Military service and combat in World War II or the Korean War had given some of them a common experience, maturing and sobering. But the mood of Northern California in the late 1960s (exciting, "laid back," less competitive, more idealistic than now) also fostered a camaraderie and a spirit captured in the phrase, "We designers against the world." These young men (and a few women) were determined to push themselves and their clients beyond conventional planning and design, toward more socially responsible and artistically satisfying solutions.

Given these high-minded goals, some activities seemed to need no economic justification, such as the summer intern program for landscape architecture students, begun in the early 1970s. Although costly, the program brought the intangible benefits of intellectual stimulation and the clarification of ideas, as practitioners assumed the roles of in-house teachers (figure 139).

The early 1970s was also a period of rapid office expansion. By 1971, with Raymond Belknap as a principal and John Furtado on the staff, an SWA brochure featured environmental analysis and planning. Michael Gilbert had been persuaded to leave a national real estate development corporation in order to restructure SWA's business organization and financial management. Soon Richard Burns, designer of SWA's office brochures, was brought in to work with Campbell in the new communications division. Engineering became a separate division. The only design capability not offered was architecture; unlike Sasaki Associates, in Watertown, Massachusetts, SWA did not employ practicing architects,

139. Hideo Sasaki with students at the SWA summer intern program, Sausalito, California, 1971.

in part to avoid their dominating the office, in part for the option to collaborate more freely with architects on the outside.

The year 1973 was one of tremendous change for SWA. First, the Employee Stock Ownership Program (whereby all the employees—over a hundred—would gain control of the firm's stock) was instituted. This program indirectly led to the severing of formal ties with Hideo Sasaki's office in Watertown, through legal tangles over what constitutes an employee, flawed negotiations, and some tragic misunderstandings.[16] Another change was the short-lived merger with James A. Roberts and Associates, a prominent environmental planning firm headed by Roberts (who had earned a Ph.D. in geography) and staffed by professionals with degrees in ecology, biology, zoology, meteorology, geography, soil science, life sciences, wildlife sciences, environmental science, forestry, and renewable natural resources. In theory, these scientists were to become integrated with SWA's planners and designers, developing creative thought and methods through collaboration. In practice, this did not happen within the short life of Sasaki, Walker, Roberts (SWR).[17]

The overt crisis, which not only prevented smooth integration of the scientists but also threatened to bankrupt the firm, was the severe nationwide recession in the housing and building industry from late 1972 to 1974. Although some environmental planning work was ongoing at the time, only the long-standing working relationships with large new-community developers, notably, the Irvine Company in Southern California and the Arvida Corporation in Florida, kept SWR alive long enough to revert to SWA, later The SWA Group. By 1975 most of the scientists were gone, while only the foresters Walter Bemis and James Culver remained principals within The SWA Group.

An underlying problem, however, was peculiar to landscape architects throughout the country: a crisis of identity. Depending on their training and inclinations, they were site planners, land use planners, applied ecologists, designers, design critics, applied scientists, catalysts, community builders, artists with fragile egos and dreams, or some combination thereof. In 1974 the inspired writer of the SWR office brochure had mentioned the higher purposes of the corporation—to create and nurture a philosophical and administrative climate conducive to the pursuit of excellence—and added a quotation from Aldo Leopold: "A thing is right when it tends to preserve the integrity, stability and beauty of the biotic community. It is wrong when it tends otherwise."[18] Few landscape architects would have disagreed with these sentiments, yet as a body of professionals, they could not agree on the core of essential professional skills and areas of understanding.

By the time the media were pursuing the hot domestic battles of the late 1960s and early 1970s—environmentalists versus designers, community participation activists versus designers, and developers and other American businessmen versus environmentalists—SWA, like other second-wave firms, was frequently caught between suddenly polarized positions. The firm was doing both environmental impact re-

140. Golden Gate National Recreation Area, Marin County, California, ca. 1975: Master plan. National Park Service, Client. The SWA Group, Planners and Landscape Architects. Kalvin Platt, Principal Planner. For an area of 90,000 acres, The SWA Group developed a master plan to preserve natural resources while providing for public recreation. The plan incorporates information and insights gleaned from over 100 public workshops and also data from the environmental atlas that SWA had prepared in the early stages of planning.

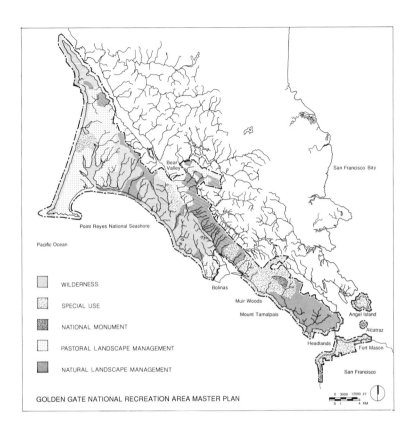

ports and new community development on virgin land (figures 140 and 141). At Promontory Point, in Newport Beach, California, the client, the newly formed California Coastal Commission, local residents, and the architects all had to be persuaded to accept a novel scheme for open space, circulation, and landscape design (figure 142). At that time, in California's High Sierra, SWA was also doing environmental studies for the U.S. Forest Service and the Mono County Planning Department, before devising a master plan for 400 square miles of the Mammoth Lakes Recreation Area.

Other second-wave offices around the country were playing similar roles, on both sides of the development-conservation fence. Even designers who became impatient with the lengthy processes of resource and site analysis could see that development and conservation did not constitute an either-or proposition but a dual necessity (figures 143 and 144). WMRT recognized that ensuring the survival of the central city was a fundamental means of saving the countryside from mindless,

Fisher-Friedman Associates, Architects.
Robert Geering, Principal Designer. The
SWA Group, Landscape Architects. Peter
Walker, Principal Designer. This plan
stemmed from the ecological evaluation
of the heavily wooded, swampy site. To
save the woods, all parking was placed
beneath the buildings, and the recreational facilities were placed out over the
small existing pond. Paths were of either
gravel or stepping-stones, allowing water
to percolate.

formless urban sprawl. What mattered was a broad vision, beyond politics and egos, that would direct the landscape architect's activities
without rancor, with knowledge, and with an eye for beauty as well as
truth (or "correctness").

Instead, for many years designers (along with developers) were cast as
the enemy. Lines were drawn when articles appeared in the professional design magazines, followed by challenges and rebuttals. A case in
point was the Eckbo-Porterfield debate of 1969–1970, in *Landscape Architecture*.[19] Both Garrett Eckbo and Neil Porterfield were by then
leaders within large multidisciplinary offices, working under second-
wave conditions. The multioffice partnership of Eckbo, Dean, Austin
and Williams had been incorporated in 1968—a bit reluctantly, Eckbo
recalls; but, to avoid the personal liabilities of large-scale practice, the
older partners had to overcome their Old Left scruples.[20] Porterfield
was then heading landscape architecture and planning at the architecture firm of HOK, in St. Louis. He was also some twenty years younger
than Eckbo, a product of the University of California, Berkeley, Pennsylvania State University (class of 1958), and the University of Pennsylvania, under Ian McHarg and Karl Linn.

Porterfield's article, "Ecological Basis for Planning a New Campus," explained his processes for planning the University of Wisconsin's new
600-acre Parkside Campus as an "ecological laboratory." He proposed
simulating natural processes so closely that even the ratio of one native
species to another (in the wild) would determine their ratios on the
campus. But Eckbo questioned these and other aspects of ecological
determinism. Ideally, he argued, both architecture and nature should inspire the landscape architect, and he invoked "the collaborative ideal
we all dreamed of."

142. Promontory Point Housing, Newport Beach, California, 1975. The Irvine Company, Developers. Fisher-Friedman Associates, Architects. Peter Geering, Principal Designer. The SWA Group, Landscape Architects. Peter Walker, Principal Designer. High-density, low-rise housing overlooking Balboa Bay is built around a series of recreational facilities, social centers, and parks with views of the bay.

143. Concord Pavilion, Concord, California, 1975. Frank O. Gehry Associates, Architects. Frank O. Gehry, Principal Designer. The SWA Group, Landscape Architects. Peter Walker, Principal Designer. An open-air performance center, the Concord Pavilion was placed in a carved-out grass bowl for sound protection. The pavilion faces the seasonally changing landscape of the California foothills.

144. Elkhorn Resort, Sun Valley, Idaho, 1976. Killingsworth, Brady & Associates, Architects. The SWA Group, Landscape Architects and Planners. Kalvin Platt, Principal Planner. Peter Walker, Principal Designer. A new resort community, Elkhorn extended the famous Sun Valley ski area into the adjacent valley. Development was kept off the hills, which form a natural backdrop for the concentrated clusters of community in the valley below.

The reply and rebuttal between these two distinguished practitioners yielded more than the buzz words *analysis paralysis* and *fantasy fatigue*. Eckbo, the witty elder statesman, became an articulate spokesman for a balance of factors in the design process—tipped slightly in favor of human needs and imagination, so that ultimately the finest works would transcend their time and place and express anonymously the aspirations of the wider culture.[21] Meanwhile, Porterfield offered intelligent arguments for favoring ecological processes and the use of native species. With many variations in tone and content, such debates have continued to this day.

It may be too soon to assess the impact of the large, corporate, multidisciplinary firm on design, environmental planning and protection, and the overall quality of our built environments. But surely the scale of these enterprises is a major factor. In the early years of Sasaki-Walker's collaborative practice, for instance, some eight to twelve professionals had worked under one roof, informally exchanging ideas and accepting the critique of one strong leader, given the wide leeway Sasaki allowed them. But Sasaki, whose understanding of business is as acute as his eye for design, knew growth was inevitable. "An office is like an organism; it has to grow, or die," he says. "It changes continually. It acts and reacts." Using the same metaphor, he has compared changes in an office to ecological change: "One species becomes more and more dominant, then finally it takes over."[22]

Precisely who becomes dominant is usually a matter of personality, ability, and chance. Then, too, American landscape architecture, particularly since World War II, has tended to mirror American business, culture, and, to some extent, politics. Until the late 1960s or early

1970s, those who dominated the field might lean toward pragmatism, but idealism still ran high, energizing their work. Things, objective fact, and built work usually dominated over context or setting. Thus, architects typically dominated landscape architects. From the late 1960s, the new tools of computers, scientific methods, environmental legislation, and a popular interest in context seemed to promise increased stature for some landscape architects, while changes in the media and advertising gave artistic efforts some attention. Corporate financial tools have offered the larger firms degrees of power undreamed of just after the war. And technological innovation—computer-aided design systems, fax machines, and other tools of communication—have aided the decentralizing of second-wave firms and also allowed smaller firms to compete with the large corporate firms.

Will these smaller firms thrive, however, without some degree of specialization—another hallmark of the large corporate office? Ironically, by the early 1980s, specialization in the previous fifteen years had produced a whole new scale of craft appropriate, for the first time, to the size and speed required by the new urban and suburban pace of development. Planning, civil engineering, campus planning and design, urban design, construction supervision, and contract administration were finally at a level of technical skill appropriate to the tasks of the modern environment. But the real ability to build had arrived at the very moment when the designers' passion and direction of the previous thirty years had seemed to run out of energy.

Even so, during the 1970s and 1980s, the large corporate offices produced a tremendous amount of built work, at very high levels of execution, compared with that of the previous twenty years—particularly in suburban housing, resorts, urban renewal, parks, and suburban commercial development. At the same time there was a noticeable reduction of intellectually challenging, culturally significant work, and little positive criticism of this more standardized work has appeared. In fact, by the late 1980s, the smaller, younger offices were attracting more attention from art and design critics, academia, and the popular media than their corporate parents. Having seen the aesthetic leadership of the corporate firms diminish in the 1980s, the committed, passionate designers left the corporate structures that had been so painstakingly developed and turned to earlier forms of practice: Church's studio or atelier; or the partnership format of Eckbo, Royston, and Williams—itself a variation on the model of Olmsted, Olmsted and Eliot.

In years to come, perhaps no single type or scale of office will be sufficient to sustain the broad scope of Olmsted's practice, from the design of private gardens to planning for metropolitan and national park systems and conserving natural resources. Meanwhile, Olmsted's personal struggles to reconcile being and doing have their counterpart in collective efforts to reconcile nature and culture. The endangered planet and the momentary existence of human beings upon it can no longer be seen as oppositions. The interdependence of both in an advanced technological age, along with the interdependence of science and art, process and product, stewardship and creation, must in time be generally recognized—and expressed in fine, memorable built work.

The growth and success of the landscape architectural profession in the past fifty years cannot eliminate the environmental impoverishment of America over the same period. This impoverishment can be related to the so-called failure of modern architecture propounded by postmodern theorists; both architecture and landscape architecture exist in the same place and time. But our inquiries have tended to confirm what may be obvious to some: that landscape architecture does not completely share the ideas or ideals of architecture. Its historic foundations and primary concerns—at least as revealed in the work of Frederick Law Olmsted, Jens Jensen, and their contemporaries—are quite distinct from those of architecture.

For landscape architecture, the decades immediately after World War II now seem to be classically tragic. Opportunities were never greater, and many paramount issues were identified correctly, if uncertainly. Economic and social forces in America altered the landscape at a magnitude and pace unequaled by any other period in history, except perhaps the post–Civil War years. The profession attracted people of great talent, intellect, and organizational ability—people who had been aware, since the early 1950s, of the great promise of the age. Yet the rate of expansion of suburban growth, the building of roads, houses, and factory and service facilities, outstripped designers' abilities to produce high-quality work on a large scale. Rather, newly made and mediocre environments became the overpowering images of the age. By not commanding the attention of the decision makers and arbiters of taste, the important alternative icons, ones of true quality, were not able to set standards for, and thus guide, the country's development. By the time the offices had gained effective size for significant quantitative production, they had become oriented toward process rather than product. The offices themselves had become a normative voice rather than one of criticism or leadership.

It seems ironic that, in a world fast moving toward a state of image supremacy over experience, it was the focused image of these landscapes that was missing throughout so much of the era. The important body of work that has been amassed has had little iconic or political weight, collectively. Since the popular garden imagery of Thomas Church in the 1940s and 1950s, there has been a decline in writing, criticism, and publication of iconic images. The public was never made fully aware of the scope of landscape architecture, and among those who were aware, attitudes have changed over the past forty years from hopeful interest to, at worst, critical wrath.

Why has a field so full of idealism and both practical and economically available solutions had so little influence and effect? The answers do not seem to lie in the arguments and dichotomies of the field itself, though insecurities that may have been both cause and effect certainly have played a role.

One basis of insecurity may have been inherited from the modern architectural movement's dictum that history is not important. While being educated for a greatly expanded contemporary role, students of design were routinely underprepared to measure their current efforts against the work of previous generations and other cultures. This has not only psychologically orphaned the young practitioners but also denied them the means to evaluate previous work in any but their own terms. The emphasis on learning about, and assimilating, increasing amounts of science and technology in the schools has limited students' access to cultural and philosophical inquiry. This has tended to remove students from debates about the political and economic forces that have controlled the direction of society. What is more, the mistaken faith that technical knowledge would give the power to lead may have reduced the designer's ability to affect society by the power of iconic example. If one is service oriented, how much scope does one have for offering philosophical guidance or cultural leadership?

In his maturity, Olmsted came to recognize that his power to lead could not be based on his administrative or technical skills alone. Rather, his artistic accomplishments, especially visible in his public parks and park systems, would become a basis of power—but only if his underlying intentions were understood and appreciated by the public. Thus, his published reports and essays, along with his precise directions for park management, were critical to his success as a landscape architect. In his later years, Olmsted repeatedly emphasized that his achievements were works of art, not merely products of craft or skillful supervision. Today, his misportrayed image of conservationist nonintervention in the landscape is among the most ironic results of contemporary landscape architects' lack of historical perspective.

Another irony lies in the incomplete assimilation of landscape architecture into the business of land development and building. While landscape architects may have become necessary (though subordinate) players on a profit-driven team, their roles as spokesmen for, or interpreters of, cultural and philosophical values have diminished. The separation of design from high culture, most noticeably from the 1960s onward, not only deprived landscape architecture of direct access to the cultural elite; it also separated the field from the information and ideas flowing in and out of the worlds of art and literature.

As departments and schools of design have grown and developed new specialties, they have lost their connected positions within the larger university communities and become separated from departments of art and art history. Sasaki, for one, found the students with bachelor's degrees in landscape architecture from the land grant colleges remarkably unworldly and unaware, despite the stature of those institutions. Typically, design students are no longer encouraged to take courses in other departments and schools of the university. Rather, specialists in ecology, economics, law, business management, systems analysis, and even art have been brought into the design schools, particularly in the leading graduate schools of design. These schools have become universities unto themselves, though quite small and perhaps less fine than their parents. In addition, the economics of these trends of internal expansion are crippling the private schools of design.

For more than a century, landscape architecture has been a field difficult to define. Over the past four decades, the field has been most often defined in terms of a balance of unlike elements. Increasingly, however, landscape architects have yearned for a more singular or simpler definition (that is, a definition more like that of "architecture"). Some believe that a purging and homogenizing of Olmsted's blend of art, science, and sociology would be clearer and more effective. But these attempts at redefinition have not worked; landscape architecture still depends on rich, varied combinations of skills, insights, and bodies of knowledge, continually recombined and redefined by the individuals who practice landscape architecture.

Today an elegant body of landscape architectural work exists. Though largely unheralded, it stands alongside the architecture of its age as a selection of useful and beautiful emblems. As a whole, these emblems only peripherally participate in the ubiquitous accumulations of "objects in space," those travesties of the Corbusian ideal that have so damaged the American built landscape. This elegant work has tried, however—often unsuccessfully—to bridge the gap between unaltered nature and modern culture. (And by "modern culture," we allude to both the best and the worst of late-twentieth-century Western, increasingly global, culture, which generally acquiesces to the overriding pursuit of private wealth and the disastrous single-purpose zoning begun by Baron Haussmann in late-nineteenth-century Paris.)

As more comprehensive histories of modern landscape architecture are written, detailed criticism and evaluation of its meaning and importance, both culturally and artistically, will become available. To date, the critical writing does not yet constitute a comprehensive theory of the profession. With more history, criticism, discussion, and reflection, perhaps with a more balanced consideration of natural processes and cultural expression, a workable and politically useful theory of environmental design may emerge.

This book has considered landscape architects and offices that are in many ways distinct in temperament, geography, and time, yet their histories are woven together by some common causes and also frayed by some common experiences, particularly the violence of change during the postwar years. These landscape architects have attempted to address the problems, the opportunities, and the spirit of the particular phase of the modern world in which they found themselves. They are connected not only by their times but also by loose ties through their education and the history of their profession, though much of their inheritance was not clearly recognized or collectively appreciated. The majority have been practitioners who tried to chart a course while being tumbled by immense events. Many have also been teachers who attempted, perhaps imperfectly, to develop new curricula, reorganize the profession, or point the way. Several have been philosophical and popular leaders who initiated or directed discussions of ends and means or who questioned the very idea of goals. All have contributed to a significant body of work and hypothesis that, though seemingly disjointed and even at times contradictory, has collectively marked their presence and characterized their time. There is an element of heroism in their efforts, for each has aimed to enrich and improve.

Over the past ten years, a number of signs indicate a more hopeful and more integrated future for the profession. A revival of formal design at Harvard University in the mid-1970s has found positive reaction in many of the other university landscape programs without the loss of their expanded environmental interests. In a number of schools, notably the universities of California (at Berkeley), Illinois (at Urbana), and Virginia, integration of the two viewpoints has been largely accomplished. The study of history has also been expanded in schools where some professional historians now focus on landscape architecture.

New firms have appeared to challenge the corporate giants, and several of these have received national recognition and even some small critical attention. The magazine *Landscape Architecture,* after a shaky transition in the late 1970s, has been revived as a forum for debate and record of the more advanced work in both areas. The procedures for the ASLA awards jury have been revised to provide a more catholic review of current professional work. Japanese and European publications have also revealed a heightened interest in both early modernist design and later examples of design-oriented American landscape architecture. Ironically, the recession of the early 1990s has strengthened these new developments in the profession, and there seems to be every reason to look forward to a hopeful and positive future.

Finally, although the works we have considered are not all masterpieces, many are works of art. Together they bear witness to a continuing quest for beauty, meaning, mystery, and the perhaps unattainable garden of myth. Could it be that a thoughtfully balanced, properly integrated field of landscape architecture will, in the hands of Ian McHarg's informed designer-artist, help bring us back to a state of grace? If such a state cannot yet be defined, surely it would be sustained by some of the classic virtues: among them, maintenance of the earth, and the dream of human integration within the rhythms of the days, the seasons, and the endlessness of cultural time.

Peter Walker
San Francisco, August 1993

Notes

Introduction

1. See Nikolaus Pevsner, *Pioneers of the Modern Movement* (London: Faber & Faber, 1936), and Henry-Russell Hitchcock and Philip Johnson, *The International Style: Architecture since 1922* (New York: W. W. Norton & Co., 1932). Hitchcock's and Johnson's brief comments (in chapter 7) on naturalistic and architectural settings for modern buildings do not constitute a body of principles for a modern style of landscape design.

2. For Olmsted's relations with Cleveland, see Laura Wood Roper, *FLO: A Biography of Frederick Law Olmsted* (Baltimore: Johns Hopkins University Press, 1973), 333–35. See also William H. Tishler, "H.W.S. Cleveland," in Tishler, ed., *American Landscape Architecture: Designers and Places* (Washington, D.C.: National Trust for Historic Preservation/American Society of Landscape Architects, 1989), 24–29.

3. Garrett Eckbo, "What do we mean by Modern Landscape Architecture?" *Journal of the Royal Architectural Institute of Canada* 27, no. 8 (August 1950): 268.

4. Ibid., 269.

5. Hideo Sasaki, "Thoughts on Education in Landscape Architecture," *Landscape Architecture* (July 1950): 159. See also Hideo Sasaki, "Landscape Architecture Education in Transition," *Forsite*, Department of City Planning and Landscape Architecture, University of Illinois, Champaign-Urbana (1951): 3–6; and Hideo Sasaki, "Landscape Architecture and the Planning Effort," *Forsite* (1953): 6–7.

6. Hideo Sasaki, "The City and the Landscape Architect," *Space*, Department of Landscape Architecture, University of California, Berkeley (1956): 19–21; and "Thoughts on Education in Landscape Architecture."

7. Lawrence Halprin, "The Community in the Landscape," *American Institute of Architects' Journal* (September 1961): 52–57.

8. Lawrence Halprin, *Cities* [1963] (Cambridge, Mass.: MIT Press, 1980), 14.

9. Lawrence Halprin to Patric Condon, *Landscape Journal* 8, no. 2 (Fall 1989): 151.

10. See Stuart Wrede and William Howard Adams, *Denatured Visions: Landscape and*

Culture in the Twentieth Century (New York: Museum of Modern Art/Abrams, 1991) (from the conference on twentieth-century architecture and landscape architecture at the Museum of Modern Art, Autumn 1988); Patrick M. Condon and Lance M. Neckar, eds., *The Avant-Garde and the Landscape: Can They Be Reconciled?* Proceedings of the Conference at the University of Minnesota, Minneapolis, Spring 1989 (Minneapolis: Landworks Press, 1990); and Marc Treib, ed., *Modern Landscape Architecture: A Critical Review* (Cambridge, Mass.: MIT Press, 1993) (from the conference at the University of California, Berkeley, Fall 1989). Other recent symposia on the work of twentieth-century landscape architects have been held at Harvard, the University of Virginia, and elsewhere. Recent publications have included monographs on Robert Burle Marx; new editions of Thomas Church, *Gardens Are for People* (New York: Reinhold, 1955; New York: McGraw-Hill, 1983) and Elizabeth B. Kassler, *Modern Gardens and the Landscape* (New York: Museum of Modern Art, 1964, 1984); and Felice Frankel

and Jory Johnson, *Modern Landscape Architecture* (New York: Abbeville Press, 1991).

11. Halprin to Condon, 151.

12. Lawrence Halprin to Melanie Simo, April 22, 1992.

13. Garrett Eckbo, "Modern Landscape Architecture Re-Visited," unpublished typescript, April 1992, a copy of which Eckbo sent to Melanie Simo.

14. Ian McHarg, in conversation with Melanie Simo, May 20, 1987, Berkeley, California.

15. See Melanie L. Simo, *Loudon and the Landscape: From Country Seat to Metropolis, 1783–1843* (New Haven: Yale University Press, 1988); George B. Tatum, "Andrew Jackson Downing: Arbiter of American Taste, 1815–1852" (Ph.D. diss., Princeton University, 1950); and Walter L. Creese, *The Crowning of the American Landscape: Eight Great Spaces and Their Buildings* (Princeton: Princeton University Press, 1985), 75–85.

16. Charles Capen McLaughlin, Editor-in-Chief, and Charles E. Beveridge, Series Editor, *The Papers of Frederick Law Olmsted* (hereafter, *FLO Papers*), vol. 1 (1822–1852) through vol. 6 (1865–1784)

(Baltimore: Johns Hopkins University Press, 1977–1992).

17. Frederick Law Olmsted (hereafter, FLO) to Elizabeth Baldwin Whitney, December 16, 1890, in Charles Capen McLaughlin, "Selected Letters of Frederick Law Olmsted" (Ph.D. Diss., Harvard University, 1960), 396–411.

18. Ibid., 401. This quotation also appears in Melvin Kalfus, *Frederick Law Olmsted: The Passion of a Public Artist* (New York: New York University Press, 1990), 53.

19. Ibid., 394–95.

20. Roper, *FLO*, 419–21.

21. See note 18.

22. FLO to Elizabeth Baldwin Whitney, December 16, 1890, in McLaughlin, "Selected Letters," 407; and FLO to Mariana Griswold Van Rensselaer, June 11, 1893, in ibid., 429.

23. FLO, *Walks and Talks of an American Farmer in England* [1852] (Ann Arbor: University of Michigan Press, ca. 1975), 52.

24. Ibid., 95.

25. Calvert Vaux to FLO, May 22, 1865, in *FLO Papers,* 5:375–78.

26. FLO to Mariana Griswold Van Rensselaer, June 11, 1893, in McLaughlin, "Selected Letters," 431.

27. See Charles E. Beveridge, "Frederick Law Olmsted's Theory of Landscape Design," *Nineteenth Century* 3, no. 2 (Summer 1977): 38–43; Frederick Law Olmsted, Jr., and Theodora Kimball, eds., *Forty Years of Landscape Architecture: Central Park* [1928] (Cambridge, Mass.: MIT Press, 1973); and *FLO Papers,* especially vols. 3, 5.

28. FLO to Board of Commissioners of Central Park, January 22, 1861, in *FLO Papers,* 3:304.

29. See biographical sketch of Andrew Haswell Green in *FLO Papers,* 3:55–59.

30. FLO to John Bigelow, February 9, 1861, in *FLO Papers,* 3:324.

31. FLO to Calvert Vaux, November 26, 1863, in *FLO Papers,* 5:150.

32. FLO to Parke Godwin, August 1, 1858, in *FLO Papers,* 3:200–201.

33. Augustus Saint-Gaudens, in Burke Wilkinson, *Uncommon Clay: The Life and Works of Augustus Saint Gaudens* (New York: Harcourt Brace Jovanovich, 1985), 242.

34. Wilkinson, *Uncommon Clay,* 258.

35. FLO to Daniel H. Burnham, October 2, 1893, in Roper, *FLO,* 450.

36. Daniel H. Burnham, quoted in Roper, *FLO,* 447.

37. FLO to William Platt, February 1, 1892, quoted in Roper, *FLO,* 433–34.

38. FLO to William A. Stiles, March 10, 1895, in McLaughlin, "Selected Letters," 443–52.

39. Charles Sprague Sargent, "Prospect Park," *Garden and Forest* 1 (July 4, 1888): 217, quoted in *FLO Papers,* 6:24.

40. See Roger B. Stein, "Artifact as Ideology: The Aesthetic Movement in Its American Cultural Context," in *In Pursuit of Beauty: Americans and the Aesthetic Movement* (New York: Metropolitan Museum of Art/Rizzoli, 1986); James Thomas Flexner, *That Wilder Image: The Native School from Thomas Cole to Winslow Homer* (Boston: Little, Brown, 1962); Neil Harris, *The Artist in American Society: The Formative Years, 1790–1860* (New York: George Braziller, 1966); and *The American Renaissance: 1876–1917* (New York: The Brooklyn Museum/Pantheon, 1979).

41. See Alfred H. Barr, *Cubism and Abstract Art* (New York, 1936); and Henri Focillon, *Vie des formes* [1934], trans. C. B. Hogan and G. Kubler, as *The Life of Forms in Art* (New York: Zone Books, 1989).

42. See, for example, Lewis Mumford, *The Brown Decades: A Study of the Arts in America (1865–1895)* [1931] (New York: Dover, 1955), 173.

43. Henry Vincent Hubbard and Thodora Kimball, *An Introduction to the Study of Landscape Design* (New York: Macmillan, 1917), 29–31.

44. See Rudi Blesh, *Modern Art USA: Man, Rebellion, Conquest, 1900–1956* (New York: Alfred A. Knopf, 1956); and Henry-Russell Hitchcock and Philip Johnson, *The International Style,* (new ed.) (New York: W. W. Norton, 1966).

45. P. D. Ouspensky, *Tertium Organum,* quoted in Fletcher Steele, "New Pioneering in Garden Design," *Landscape Architecture* (April 1930): 160.

Chapter 1

1. The landscape architects cited here are all featured or mentioned in William H. Tishler, ed., *American Landscape Architecture: Designers and Places* (Washington, D.C.: Preservation Press, 1989).

2. Lewis Mumford, in Clarence S. Stein,

Toward New Towns for America (Liverpool: University Press of Liverpool,
1951), 18–19.

3. Stein, *Toward New Towns for America,* 62.

4. Ibid., 45.

5. Ebenezer Howard, *Tomorrow: A Peaceful
Path to Real Reform* [1898] (London: Fa-
ber and Faber, 1967), 158–59. See also
Marshall Stalley, ed., *Patrick Geddes:
Spokesman for Man and the Environment*
(New Brunswick, N.J.: Rutgers University
Press, 1972).

6. See Marc A. Weiss, *The Rise of the Community Builders: The American Real Estate
Industry and Urban Land Planning* (New
York: Columbia University Press,1987),
4–12.

7. Henry Wright, *Rehousing Urban America*
(New York: Columbia University Press,
1935), 61.

8. Lewis Mumford to Patrick Geddes, December 4, 1924, in Mumford, *Findings
and Keepings* (New York: Harcourt Brace
Jovanovich, 1975), 78.

9. Mumford's role as poet is not revealed in
the excerpt of his letter to Geddes, cited
in ibid. See Donald L. Miller, *Lewis Mum-*
ford: A Life (New York: Weidenfeld & Ni-
colson, 1989), 207.

10. Lewis Mumford, *The Culture of Cities*
(New York: Harcourt, Brace: 1938), 351.

11. Other RPAA members included Tracy
Augur, Clarence Perry, Russell Black, Nils
Hammarstrand, William T. Johnson, Joseph K. Hart, Robert Bruere, and Sullivan
Jones. See Carl Sussman, *Planning the
Fourth Migration: The Neglected Vision of
the Regional Planning Association of America* (Cambridge, Mass.: MIT Press, 1976),
17–23.

12. Clarence Stein, "Henry Wright, 1878–
1936," *American Architect and Architecture*
(August 1936): 23.

13. "Cooperative Group Planning," *Architectural Record* (November 1913): 467–75.

14. Henry Wright, "The Autobiography of
Another Idea," *Western Architect* 39 no. 9
(September 1930): 139.

15. Lewis Mumford, Introduction to Stein,
Toward New Towns for America, 13.

16. Stein, "Henry Wright," 23.

17. Douglas Haskell, "For Architects Only,"
Architectural Forum (July 1954): 168.

18. Roy Lubove, *Community Planning in the
1920s* (Pittsburgh: University of Pittsburgh Press, 1963), 32; and Lewis Mumford, "A Modest Man's Enduring
Contributions to Urban and Regional
Planning" [on Stein], *Journal of the American Institute of Architects* (December
1976): 19.

19. See Bertram Goodhue, Introduction to
Carleton M. Winslow, *The Architecture
and the Gardens of the San Diego Exposition* (San Francisco: Paul Elder, 1916).

20. Clarence Stein, "A Triumph of the Spanish Colonial Style," in Winslow, *Architecture,* 11.

21. Stein, "Henry Wright," 24.

22. Clarence Stein, quoted in Mumford, "A
Modest Man's Enduring Contributions,"
24.

23. Stein, *Toward New Towns for America,* 23–
26.

24. Marjorie Sewell Cautley (1891–1954)
was born in San Francisco. As a child
growing up in New York City, she took
art lessons at the Pratt Institute. After
graduating in 1917 from Cornell University with a B.S. in landscape architecture,
she began to design private gardens in
the New York metropolitan area. In the
1930s she served as landscape consultant

323 Notes to Pages 33–43

to the state of New Hampshire, working on park projects. She also served as lecturer in the Department of Architecture and Planning at the Massachusetts Institute of Technology and at the Columbia School of Architecture. In 1943 she earned an M.F.A. degree from the University of Pennsylvania. A member of the ASLA from 1925 to 1950, Cautley died in 1954.

How Cautley came into contact with Stein and Wright remains a mystery. Perhaps, as Nell Walker has suggested, one of her *Country Life* articles on residential landscape design, published in 1922, came to their attention. See "Marjorie Sewell Cautley: Landscape Architect for the Early American Garden Cities," written for Melanie Simo's Radcliffe seminar, Fall 1984. In archives of the Radcliffe Seminars, Radcliffe College, Cambridge Massachusetts; "Marjorie Sewell Cautley," in *American Women, 1935–40* (1981); Obituary in *Landscape Architecture* (October 1954), 40; and Cautley, *Garden Design* (New York: Dodd, Mead and Co., 1935).

25. Lewis Mumford, *Sketches from Life* (New York: Dial, 1982), 410–21.

26. Ibid.

27. Lewis Mumford, *Green Memories* (New York: Harcourt, Brace, 1947), 30.

28. Frederick J. Osborn, Introduction to Howard, *Tomorrow,* 26.

29. Walker, "Marjorie Sewell Cautley," 14.

30. Geddes Smith, quoted in Stein, *Towards New Towns for America,* 44.

31. Clarence Stein, Introduction to a reprint of Benton MacKaye's "An Appalachian Trail: A Project in Regional Planning," *AIA Journal* (October 1921), cited by Sussman, *Planning,* 15; and Stein, "Dinosaur Cities," reprinted from *Survey Graphic* 7 (May 1925): 134–38, in Sussman, *Planning,* 74.

32. Wright, *Rehousing Urban America,* 86–87.

33. Like Thomas Carlyle, John Ruskin, William Morris, and Henry Adams, Stein felt some revulsion from modernism—that is, from the intertwined developments of capitalism, industry, technology, and their socioeconomic and cultural manifestations. He had to accept modern conditions and tools, but for a long time he rejected modern design, perhaps because

of its association with the very forces that garden cities were meant to counteract. For a discussion of Adams's critique of modern culture and references to Carlyle, Ruskin, and Morris, see T. J. Jackson Lears, *No Place of Grace: Antimodernism and the Transformation of American Culture, 1880–1920* (New York: Pantheon, 1981),

34. For accounts of their separation, see Mumford, "A Modest Man's Enduring Contributions," 28, and Miller, *Lewis Mumford,* 365.

35. Henry Churchill, "Henry Wright: 1878–1936," *Journal of the American Institute of Planners* 26, no. 4 (November 1960): 293–301.

36. Henry Wright to Lewis Mumford, ca. 1933, quoted in Mumford, "A Modest Man's Enduring Contributions," 22.

37. Stein and Wright were site planners and consulting architects at Chatham Village (1930–1935). Stein was also consulting architect at Baldwin Hills (1938–1942). For a recent evaluation of Baldwin Hills (which won the AIA's 25-Year Award in 1972), see George Rand, "Evaluation:

Three California Pioneers," *Architecture* (July 1985): 88–89.

38. Churchill ("Henry Wright," 297) praised Wright's site planning abilities, noting that he was endowed with "a most delicate feeling for contours."

39. Marjorie Cautley, "Planting at Radburn," *Landscape Architecture* (October 1930): 23–29.

40. Stein, [Toward New Towns for America,] 62.

41. Lewis Mumford, *Art and Technics* (New York: Columbia University Press, 1952), 11, and *Technics and Civilization* (New York: Harcourt, Brace & Co., 1934), 345. See also Stanislaus von Moos, "The Visualized Machine Age or: Mumford and the European Avant-Garde," in Thomas P. Hughes and Agatha C. Hughes, eds., *Lewis Mumford, Public Intellectual* (New York: Oxford University Press, 1990), 181–232.

42. Lewis Mumford, "The Fate of Garden Cities," *AIA Journal* 15, no. 2 (February 1927): 37–39.

43. Siegfried Giedion, *Mechanization Takes Command* [1948], new ed. (New York: W. W. Norton & Co., 1975), 347–48.

44. Catherine Bauer to Lewis Mumford, September 2, 1934, quoted in Miller, *Lewis Mumford,* 333–34. Bauer, principal adviser and executive secretary of the Housing Labor Conference in Philadelphia, became a vigorous advocate of community participation while working with architect Oscar Stonorov and the American Federation of Full-Fashioned Hosiery Workers on the Carl Mackey Houses, a New Deal program. Later Bauer rose to director of research and information in the U.S. Housing Authority and helped to draft the pioneering Wagner-Steagall bill (which led to the U.S. Housing Act of 1937). For her later, strong reservations about the results of that bill—standard public housing projects—see Bauer, "The Dreary Deadlock of Public Housing," *Architectural Forum* (May 1957): 141.

45. Lewis Mumford, quoted in Miller, *Lewis Mumford,* 90.

46. Clarence Stein, "Communities for the Good Life," *AIA Journal* (July 1956): 11–18; and the notice of Stein's Gold Medal, *AIA Journal* (May 1956): 210.

Chapter 2

1. Isamu Noguchi, *A Sculptor's World* (New York: Harper & Row, 1968), 167.

2. Roberto Burle Marx, "A Garden Style in Brazil to Meet Contemporary Needs," *Landscape Architecture* (July 1954): 208.

3. José Gomez Sicre, *4 Artists of the Americas* (Washington, D.C.: Pan American Union, 1957), 9. See also William Howard Adams, *Roberto Burle Marx: The Unnatural Art of the Garden* (New York: Museum of Modern Art, 1991); and Sima Eliovson, *The Gardens of Roberto Burle Marx* (New York: Abrams/Sagapress, 1991).

4. P. M. Bardi, *The Tropical Gardens of Burle Marx* (New York: Reinhold, 1964), 16.

5. Ibid., 86.

6. Burle Marx, "A Garden Style in Brazil," 202.

7. Frederick L. Gregory, "Roberto Burle Marx, The One-Man Extravaganza," *Landscape Architecture* 71 (May 1981): 347.

8. Norman K. Johnson, "Keeping Up with Roberto," *Garden Design* 2, no. 1 (Spring 1983): 28.

9. Roberto Burle Marx, quoted in a *New York Times* article, reprinted as "Fighting for Brazil's Green Treasure," *San Francisco Chronicle*, August 22, 1980.

10. For a comparison of Le Nôtre and Burle Marx on different grounds, see Adams, *Roberto Burle Marx*, 28.

11. For information on Ferdinand Bac and Les Columbières, see Michel Racine, Ernest J.-P. Boursier-Mougenot and Françoise Binet, *The Gardens of Provence and the French Riviera* (Cambridge, Mass.: MIT Press, 1987). See also several reproductions of Bac's watercolor drawings of his own gardens, in Albert Maumené, "Résidences méditerranéennes d'esprit différent," *Vie à la campagne* March 1, 1933, 100–109.

12. Andrea O. Dean, "Luis Barragán, Austere Architect of Silent Spaces," *Smithsonian* 11, no. 8 (November 1980): 158.

13. Ferdinand Bac, *La Volupté romaine* (Paris, 1922). This novel was illustrated by Bac, whose visual expression was lyrical and fluid but not surreal.

14. See, for example, Emilio Ambasz, *The Architecture of Luis Barragán* (New York: Museum of Modern Art, 1976); Marie-Pierre Toll, "Labyrinth of Light and Color," *House and Garden* (April 1984): 125–31; and note 12.

15. Paul F. Damaz, *Art in Latin American Architecture* (New York: Reinhold, 1963), 68.

16. Ibid., 42–44, 68–79. See also I. E. Myers, *Mexico's Modern Architecture* (New York: Architectural Book Publishing Co., 1952): 10–22; and Esther Born, *The New Architecture in Mexico* (New York: Architectural Record/William Morrow, 1937), 32–35.

17. José Villagrán García, in Clive B. Smith, *Builders in the Sun: Five Mexican Architects* (New York: Architectural Book Publishing Co., 1967), 10. For a reappraisal of the work of Villagrán García and his colleagues, see Enrique X. de Anda Alanis, *La Arquitectura de la Revolución Mexicana: Corrientes y Estilos en la Decada de los Veinte* (Mexico City: Universidad Nacional Autonoma de Mexico, 1990).

18. Luis Barragán, in Damian Bayon, "An Interview with Luis Barragán," *Landscape Architecture* (November 1976): 533.

19. Isamu Noguchi, *A Sculptor's World* (New York: Harper & Row, 1968), 30.

20. Buckminster Fuller, in Noguchi, *Sculptor's World*, 7.

21. Noguchi, *Sculptor's World*, 39.

22. Ibid., 13–16. See also Sam Hunter, *Isamu Noguchi* (New York: Abbeville Press, 1978); Nancy Grove, *Isamu Noguchi, Portrait Sculpture* (Washington, D.C.: Smithsonian Institution Press, 1989); and Dore Ashton, *Noguchi, East and West* (New York: Alfred A. Knopf, 1992).

23. Isamu Noguchi, in "Isamu Noguchi," *California Arts and Architecture* (November 1950): 24–47.

24. Isamu Noguchi, "Towards a Reintegration of the Arts," *College Art Journal* 9, no. 1 (Autumn 1949): 59–60.

25. Isamu Noguchi, in John Gruen, "The Artist Speaks: Isamu Noguchi," *Art in America* 56, no. 2 (March–April, 1968): 31.

26. Nancy Grove in ibid., 92. Grove explains that MacMahon loaned Noguchi $500 to help him travel to the Far East in 1930.

27. See "Letters," *Landscape Architecture* 80, no. 11 (November 1990): 10–14. See also Andrea O. Dean, "Bunshaft and Noguchi: An Uneasy But Highly Productive Architect-Artist Collaboration," *AIA Journal* (October 1976): 52–54.

28. See Peter Walker, "A Levitation of Stones," *Landscape Architecture* 80, no. 4 (April 1990): 36–39. This issue of *Landscape Architecture* features the landscape design work of Noguchi.

29. Noguchi, *A Sculptor's World,* 171.

Chapter 3

1. See, for example, "Thomas Church: His Gardens," *Architectural Forum* 83 (August 1945): 111–18; William McCance and H. F. Clark, "The Influence of Cubism on Garden Design," *Architectural Design* 30 (March 1960): 112–17; and Michael Laurie, "Thomas Church and the Evolution of the California Garden," *Landscape Design* 101 (February 1973): 8–10.

2. Thomas Church, "Evening Discussion with the Northern California Chapter of the ASLA, February 9, 1971," transcript courtesy of Michael M. Laurie, in *Thomas Church, Landscape Architect,* 2 vols., interviews conducted by Suzanne B. Riess, Regional Oral History Office, Bancroft Library, University of California, Berkeley, 1978. Church died in 1978.

3. James Rose, "Garden Details," *California Arts and Architecture* (July 1941): 28–29.

4. See Pam-Anela Messenger, "The Art of Thomas Dolliver Church" (M.L.A. thesis, University of California at Berkeley, 1976): Bibliography.

5. Joseph E. Howland, "Reflections on Tommy Church and His Gardens," *Landscape Architecture* 71 (July 1981): 463–68.

6. Church, "Evening Discussion."

7. Kevin Starr, *Americans and the California Dream* (New York: Oxford University Press, 1973), Preface.

8. See Pam-Anela Messenger, "The Art of Thomas Dolliver Church"; and A. Cort Sinnes, "Tommy's World," *Garden Design* 1, no. 3 (Winter 1982): 61–67.

9. Geraldine Knight Scott, recollections, in Michael Laurie, with David Streatfield, *75 Years of Landscape Architecture at Berkeley* (privately printed for the Department of Landscape Architecture, University of California, Berkeley, 1988), 20–21.

10. Robin Karson, *Fletcher Steele, Landscape Architect* (New York: Harry N. Abrams/Sagapress, 1989), 10–11.

11. Thomas Church, quoted in Carroll Calkins, "Thomas D. Church, The Influence of 2,000 Gardens," *House Beautiful* 109 (March 1967): 142.

12. Thomas Church, "A Study of Mediterranean Gardens, and Their Adaptability to California Conditions, 1926–27," in Loeb Library, Harvard Graduate School of Design.

13. Thomas Church, "The Small California Garden, Chapter 1: A New Deal for the Small Lot," *California Arts and Architecture* (May 1933): 32.

14. Hillside Club pamphlet, 1906–1907, Anonymous, illustrated with drawings by Bernard Maybeck, and probably written with contributions by Maybeck and his fellow club member, Charles Keeler. See Keeler, *The Simple Home* (San Francisco: Paul Elder and Co., 1904); and Kenneth H. Cardwell, *Bernard Maybeck, Artisan, Architect, Artist* (Salt Lake City: Gibbs M. Smith, 1977).

15. Lewis Mumford, "Skyline," *New Yorker,* October 11, 1947, excerpted in "What Is Happening to Modern Architecture?" *Museum of Modern Art Bulletin* (New York) 15, no. 3 (Spring 1948): 2.

16. Thomas Church, *Gardens are for people* (New York: Reinhold, 1955), 88.

17. Garden for Mr. and Mrs. Jerd Sullivan, *House and Garden* 79 (April 1941): 44. Robert Royston dates this garden from about 1937. Royston, in conversation with Melanie Simo and Roger Scharmer, March 31, 1988, Mill Valley, California.

18. Lawrence Halprin, interviewed by Suzanne Riess, in *Thomas Church, Landscape Architect*, 2:748.

19. Jean Wolff, "A Garden and Flower Care Expert Analyses her Thomas Church Garden," an oral history conducted by Suzanne B. Riess in *Thomas Church, Landscape Architect, Volume I*, Regional Oral History Office, The Bancroft Library, University of California, Berkeley, 1978. Courtesy of The Bancroft Library.

20. See Stacey Moss, *The Howards: First Family of Bay Area Modernism*, catalogue of an exhibition, May 14–August 7, 1988, Oakland (California) Museum; Jermayne MacAgy, Alice C. Kent, and Robert B. Howard, *Autobiography: From the Notebooks and Sculpture of Adaline Kent* (privately published, 1958); and Thomas Albright, *Art in the San Francisco Bay Area, 1945–1980* (Berkeley: University of California Press, 1985).

21. Jacques Schnier, quoted in Moss, *The Howards*, 36.

22. See the interviews conducted by Suzanne Riess in *Thomas Church, Landscape Architect*, particularly those with Ruth Jaffe, June Meehan Campbell, Roger Sturtevant, Lawrence Halprin, and Elizabeth Roberts Church.

23. See Church, *Gardens are for people*, 222–23.

24. Ibid., 231–35.

25. Lawrence Halprin, interviewed by Suzanne Riess, in *Thomas Church, Landscape Architect*, 2:752.

26. Lawrence Halprin, in conversation with Melanie Simo, November 6, 1991, San Francisco.

27. Thomas Church and William Wurster, Description of Model 10, *Contemporary Landscape Architecture and Its Sources*, catalog of the exhibition, February 12–March 22, 1937, San Francisco Museum of Art, 34.

28. Lawrence Halprin, interviewed by Suzanne Riess, in *Thomas Church, Landscape Architect*, 2:740ff.

29. See Suzanne Riess, *Thomas Church, Landscape Architect*, vol. 2: interviews with

Jack Wagstaff (a University of California, Santa Cruz, campus architect) and Betsy Church. Wagstaff's interview contains a memorandum by Church regarding the principles of planning the Santa Cruz campus.

Chapter 4

1. Robert Royston, "Looking Down on the San Francisco Bay Area," *Landscape Architecture* (July 1974): 234–43.

2. Garrett Eckbo, syllabus for "Architecture 190ab, Landscape Design," University of Southern California [ca. 1948], among Eckbo's files, at his home in Berkeley.

3. Robert Royston, "A Brief History," *Landscape Australia* 8, no. 1 (Autumn 1986): 34–38. Later, Royston became a frequent guest lecturer at North Carolina State University, Louisiana State University, Harvard, and elsewhere. Eckbo was chairman of the University of California at Berkeley's department of landscape architecture, 1965–1969.

4. Robert Royston, conversation with Melanie Simo, October 23, 1991, Mill Valley, California. See Institute of Urban and Regional Development, "The Environmental

Simulation Laboratory," brochure (Berkeley: University of California, n.d. [ca. 1969]).

5. Biographical information from Melanie Simo's interviews and conversations with Garrett Eckbo in Berkeley, January 1987–1992.

6. Eckbo's original plan and bird's-eye view are preserved in the archives of the Department of Landscape Architecture, University of California, Berkeley. His history notebook is among his personal files in Berkeley.

7. In 1987, Eckbo lent Melanie Simo his annotated copy of Henry Vincent Hubbard and Theodora Kimball, *Introduction to the Study of Landscape Design* (New York: Macmillan, 1917). See Melanie Simo, "The Education of a Modern Landscape Designer" [on Eckbo], *Pacific Horticulture* (Winter 1988): 19–30.

8. Garrett Eckbo to the editor, *Landscape Architecture* (January 1980): 29.

9. Elbert Peets, "The Landscape Priesthood," *American Mercury* (January 1927): 94–99. See also Garrett Eckbo, *Landscape for Living* (New York: F. W. Dodge Corporation, 1950), 23–25.

10. See, for example, "Garrett Eckbo, "Architecture and Landscape, Landscape and Architecture," *Places* 4, no. 4 (1987): 49–51; and Eckbo, "Italy Revisited," *Garden Design* (March 1982): 46–55.

11. Garrett Eckbo, "Small Gardens in the City," *Pencil Points* (September 1937): 573–86.

12. See Eckbo, *Landscape for Living,* figs. 138–41.

13. Garrett Eckbo, conversations with Melanie Simo, Summer 1991.

14. "Valencia Gardens," *Pencil Points* (January 1944): 26–36. See also *Landscape Design,* catalog of an exhibition at the San Francisco Museum of Art, Spring 1948 (San Francisco: Museum of Art, 1948), 34.

15. Robert Royston, conversation with Melanie Simo, May 19, 1987, Mill Valley, California.

16. Robert Royston, interview with Suzanne Riess, in Riess, ed., *Thomas Church, Landscape Architect,* 2 vols. (unpublished document, produced for the Bancroft Library series of oral histories, University of California, at Berkeley, ca. 1978). For further biographical information, see Robert Royston, "Point of View," *Landscape Ar-*

chitecture (November–December 1986): 66–67.

17. Robert Royston, notes on landscape architectural education (untitled), in *Axis* (June 1947), annual student publication of the Department of Landscape Architecture, University of California, at Berkeley, pp. 4–5.

18. Eckbo, *Landscape for Living,* 1.

19. Ibid., 254.

20. Ibid., figs. 229–70. See also Roger Montgomery, "Mass Producing Bay Area Architecture," in Sally Woodbridge, ed., *Bay Area Houses,* new ed. (Salt Lake City: Peregrine Smith, 1988), 229–54; and Esther McCoy, *The Second Generation* (Salt Lake City: Peregrine Smith, 1984), 118–30.

21. Esther McCoy, "Arts and Architecture Case Study Houses," in Elizabeth A. T. Smith, ed., *Blueprints for Modern Living: History and Legacy of the Case Study Houses* (Los Angeles: Museum of Contemporary Art/Cambridge, Mass.: MIT Press, 1989), 23. Eckbo, Royston, and Williams designed a garden for Case Study House 16, by Rodney A. Walker, *Arts & Architecture* (June, August, and

September 1946). Richard Haag's garden for Case Study House 19, by Don Knorr, appeared in *Arts & Architecture* (August, September, and December 1957).

22. Edward Williams, "Prize-Winning Landscape Firm," *Independent-Journal* (Marin County, California), January 19, 1952, sec. M:8.

23. Arline Williams Eckbo, in conversations with Melanie Simo, summer 1991.

24. "Landscape Architecture, A Professional Adventure in Use of Outdoor Space" [profile of Eckbo, Royston & Williams], *Architect and Engineer* (September 1946): 20–22.

25. Royston, conversation with Simo, October 23, 1991; and Christopher Degenhardt, "Edward A. Williams, FASLA, 1914–1984," *Landscape Architecture News Digest* [*LAND*] (December–January 1985): 7.

26. See, for instance, the K. E. Appert residence in *Architectural Record* (November 1951): 124–28.

27. See James M. Fitch and F. F. Rockwell, *A Treasury of American Gardens* (New York: Harper & Brothers, 1956), 146; and Garrett Eckbo, *The Art of Home Landscaping*

(New York: F. W. Dodge Corporation, 1956), 131.

28. See Kenneth H. Cardwell, *Bernard Maybeck, Artisan, Architect, Artist* (Salt Lake City: Peregrine Smith, 1977); and Charles Keeler, *The Simple Home* (1904) Salt Lake City: Peregrine Smith, 1979).

29. "Northern California Chapter of the A.I.A.," *Arts & Architecture* (April 1929): 83.

30. "Geometry in the Patio," *San Francisco Chronicle,* July 10, 1949. For background, see Thomas Albright, *Art in the San Francisco Bay Area, 1945–1980* (Berkeley: University of California Press, 1985).

31. Alfred Frankenstein, "Architects Take the Lead at Art Festival," *San Francisco Chronicle,* October 17, 1951, p. 7.

32. J. Robert Oppenheimer, quoted in Belle Krasne, "Art," *Arts & Architecture* (January 1955): 4.

33. Robert Royston, "Thoughts on Landscape Architecture," *Landscape Australia* 8, no. 2 (May 1986): 152; and Royston, conversation with Melanie Simo, October 23, 1991, Mill Valley, California.

34. Michael Laurie, "University of California

[Berkeley]," *Landscape Architecture* (January 1965): 91.

35. Edward Williams, *Open Space: The Choices Before California* (San Francisco: Diablo Press, 1969) (a publication of the 1965 document).

36. See Manuel Castells, *The Informational City: Information Technology, Economic Restructuring and the Urban-Regional Process* (Cambridge, Mass.: Basil Blackwell, 1991); and Sharon Zukin, *Landscapes of Power: From Detroit to Disney World* (Berkeley: University of California, 1991).

37. Garrett Eckbo to the editor, *Landscape Architecture* (July 1981): 440.

Chapter 5

1. Lewis Mumford, *The City in History* (1961) (Harmondsworth, Middlesex, England: Penguin, 1973), 601.

2. Ibid., 575.

3. Ibid., 635–36.

4. André Malraux, *Le Musée imaginaire de la sculpture mondiale* (Paris: Gallimard, 1952–1954), trans. Stuart Gilbert and Francis Price as *Museum without Walls* (Garden City, N.Y.: Doubleday, 1967).

5. Lawrence Halprin, *New York, New York,* privately printed, by Lawrence Halprin & Associates, for the City of New York (John V. Lindsay, Mayor) and Housing and Development Administration (Jason R. Nathan, Administrator) (San Francisco, 1968).

6. Friedrich Nietzsche, *Also Sprach Zarathustra* (1882–1885), trans. Thomas Common as *Thus Spake Zarathustra* (New York: Modern Library, 1960).

7. George Rand, quoted in Halprin, *New York,* 47.

8. Halprin, *New York,* 108–9, 2–3.

9. Lawrence Halprin, conversation with Melanie Simo, August 1, 1988, San Francisco; and *Lawrence Halprin: Changing Places,* catalogue of an exhibition at the San Francisco Museum of Modern Art, July 3–August 24, 1986 (San Francisco: Museum of Modern Art, 1986), 114.

10. See Lawrence Halprin to the Editor, *Landscape Architecture* (September 1979): 466.

11. Lawrence Halprin to the editor, *Landscape Architecture* (April 1961): 138.

12. See Teddy Kollek, "Re-viewing Jerusa-

lem," in *Lawrence Halprin: Changing Places,* 104–13.

13. Lawrence Halprin to Jim Burns, November 1985, in Burns, "The *How* of Creativity: Scores and Scoring," in *Lawrence Halprin: Changing Places,* 53.

14. Roger Osbaldeston, "Lawrence Halprin," in *Contemporary Architects,* ed. Muriel Emanuel (New York: St. Martin's Press, 1980), 378.

15. See Theodore Roszak, *The Making of a Counter Culture* (Garden City, N.Y.: Doubleday, 1969).

16. Charles Moore, "Still Pools and Crashing Waves," in *Lawrence Halprin: Changing Places,* 22.

17. Angela Danadjieva, "Danadjieva on the Creative Process," and Margaret Marshall, "How the Impossible Came to Be," *Landscape Architecture* (September 1977): 404–6, 399–402; and *Lawrence Halprin/PROCESS: Architecture 4* (Tokyo: Process Architecture Publishing Company, 1978), 227–39. Marshall's article emphasizes the combined efforts of the landscape architects, the several planning and design consultants, and federal, state, and city officials.

18. See Thomas Aidala, "The FDR Memorial: Halprin Redefines the Monumental Landscape," *Landscape Architecture* (January 1979): 42–52; and J. William Thompson, "Master of Collaboration" [a profile of Halprin], *Landscape Architecture* (July 1992): 59–68.

19. See the exchange of letters between Patrick Condon and Lawrence Halprin in *Landscape Journal* 8, no. 2 (Fall 1989): 151–52, initiated by Condon's article, "Cubist Space, Volumetric Space, and Landscape Architecture," in *Landscape Journal* 7, no. 1 (Spring 1988): 1–14.

20. Lawrence Halprin, *RSVP Cycles* (New York: George Braziller, 1969), 148.

21. See Jim Burns, "Sea Ranch: Resisting Suburbia," *Architecture* (December 1984): 56–63; and Allen Freeman, "Vernacular Village of Low-Income Houses at Sea Ranch," *Architecture* (October 1987): 64–67. See also Halprin's and his colleagues' recollections and assessments of Sea Ranch in *Progressive Architecture* (February 1993): 85–99.

22. See Allen Freeman, "'Fine Tuning' a Landmark of Adaptive Use," *Architecture* (November 1986): 67; and *Lawrence Halprin/*

PROCESS: Architecture 4, 103–18.

23. See John Morris Dixon, "Riis Plaza: Three Acres Filled with Life," *Architectural Forum* (July–August 1966): 68–73. Friedberg was born in 1931 in Brooklyn, New York. He received the B.S. degree in 1954 from Cornell University. He has been director of the Urban Landscape Architecture Program at City College of New York since he founded the program in 1971. See also *M. Paul Friedberg: Landscape Design/ PROCESS: Architecture 82* (Tokyo: Process Architecture Publishing Company, 1989).

24. Allen Freeman, "Evaluation: Neglected Relic of the '60s," *Architecture* (December 1985): 48–53.

25. See *Robert Zion: A Profile in Landscape Architecture/PROCESS: Architecture 94* (Tokyo: Process Architecture Publishing Company, 1991). Born in 1921, Zion received the A.B., the I.A., the M.B.A., and the M.L.A. degrees from Harvard. He was awarded the Charles Eliot Traveling Fellowship in 1951 and worked for I. M. Pei before opening his own practice in New York City in 1954.

26. See Carol H. Krinsky, "Architecture in New York City," in Leonard Wallock, ed., *New York, Culture Capital of the World, 1940–1965* (New York: Rizzoli, 1988), 118–19; and *Robert Zion: A Profile in Landscape Architecture*, 143.

27. Lawrence Halprin, "The Landscape Architect and the Planner," in Sylvia Crowe, ed., *Space for Living* (Amsterdam, 1961), 46–50.

28. See, for instance, "Lawrence Halprin, "The Community in the Landscape," *AIA Journal* (September 1961): 52–57.

29. Lawrence Halprin, conversation with Melanie Simo, November 6, 1991, San Francisco.

30. Lawrence Halprin, "The Shape of Erosion," *Landscape Architecture* (January 1962): 87–88.

31. Halprin, conversation with Simo, November 6, 1991. See also Halprin, conversation with Ching-yu Chang, in Chang, ed., *Lawrence Halprin/ PROCESS:Architecture 4*, 247.

32. Halprin, conversation with Simo, November 6, 1991.

33. Leo Marx, "Lewis Mumford: Prophet of Organicism," in Thomas P. Hughes and Agatha C. Hughes, eds., *Lewis Mumford, Public Intellectual* (New York: Oxford University Press, 1990), 164–80.

Chapter 6

1. Dan Kiley, in conversations with Peter Walker and his students, in a graduate seminar at Harvard, 1978–1979 (hereafter, "Harvard Seminar").

2. John Russell, *Henry Moore* (Baltimore: Penguin 1973), 44.

3. Henry Moore, in Deborah E. Scott and Deborah Leveton, eds., *The Nelson Atkins Museum of Art/Henry Moore Sculpture Garden* (Kansas City, Mo., 1989), 11.

4. Dan Kiley, in Scott and Leveton, *Nelson Atkins Museum of Art*, 4.

5. See, for example, Dan Kiley, "Nature: The Source of All Design," *Landscape Architecture* (January 1963): 127; Kiley, "My Design Process," in *PROCESS: Architecture 33/Landscape Design: Works of Dan Kiley* (Tokyo: Process Architecture Publishing Company, 1982), 15–20; and Kiley, "What is Design?" in *PROCESS: Architecture 108/Dan Kiley: Landscape Design II* (1993), 8–14.

6. Stuart Dawson, conversation with Melanie Simo, December 13, 1988, Watertown, Massachusetts. Dawson received his B.F.A. in landscape architecture at the University of Illinois in 1957. See below, chapter 8.

7. Dan Kiley, "Harvard Seminar"; Kiley, in Warren T. Byrd, Jr., and Reuben M. Rainey, eds., *The Work of Dan Kiley: A Dialogue on Design Theory*, Proceedings of the First Annual Symposium on Landscape Architecture, University of Virginia, February 6, 1982 (Charlottesville, Va., 1983) (hereafter "UVA Symposium"), 28.

8. Robert Frost, "New Hampshire," in *The Poetry of Robert Frost* (New York: Holt, Rinehart and Winston, 1969), 164.

9. Dan Kiley, in Susan Webster, Alan Goodheart and Michael Laurie, "A Conversation with Dan Kiley," *Landmark*, a student publication of the Department of Landscape Architecture, University of California, at Berkeley, 1965: 10 (hereafter, "Conversation at Berkeley").

10. Kiley, "UVA Symposium," 28.

11. Henry David Thoreau, "Walking," in *The Portable Thoreau*, ed. Carl Bode (New York: Viking, 1960), 592, 602.

12. Kiley, "Harvard Seminar."

13. Ibid.

14. Kiley, "UVA Symposium," 8.

15. See William Grundmann, "Warren T. Manning," in *American Landscape Architecture, Designers and Places*, ed. William H. Tishler (Washington, D.C.: National Trust for Historic Preservation, 1989), 56–59.

16. Elbert Peets, "The Landscape Priesthood," *American Mercury* (January 1927): 94–99.

17. Frederick Law Olmsted, quoted in Melvin Kalfus, *Frederick Law Olmsted: The Passion of a Public Artist* (New York: New York University Press, 1990), 314.

18. Shary Page Berg, "Frederick Law Olmsted, Jr.," in *American Landscape Architecture, Designers and Places*, 62.

19. Fletcher Steele, "New Pioneering in Garden Design," *Landscape Architecture* (April 1930): 159–77.

20. Norman T. Newton, "Modern Trends—What Are They?" *Landscape Architecture* (July 1932): 302.

21. See Garrett Eckbo, "Small Gardens in the City," *Pencil Points* (September 1937): 573–86; Eckbo, "Sculpture and Landscape Design," *Magazine of Art* 31 (April 1938): 202–8; and James Rose, "Freedom in the Garden: A Contemporary Approach," *Pencil Points* (October 1938). See also below, notes 22 and 23.

22. Garrett Eckbo, Daniel U. Kiley, and James C. Rose, "Landscape Design in the Urban Environment," *Architectural Record* (May 1939): 70.

23. Ibid., 71. See also their subsequent articles in *Architectural Record* for August 1939 and February 1940.

24. Kiley, "Harvard Seminar" and "UVA Symposium," 24.

25. Kiley, "Harvard Seminar." See also Robin Karson, "Conversation with Kiley," *Landscape Architecture* (March–April 1986): 50–57.

26. See Carleton Knight III, "J. Irwin Miller: Patron, Client, But Always a Businessman," *Architecture* 73, no. 4 (June 1984): 62–67. This issue of *Architecture* focuses on Columbus, Indiana, and several of its buildings—the work of leading architects of the mid- to late twentieth century.

27. Kiley, "Conversation at Berkeley," 10.

28. Kiley, "UVA Symposium," 25.

29. Frederick Gutheim, "Natural Responses to Architectural Statements," in *PROCESS:*

Architecture 33/Landscape Design: Works of Dan Kiley (1982), 64.

30. Kiley, "Harvard Seminar."

Chapter 7

1. Albert Einstein, paraphrased in Lincoln Barnett, *The Universe and Dr. Einstein* (New York: William Sloane Associates, 1948), 52.

2. Hideo Sasaki, in Stanley White, ed., *The Teaching of Landscape Architecture* (East Lansing, Michigan, 1953), unpublished mimeographed copy, Frances Loeb Library, Harvard Graduate School of Design (hereafter, HGSD), 82.

3. Stanley White, in White, *Teaching,* 4.

4. See Hideo Sasaki, review of Thomas Church, *Gardens are for people* (1955), *Landscape Architecture* (January 1956): 109.

5. Sasaki was well aware of the vulnerability of Japan's integrated environment in the immediate postwar years. In a review of several books, including *The Architecture of Japan* (1955) by Arthur Drexler and *Japan's New Architecture* (1956) by Shinji Koike, with Ryuichi Hamaguchi, Sasaki posed several questions, among them,

"Can Japan continue to retain its orderly development in the face of current democratic upheaval?" See note 6.

6. Hideo Sasaki, book review, in *Landscape Architecture* (January 1957): 372.

7. Stanley White, in *Proceedings of the National Council on Instruction in Landscape Architecture* (Lisle, Ill.: Morton Arboretum, 1959), 21.

8. Hideo Sasaki, in Gary O. Robinette, *Landscape Architectural Education* (Dubuque, Iowa: Kendall/Hunt Publishing Co., 1973, 1: 83 (hereafter *L.A. Education*).

9. White, *Proceedings, NCILA,* 21.

10. See *The Letters of E. B. White,* ed. Dorothy L. Guth (New York: Harper & Row, 1976); and Scott Elledge, *E. B. White, A Biography* (New York: W. W. Norton & Co, 1984).

11. White, *Teaching of Landscape Architecture,* 26.

12. Malcolm Cairns and Gary Kesler, "Stanley White, Teacher," *Landscape Architecture* (January–February 1985): 87.

13. White, *Proceedings NCILA* (1957), Asilomar, Pacific Grove, California, 51.

14. E. B. White, *Letters,* 6.

15. E. B. White, in Elledge, *E. B. White,* 300.

16. Robinette, *L.A. Education,* 1: 76–92.

17. White, *Teaching of Landscape Architecture,* 42; Robinette, *L.A. Education,* 2: 8; 134.

18. White, *Teaching of Landscape Architecture,* 95.

19. A mimeographed copy of this document is kept in the Frances Loeb Library, HGSD.

20. Hideo Sasaki, conversation with George Waters and Melanie Simo, January 18, 1988, Lafayette, California. See also Melanie Simo, "A Conversation with Hideo Sasaki," *Pacific Horticulture* (Winter 1988): 18.

21. Robinette, *L.A. Education,* 1: 86–91.

22. Stanley White, "The Case for Landscape Architecture," *Forsite,* student publication of the Department of Landscape Architecture, University of Illinois (1952): 27–29.

23. See Julius Gy. Fabos, Gordon T. Milde, and V. Michael Weinmeyer, *Frederick Law Olmsted, Sr.* (Amherst, Mass.: University of Massachusetts Press, 1968). The traveling exhibition of Olmsted's work was also financially assisted by the American Society of Landscape Architects and the society's Boston chapter.

24. Hideo Sasaki, conversation with Melanie Simo, June 14, 1988, Lafayette, California.

25. White, *Teaching of Landscape Architecture,* 9.

26. Hideo Sasaki, "Thoughts on Education in Landscape Architecture," *Landscape Architecture* (July 1950): 158–60.

27. Bremer Pond, in Robinette, *L.A. Education,* 1: 60.

28. Joseph Volpe to Garrett Eckbo, spring 1963. In 1987, Eckbo lent this letter to Melanie Simo; from Eckbo's files at his home in Berkeley, California.

29. Richard Haag to Melanie Simo, August 1991. Born in 1923 in Jeffersontown, Kentucky, Haag studied landscape architecture at the University of Illinois under Stanley White and Hideo Sasaki. He received the B.S.L.A. degree from the University of California, Berkeley, in 1950, and the M.L.A. degree from Harvard, in 1952. He spent two years in Japan on a Fulbright scholarship and worked for Dan Kiley, Theodore Osmundson, and Lawrence Halprin before opening his own office in 1957 in San Francisco. Since 1958, he has practiced in Seattle and taught at the University of Washington.

30. See Richard Haag, "Edible Landscape," *Landscape Architecture* (November 1980): 634–37; Haag, "The Garden in the Collective Unconscious, or Design with DNA," in *Meanings of the Garden,* ed. Mark Francis and Randolph T. Hester, Jr., Proceedings of a Conference at the University of California, Davis, May 14–17, 1987, 47–49; Lawrence Kreisman, *The Bloedel Reserve, Gardens in the Forest* (Bloedel Reserve, Bainbridge Island, Wash.: Arbor Fund, 1988); and "Gas Works Park," *Landscape Architecture* (September 1981): 594–96.

31. Charles Harris, "The Affective Domaine in Landscape Architecture Education," *HGSD News* (May 1977). See also Charles Harris, "The Once-Lonely Turf: New directions for landscape architecture at Harvard from 1958 to 1970," in Margaret Henderson Floyd, *Architectural Education and Boston: Centennial Publication of the Boston Architectural Center, 1889–1989* (Boston: Boston Architectural Center, 1989), 105–107.

32. Sasaki, conversation with Simo.

33. Sasaki, conversation with Waters and Simo.

34. Stanley White, "The Rockies and the Arid West," *Landscape Architecture* (April 1961): 160.

35. Sasaki, conversation with Waters and Simo.

Chapter 8

1. Hideo Sasaki, conversation with George Waters and Melanie Simo, January 18, 1988, Lafayette, California. See also Melanie Simo, "A Conversation with Hideo Sasaki," *Pacific Horticulture* 49, no. 4 (Winter 1988): 16–25.

2. Philip Will, quoted in a profile by Paula Treder and Kathryn Morgan-Ryan, *House and Home* (June 1960): 142.

3. Hideo Sasaki, "Urban Renewal and Landscape Architecture," *Landscape Architecture* (January 1955): 100–101.

4. Grady Clay, "Landscape, USA: Who Did It?" *Landscape Architecture* (October 1957): 43.

5. Macklin L. Hancock received the B.S.A. degree in horticulture, in 1949, from the University of Toronto. He also studied landscape architecture at the Harvard Graduate School of Design in 1949–1950 and 1951–1952. See Hancock, "Comprehensive Environmental Design: The Landscape Architect and Education," an address to the National Conference of Instruction in Landscape Architecture (NCILA), Harvard University Graduate School of Design, July 2, 1965, in *Proceedings, NCILA* (1965), 2: 1–15.

6. Walter Gropius, "Address upon Receiving the Honorary Degree of Doctor of Humane Letters at Columbia University, March 21, 1961," *Arts and Architecture* (May 1961): 29.

7. Duane Niederman, of The SWA Group, conversation with Melanie Simo, February 23, 1990, Deerfield Beach, Florida.

8. Hideo Sasaki, conversation with Melanie Simo, June 14, 1988, Lafayette, California; William J. Johnson, conversation with Melanie Simo, August 3, 1990, San Francisco. A graduate of Michigan State University (B.S.L.A.) and Harvard (M.L.A.), William J. Johnson also received the Charles Eliot Traveling Fellowship from Harvard, in 1957. In Ann Arbor, Michigan, in 1962–63, he cofounded the partnership of Johnson, Johnson and Roy, which soon became JJR, a multioffice corporate firm with strengths in campus planning, urban design, natural resource management, and historic preservation. A professor of landscape architecture at the University of Michigan, Ann Arbor, from 1958 to 1989, Johnson also served as dean of that university's School of Natural Resources from 1975 to 1983. He is currently a partner of Peter Walker William Johnson and Partners, based in San Francisco.

9. Sasaki, conversation with Simo. June 14, 1988.

10. Stuart O. Dawson, conversation with Melanie Simo, December 13, 1988, Watertown, Massachusetts.

11. Richard Dober, "Specialists's Services in Land Design," *Progressive Architecture* (July 1960): 128.

12. Stuart O. Dawson received the B.F.A. in landscape architecture, with Honors, from the University of Illinois in 1957, and the M.L.A. from Harvard in 1958. A designer with Sasaki Associates (formerly, Sasaki, Walker and Associates; and Sasaki, Dawson, Demay Associates) since 1957, he has been a partner or principal with the firm since 1962. He has also served as a visiting critic and lecturer at Harvard, Cornell, MIT, the Rhode Island School of Design, the University of Pennsylvania, and several other universities in the United States.

Peter Walker received the B.S.L.A. degree from the University of California, Berkeley, in 1955. From Harvard, he received the M.L.A. degree and the Jacob Weidenmann Prize in 1957. Cofounder of Sasaki, Walker and Associates in 1957, he led the West Coast office of that firm, which became The SWA Group in 1973–1974. Serving as adjunct professor of landscape architecture at Harvard, he directed the Urban Design program in 1977–1978 and chaired the department of landscape architecture from 1978 to 1981. Formerly the Charles Eliot Professor of Landscape Architecture at Harvard, Walker has also served as guest critic and lecturer at other universities in the United States. He is currently a partner of Peter Walker William Johnson and Partners, based in San Francisco.

Masao Kinoshita received the Bachelor of Architecture degree from Cornell in 1955 and the Master of Architecture degree in Urban Design from Harvard in 1961. Before joining Sasaki Associates, Kinoshita had worked for architects Isoya Yoshida (in Tokyo, Japan) and Eero Saarinen and Associates (in Birmingham, Michigan). While a principal and designer at the Watertown office of Sasaki Associates, Kinoshita also served as visiting critic at the universities of Harvard, Yale, and Syracuse. He is a recipient of the Charles Goodwin Sands Medal and the Robert James Eidlitz Fellowship.

13. Sasaki, conversation with Waters and Simo.

14. Jory Johnson, in Felice Frankel and Jory Johnson, *Modern Landscape Architecture* (New York: Abbeville Press, 1991), 30.

15. Hideo Sasaki, personal communication to Melanie Simo, February 1, 1992.

16. Hideo Sasaki, in *Landscape Architecture* (January 1957): 372.

17. Sasaki, conversation with Waters and Simo.

18. Hideo Sasaki, conversation with Melanie Simo, August 27, 1991, Lafayette, California; Aymar Embury II, "The New University of Colorado Buildings, Boulder, Colorado," *Architectural Forum* (September 1919): 71–80; and John Morris Dixon, "Colorado University: Respect for a Robust Environment," *Architectural Forum* (October 1966): 54–63.

19. Hideo Sasaki, quoted in "Cutting the Slab Down to Size," *Progressive Architecture* (November 1966).

20. William C. Muchow, telephone conversation with Melanie Simo, August 26, 1991.

21. Hideo Sasaki, conversation with Simo, August 27, 1991.

22. William C. Muchow, conversation with Melanie Simo, September 10, 1991, San Francisco.

23. Sasaki, conversation with Simo, August 27, 1991.

Chapter 9

1. Harlow Whittemore, in *Proceedings of the National Conference on Instruction in Landscape Architecture,* Asilomar, Pacific Grove, California, July 5–7, 1957, 39.

2. Lawrence Halprin, in ibid., 30.

3. Ian McHarg, in ibid., 41.

4. Ibid., 37.

5. Ian McHarg, speaking with Garrett Eckbo, before a gathering of the ASLA, Northern California Chapter, May 27, 1987, Oakland, California.

6. Ian McHarg, conversation with Melanie Simo, May 20, 1987, Berkeley, California.

7. Ian McHarg, "The Humane City: Must the Man of Distinction Always Move to the Suburbs?" *Landscape Architecture* (January 1958): 103–7.

8. James B. Conant, *On Understanding Science: An Historical Approach* (New Haven: Yale University Press, 1947), 3–4.

9. See chapter 7.

10. Hideo Sasaki, "Introduction to the NCILA Conference," *Proceedings, NCILA,* Graduate School of Design, Harvard University, Cambridge, Massachusetts, July 2–3, 1965, v.

11. Stanley White, ed., *The Teaching of Landscape Architecture,* Report to the NCILA, East Lansing, Michigan, June 25, 1953, 70, 89. See also Carl Steinitz, Paul Parker, and Lawrie Jordan, "Hand-Drawn Overlays: Their History and Prospective Uses," *Landscape Architecture* (September 1976): 444–55.

12. Robert F. White, in White, *Teaching,* 69.

13. Hideo Sasaki, conversation with George Waters and Melanie Simo, January 18, 1988, Lafayette, California.

14. Raymond K. Belknap and John Furtado, *Three Approaches to Environmental Resource Analysis,* prepared by the Landscape Architecture Research Office, Graduate School of Design, Harvard University (Washington, D.C.: Conservation Foundation, November 1967).

15. Ibid., 31–58.

16. Ibid., 87.

17. Thomas Mierzwa, in *Connection,* student publication of the Harvard Graduate School of Design, 5, nos. 2–3 (Winter–Spring 1968), quoted in Gary Robinette, *Landscape Architectural Education* (Dubuque, Iowa: Kendall/Hunt Publishing Co./ASLA, 1973), 1: 74. See also Ervin H. Zube, "Scenic Resources and the Landscape Continuum: Identification and Measurement" (Ph.D. diss., Clark University, 1973); and Robert H. Twiss, Jr., "An Approach to the Study of Natural Resources Policy: The Porcupine Mountains Controversy" (Ph.D. diss., University of Michigan, 1962).

18. See Carl Steinitz, "Landscape Resource Analysis, The State of the Art," *Landscape Architecture* (January 1970): 101–5; Steinitz, *Defensible Processes for Regional Landscape Design* (Washington, D.C.: ASLA, 1979); and Steinitz, "GIS: A Personal Historical Perspective," *GIS Europe* 2, no. 5 (June 1993): 19–22.

19. Ian McHarg, *Design with Nature* (New York: American Museum of Natural History, 1969), 1–5.

20. Edward J. Milne, "Providence Tomorrow?" *Rhode Islander, Providence Sunday Journal Magazine,* June 11, 1950, 3–6.

21. Ian McHarg, conversation with Melanie Simo, May 20, 1987, Berkeley, California.

22. Ian McHarg, "An Ecological Method of Landscape Architecture," *Landscape Architecture* (January 1967): 107.

23. Ian McHarg, "The Court House Concept," *Architect's Yearbook 8* (London, 1957), 74–102; and McHarg, conversation with Simo.

24. Ian McHarg, conversation with Simo.

25. Ian McHarg, "Can We Afford Open Space?" *Architect's Journal,* (London), March 8–15, 1956, 261–68.

26. Anne Spirn, guest commentator in Peter Walker's seminar, "Landscape Architecture and Modern Art," Harvard Graduate School of Design, Fall 1980.

27. Ian McHarg, "Is Man a Planetary Disease?" *Journal of the Royal Institute of British Architects* (July 1970): 305; and McHarg, *Design with Nature,* 44–45.

28. Ian McHarg, conversation with Margaret Mead, broadcast of the program, "The House We Live In," on station WCAU-TV, Philadelphia, November 6, 1960, vol. 1 of the two-volume transcripts, Wurster Hall Library, University of California, Berkeley.

29. Ian McHarg, conversation with Paul Tillich, "The House We Live In," November 20, 1960, vol. 1.

30. Alan Watts, conversation with Ian McHarg, "The House We Live In," December 11, 1960, vol. 1.

31. Ian McHarg, conversation with Hans Selye, "The House We Live In," January 15, 1961, vol. 1.

32. See "How to Design with Nature," *Time,* October 10, 1969, 70–71; and "Ian McHarg vs. Us Anthropocentric Clods," *Life,*

August 15, 1969, 48B–48D; and Ian McHarg, "Man, Planetary Disease," *Vital Speeches of the Day,* August 1, 1971, 634–40.

33. David A. Wallace, ed., *Metropolitan Open Space and Natural Process* (Philadelphia: University of Pennsylvania Press, 1970), 4.

34. See Grady Clay, "On Baltimore's Inner Harbor," *Landscape Architecture* (November 1982): 48–53; and Simpson Lawson, "Baltimore Re-Examined," *AIA Journal* (November 1982): 56–63.

35. See, for example, Ian McHarg and David A. Wallace, "Plan for the Valleys vs. Spectre of Uncontrolled Growth," *Landscape Architecture* (April 1965): 179–81; McHarg, *Design with Nature,* 79–93; and William H. Whyte, *The Last Landscape* (Garden City, N.Y.: Doubleday, 1968), 182–88.

36. Ian McHarg, "Open Space from Natural Processes," in David A. Wallace, *Metropolitan Open Space and Natural Process,* 17, note 4.

37. See McHarg, *Design with Nature;* Wallace, McHarg, Roberts and Todd, *A Report on the Master Planning Process for a New*

Residential Community, Amelia Island, Florida (privately printed, 1971); and William H. Roberts and Jonathan Sutton, "Seeking the Right Environmental Fit for a New Resort Community at Amelia Island, Florida," *Landscape Architecture* (April 1973): 239–50.

38. Ian McHarg and Jonathan Sutton, "Ecological Plumbing for the Texas Coastal Plain," *Landscape Architecture* (January 1975): 81.

39. Ibid., 78. The $50 million grant, awarded in 1971, was made largely because "the ecological study was conducted simultaneously as a planning and environmental impact analysis." (page 81). For more on "The Woodlands," see Anne Whiston Spirn, *The Granite Garden, Urban Nature and Human Design* (New York: Basic Books, 1984); and Narendra Juneja and James Veltman, "Natural Drainage in the Woodlands," in *Stormwater Management Alternatives,* ed. J. Toby Tourbier and Richard Westmacott (Newark: Water Resources Center, University of Delaware, 1980).

40. Ian McHarg, in Farney, "Land Politics," 16.

41. Ian McHarg, "School News: A New Role for Landscape Architects," *Landscape Architecture* (April 1964): 227.

42. McHarg, in "Ian McHarg vs. Us Anthropocentric Clods," 48D.

43. Ian McHarg, conversation with Melanie Simo, April 13, 1987, Berkeley, California.

44. Heidi Landecker, "In Search of an Arbiter" (profile of Ian McHarg), *Landscape Architecture* (January 1990): 90.

45. For the evolution of Olmsted's self-image as an artist, see the Introduction to this book; Olmsted's letters to Calvert Vaux, especially that dated June 8, 1865, in *The Papers of Frederick Law Olmsted,* vol. 5: 1863–1865, ed. Victoria P. Ranney (Baltimore: Johns Hopkins, 1990), 390–91; F. L. Olmsted, "Montreal: A Mountaintop Park and Some Thoughts on Art and Nature" (1881), in S. B. Sutton, ed., *Civilizing American Cities* (Cambridge, Mass.: MIT Press, 1971), 197–220; and Frederick Law Olmsted, "The Spoils of the Park" (1882), in Frederick Law Olmsted, Jr., and Theodora Kimball, eds., *Forty Years of Landscape Architecture: Central Park* (Cambridge, Mass.: MIT Press, 1973), 117–55.

Chapter 10

1. "Winners in the 1978 Professional Design Competition of the ASLA," *Landscape Architecture* (July 1978): 291.

2. Albert Fein, *A Study of the Profession of Landscape Architecture, Technical Report* (McLean, Va.: ASLA, 1972).

3. Ibid., sec. 5:3.

4. Ibid., sec. 3.

5. Ibid., sec. 1:52.

6. Ibid., sec. 1:26, 94; sec. 5:7.

7. Eero Saarinen, extracts from letters and lectures, in *Eero Saarinen on His Work*, ed. Aline B. Saarinen (New Haven: Yale University Press, 1962), 13.

8. "Report by the Special Committee on Education, AIA," *AIA Journal* (April 1963).

9. "ASLA Responds to 'Centennial Challenges,'" *Landscape Architecture* (October 1964): 15–17.

10. "The 1964 AIA Honor Awards," *AIA Journal* (July 1964): 21.

11. "The 1968 AIA Honor Awards," *AIA Journal* (June 1968): 84.

12. For background on corporate design practices, see Dudley Hunt, Jr., "Corporate Architectural Practice," *Architectural Record* (May 1963): 163–66; "Bigger Jobs, Mounting Pressures," *Landscape Architecture* (October 1965): 13–14; and Lane L. Marshall, "Ed Able on the Growth of a Profession," *Landscape Architecture* (September–October 1986): 121. For information on specific firms, see James D. Van Trump, "Figures in a Landscape, Simonds and Simonds of Pittsburgh," *Landscape Architecture* (January 1964): 127–29; "JJR," *Landscape Architecture* (October 1969): 41–46; and Nilo Lindgren, "Riding a Revolution, 1 and 2" [on stages of reorganization in Lawrence Halprin's office], *Landscape Architecture* (April 1974): 133–47.

13. Ian McHarg, conversation with Melanie Simo, May 20, 1987, Berkeley, California.

14. Michael Laurie, review of *Design with Nature, Landscape Architecture* (April 1971): 206.

15. Roger Yee, "Planning for the brave new world," *Progressive Architecture* (June 1974): 88–97.

16. See Melanie Simo, "From Sasaki, Walker and Associates to The SWA Group, 1957–1974," in *PROCESS: Architecture 85, Peter Walker: Landscape as Art* (Tokyo: Process Architecture Publishing Company, 1989), 18–21.

17. Information on Sasaki, Walker & Associates, SWR, and SWA is derived, in part, from several office brochures, dating from May 1963 to the present; and from Melanie Simo's interviews with current SWA principals. See Melanie Simo, "The SWA Group: A Retrospective," in *PROCESS: Architecture 103, Landscape Design and Planning at the SWA Group* (Tokyo: Process Architecture Publishing Company, 1992), 8–11.

18. Aldo Leopold, *A Sand County Almanac* (1949), quoted in the SWR office brochure for 1974, archives of The SWA Group, Sausalito, California.

19. See Neil Porterfield, "Ecological Basis for Planning a New Campus," *Landscape Architecture* (October 1969): 31–33; "An Eckbo-Porterfield Exchange," *Landscape Architecture* (April 1970): 200–202; and Garrett Eckbo, "The Designer as Anonymous Transformer," *Landscape Architecture* (October 1970): 16.

20. Garrett Eckbo, conversations with Melanie Simo, spring 1991, Berkeley, California.

21. See note 19; Garrett Eckbo, "The Personalized/Anonymous Landscape," *American Institute of Architects' Journal* 43 (May 1965): 39–43.

22. Hideo Sasaki, conversation with Melanie Simo, June 14, 1988, Lafayette, California.

Further Reading

Introduction

Imbert, Dorothée. *The Modernist Garden in France*. New Haven, Conn.: Yale University Press, 1993.

Kouwenhoven, John A. *The Arts in Modern American Civilization*. New York: W. W. Norton, 1967.

Marx, Leo. *The Machine in the Garden: Technology and the Pastoral Ideal in America*. New York: Oxford University Press, 1964.

Toulmin, Stephen. *Cosmopolis: The Hidden Agenda of Modernity*. New York: Free Press, 1990.

Zaitzevsky, Cynthia. *Frederick Law Olmsted and the Boston Park System*. Cambridge, Mass.: Harvard University Press, 1982.

Chapter 1

Bauer, Catherine. *Modern Housing*. Boston: Houghton Mifflin, 1934.

Calthorpe, Peter. *The Next American Metropolis: Ecology, Community, and the American Dream*. New York: Princeton Architectural Press, 1993.

Rowe, Peter G. *Modernity and Housing*. Cambridge, Mass.: MIT Press, 1993.

Sherwood, Roger. *Modern Housing Prototypes*. Cambridge, Mass.: Harvard University Press, 1978.

Stilgoe, John R. *Origins of the American Suburb, 1820–1939*. New Haven, Conn.: Yale University Press, 1988.

Chapter 2

Karl, Frederick R. *Modern and Modernism: The Sovereignty of the Artist, 1885–1925*. New York: Atheneum, 1985.

Kubler, George. *The Shape of Time: Remarks on the History of Things*. New Haven, Conn.: Yale University Press, 1962.

Paz, Octavio. *Labyrinth of Solitude: Life and Thought in Mexico*. New York: Grove Press, 1961.

Chapter 3

Streatfield, David. "Western Expansion." In Walter T. Punch, ed., *Keeping Eden: A History of Gardening in America*. Boston: Bulfinch Press/Little, Brown/ Massachusetts Horticultural Society, 1992.

Whyte, William H., Jr. *The Organization Man*. New York: Simon & Schuster, 1956.

Wyatt, David. *The Fall into Eden: Landscape and Imagination in California.* Cambridge: Cambridge University Press, 1986.

Chapter 4

Agee, James, and Walter Evans. *Let Us Now Praise Famous Men.* Boston: Houghton Mifflin, 1941.

Chermayeff, Serge. *Design and the Public Good: Selected Writings, 1930–1980.* Cambridge, Mass.: MIT Press, 1982.

Scott, Mel. *The San Francisco Bay Area: A Metropolis in Perspective.* Berkeley: University of California Press, 1985.

Chapter 5

Jacobs, Jane. *The Death and Life of Great American Cities.* New York: Random House, 1961.

Jung, C. G., ed. *Man and His Symbols.* Garden City, N.Y.: Doubleday, 1964.

Tunnard, Christopher. *The City of Man.* New York: Scribner, 1953.

Chapter 6

Baubion-Mackler (photographer). *French Royal Gardens.* Text by Vincent Scully. New York: Rizzoli, 1992.

Thoreau, Henry David. *Walden and Other Writings.* New York: Random House, 1937.

Van der Post, Laurens. *The Lost World of the Kalahari.* New York: Morrow, 1958.

Chapter 7

Barzun, Jacques. *The House of Intellect.* New York: Harper & Brothers, 1959.

Marx, Leo. *The Pilot and the Passenger: Essays on Literature, Technology and Culture in the United States.* New York: Oxford University Press, 1988.

White, E. B. *One Man's Meat.* New York: Harper & Brothers, 1944.

Whitehead, Alfred North. *Science and the Modern World.* New York: Macmillan, 1925.

Chapter 8

Banerjee, Tridib, and Michael Southworth, eds., *City Sense and City Design: Writings and Project of Kevin Lynch.* Cambridge, Mass.: MIT Press, 1990.

Galbraith, John Kenneth, *The Affluent Society.* Boston: Houghton Mifflin, 1958.

Hitchcock, Henry-Russell, and Arthur Drexler, eds. *Built in USA: Post-War Architecture.* New York: Museum of Modern Art/London: Thames and Hudson, 1952.

Chapter 9

Bronowski, J. *Science and Human Values.* New York: Harper and Brothers, 1959.

Eiseley, Loren. *The Immense Journey.* New York: Random House, 1957.

Escritt, L. B. *Regional Planning: An Outline of the scientific data relating to planning in Great Britain.* London: George Allen & Unwin, 1943.

Gore, Al. *Earth in the Balance: Ecology and the Human Spirit.* Boston: Houghton Mifflin, 1992.

Thomas, Lewis. *Lives of a Cell: Notes of a Biology Watcher.* New York: Viking, 1974.

Chapter 10

Chermayeff, Serge, and Christopher Alexander. *Community and Privacy.* Garden City, N.Y.: Doubleday, 1963.

Harvey, David. *The Condition of Postmodernity.* Cambridge, Mass.: Basil Blackwell, 1989.

Simonds, John Ormsbee. *Earthscape: A Manual of Environmental Planning and Design.* New York: Van Nostrand Reinhold, 1978.

Stokes, Samuel N., and A. Elizabeth Watson and contributing authors,

Genevieve P. Keller and J. Timothy
Keller. *Saving America's Countryside: A
Guide to Rural Conservation*. Baltimore:
Johns Hopkins University Press/National
Trust for Historic Preservation, 1989.

Epilogue

Francis, Mark, and Randolph T. Hester, Jr.,
eds. *The Meaning of Gardens: Idea, Place,
Action*. Cambridge, Mass.: MIT Press,
1990.

Jensen, Jens. *Siftings* (1939). A new
edition, with a Foreword by Charles E.
Little and an Afterword by Darrel G.
Morrison. Baltimore: Johns Hopkins
University Press, 1990.

Van Valkenburgh, Michael R., et al.,
*Transforming the American Garden: 12
New Landscape Designs*. Catalogue of an
exhibition at The Architectural League
of New York; the Harvard Graduate
School of Design, and other places.
Cambridge, Mass.: Harvard Graduate
School of Design, 1986.

Illustration Credits

Color Plates

Frontispiece: Pepsico Headquarters, Purchase, New York. Edward D. Stone, Jr., Landscape Architect. Russell Page, Landscape Architect and Garden Designer (for areas not shown here). Photo © Felice Frankel.

Plate 1: Photo © Felice Frankel.

Plate 2: Photo © Felice Frankel.

Plate 3: Photo © Michael Moran.

Plate 4: Photo by Armando Salas Portugal.

Plate 5: Photo © Felice Frankel.

Plate 6: Photo © Felice Frankel.

Plate 7: Photo by Lawrence Halprin.

Plate 8: Photo © Felice Frankel.

Plate 9: Photo © Felice Frankel.

Plate 10: Photo © Felice Frankel.

Plate 11: Photo by Robert Tetlow.

Plate 12: Photo by Peter Walker.

Figure 1: Courtesy National Park Service, Frederick Law Olmsted National Historic Site.

Figure 2: Stourhead, Wiltshire, England. Formerly, seat of Henry Hoare and his descendants; now owned by the National Trust (England). Henry Hoare II, Principal Landscape Designer. Pantheon by Henry Flitcroft, Architect. Photo by Melanie Simo.

Figure 3: Photo by Melanie Simo.

Figure 4: Photo by Melanie Simo.

Figure 5: Asher B. Durand, *View Towards Hudson Valley*, 1851. Oil on canvas, 33⅛ × 48⅛ inches. Courtesy, Wadsworth Atheneum, Hartford. The Ella Gallup Sumner and Mary Catlin Sumner Collection Fund.

Figure 6: Photo by Melanie Simo.

Figure 7: From *Official Views of the World's Columbian Exposition* (Chicago, 1893). Courtesy of the Frances Loeb Library, Graduate School of Design, Harvard University.

Figure 8: From *Official Views of the World's Columbian Exposition* (Chicago, 1893). Courtesy of the Frances Loeb Library, Graduate School of Design, Harvard University.

Figure 9: Courtesy National Park Service, Frederick Law Olmsted National Historic Site.

Figure 10: From *Pencil Points*, March 1941, page 74. Reprinted with permission of *Progressive Architecture*, Penton Publishing. Courtesy of the Frances Loeb Library, Graduate School of Design, Harvard University.

Figure 31: Photo by Armando Salas Portugal.

Figure 32: Photo by Armando Salas Portugal.

Figure 33: Photo by Armando Salas Portugal.

Figure 34: Photo by Pamela Palmer.

Figure 35: Stage set design for Martha Graham, *Errand into the Maze* (1947). Isamu Noguchi, designer. Photo by Rudolph Burckhardt. Courtesy of the Isamu Noguchi Foundation, Inc.

Figure 36: Isamu Noguchi, *Contoured Playground* (model), 1941. Photo by Rudolph Burckhardt. Courtesy of The Isamu Noguchi Foundation, Inc.

Figure 37: Photo by Melanie Simo.

Figure 38: Photo by Melanie Simo.

Figure 39: Photo by Melanie Simo.

Figure 40: Courtesy of The Isamu Noguchi Foundation, Inc.

Figure 41: Courtesy Elizabeth Roberts Church.

Figure 42: Drawing by Thomas Church. Courtesy, Elizabeth Roberts Church.

Figure 43: Joan Miró, *Landscape (The Hare) (Paysage [Le Lièvre])*. Autumn 1927. Oil on canvas, 51 × 76⅝″ (129.6 ×

194.6 cm). The Solomon R. Guggenheim Museum, New York. Photo: Robert E. Mates. Copyright The Solomon R. Guggenheim Foundation, New York.

Figure 44: Photo by Rondal Partridge. Courtesy Elizabeth Roberts Church.

Figure 45: Drawings by Thomas Church. Courtesy Elizabeth Roberts Church.

Figure 46: Photo by Rondal Partridge. Courtesy Elizabeth Roberts Church.

Figure 47: Drawing by Lawrence Halprin. Courtesy Elizabeth Roberts Church.

Figure 48: Drawing by Lawrence Halprin. Courtesy Elizabeth Roberts Church.

Figure 49: Photo by Rondal Partridge. Courtesy, Elizabeth Roberts Church.

Figure 50: Drawing by Thomas Church. Courtesy Elizabeth Roberts Church.

Figure 51: Photo by Rondal Partridge. Courtesy Elilzabeth Roberts Church.

Plate 52: Jean Arp (1887–1966), *Vase— Bust*, 1930. Relief in carved and painted wood, 12 × 8¼ inches. Courtesy, The Philadelphia Museum of Art: A. E. Gallatin Collection.

Figure 53: Photo by Melanie Simo.

Figure 54: Drawing by Thomas Church. Courtesy Elizabeth Roberts Church.

Figure 55: Photo by Rondal Partridge. Courtesy Elizabeth Roberts Church.

Figure 56: John Funk and Joseph Allen Stein, Architects. Nicholas Cirino, Civil Engineer. Eckbo, Royston, and Williams, Landscape Architects. Courtesy Garrett Eckbo.

Figure 57: Courtesy Robert Royston.

Figure 58: Courtesy Garrett and Arline Eckbo.

Figure 59: Courtesy Garrett Eckbo.

Figure 60: Ludwig Mies van der Rohe, German Pavilion, Barcelona: Floor Plan. Final scheme. Made for publication in 1929. Ink, pencil on paper, 22½ × 38½″ (57.6 × 98.1 cm). The Mies van der Rohe Archive, The Museum of Modern Art, New York. Gift of the architect.

Figure 61: Courtesy Garrett Eckbo.

Figure 62: Courtesy Garrett Eckbo.

Figure 63: Courtesy Robert Royston.

Figure 64: Courtesy Robert Royston.

Figure 65: Courtesy Robert Royston.

Figure 66: Alcoa Garden at the Eckbo Residence, Laurel Canyon, Hollywood

Hills, Los Angeles, California, ca. 1960. Home of Garrett and Arline Eckbo, 1950–1965. Alison E. Peper, playing guitar. Garrett Eckbo, Landscape Architect. Courtesy Garrett Eckbo.

Figure 67: Laszlo Moholy-Nagy, *Construction*. Lithograph. 60.2 × 44.1 cm. Courtesy of The Busch-Reisinger Museum, Harvard University Art Museums.

Figure 68: Courtesy Robert Royston.

Figure 69: Courtesy Robert Royston.

Figure 70: Drawing by Robert Royston. Courtesy Robert Royston.

Figure 71: Courtesy, Department of Landscape Architecture, Graduate School of Design, Harvard University.

Figure 72: Photo by Glenn M. Christiansen. Courtesy *Sunset* Magazine.

Figure 73: From *The Architectural Review* (January 1939). Reproduced by permission of *The Architectural Review*. Courtesy of the Frances Loeb Library, Graduate School of Design, Harvard University.

Figure 74: Photo by Lawrence Halprin. Courtesy Lawrence Halprin.

Figure 75: Courtesy Lawrence Halprin.

Figure 76: Photo by Lawrence Halprin. Courtesy Lawrence Halprin.

Figure 77: Courtesy Lawrence Halprin.

Figure 78: Photo by Lawrence Halprin. Courtesy Lawrence Halprin.

Figure 79: Photo by Brian Laczko. Courtesy Lawrence Halprin.

Figure 80: Drawing by Lawrence Halprin. Courtesy Lawrence Halprin.

Figure 81: Courtesy Lawrence Halprin.

Figure 82: Photo by Lawrence Halprin. Courtesy Lawrence Halprin.

Figure 83: Photo by David Hirsch. Courtesy M. Paul Friedberg.

Figure 84: Photo by David Hirsch. Courtesy M. Paul Friedberg.

Figure 85: Courtesy Robert Zion.

Figure 86: Photo by Clemens Kalischer.

Figure 87: Courtesy Dan Kiley.

Figure 88: Photo by Aaron Kiley. Courtesy Dan Kiley.

Figure 89: Photo by Alan Ward.

Figure 90: Photo by Gerald Campbell.

Figure 91: Courtesy Dan Kiley.

Figure 92: Photo by Alan Ward.

Figure 93: Photo by Alan Ward.

Figure 94: Courtesy Dan Kiley.

Figure 95: Photo by Peter Walker.

Figure 96: Photo by Alan Ward. Courtesy Dan Kiley.

Figure 97: Photo by Peter Hornbeck. Courtesy Department of Landscape Architecture, Graduate School of Design, Harvard University.

Figure 98: Courtesy Department of Landscape Architecture, Graduate School of Design, Harvard University.

Figure 99: Drawing by Stanley White. Courtesy Charles W. Harris.

Figure 100: Courtesy Stuart O. Dawson.

Figure 101: Courtesy Stuart O. Dawson.

Figure 102: Photo by Carlisle Becker. Courtesy Stuart O. Dawson.

Figure 103: Courtesy Stuart O. Dawson.

Figure 104: Photo © Mary Randlett. Courtesy Richard Haag.

Figure 105: Courtesy Richard Haag.

Figure 106: Photo by Melanie Simo.

Figure 107: Courtesy Sasaki Associates.

Figure 108: Courtesy Stuart O. Dawson and Sasaki Associates.

Figure 109: Courtesy Sasaki Associates.

Figure 110: Photo by David Smith. Courtesy William J. Johnson.

Figure 111: Courtesy William J. Johnson.

Figure 112: Courtesy William J. Johnson.

Figure 113: Courtesy Sasaki Associates.

Figure 114: Courtesy Deere and Company.

Figure 115: Photo by Ralph Hutchins, Hutchins Photography, Inc.

Figure 116: Photo by Steve Proehl.

Figure 117: Photo by Gerald Campbell. Courtesy The SWA Group.

Figure 118: Photo by Gerald Campbell. Courtesy The SWA Group.

Figure 119: Photo by Gerald Campbell. Courtesy The SWA Group.

Figure 120: Photo by Gerald Campbell. Courtesy The SWA Group.

Figure 121: Photo © Felice Frankel.

Figure 122: Courtesy The SWA Group.

Figure 123: Courtesy Sasaki Associates.

Figure 124: Photo by James H. Roberts. Courtesy Hideo Sasaki.

Figure 125: Photo by Rush J. McCoy. Courtesy Hideo Sasaki.

Figure 126: Photo by Mark Stern.

Figure 127: Courtesy Carl Steinitz.

Figure 128: Courtesy Carl Steinitz.

Figure 129: Courtesy Carl Steinitz.

Figure 130: Photo by H. Raymond Ball. Courtesy *Rhode Islander Magazine,* Providence Journal Company.

Figure 131: Published in the *Rhode Islander Magazine,* June 11, 1950. Courtesy Frances Loeb Library, Graduate School of Design, Harvard University.

Figure 132: From Ian McHarg, *Design with Nature* (1969), page 18. Photo Courtesy Litton Industries.

Figure 133: From Ian McHarg, *Design with Nature* (1969), page 60. Reproduced by permission of John Wiley and Sons, publishers of the 1992 edition.

Figure 134: From Ian McHarg, *Design with Nature* (1969), page 39. Reproduced by permission of John Wiley and Sons, publishers of the 1992 edition.

Figure 135: Courtesy EDAW, Inc.

Figure 136: Courtesy POD/Sasaki Associates.

Figure 137: Courtesy The SWA Group.

Figure 138: Photo by Gerald Campbell. Courtesy The SWA Group.

Figure 139: Photo by Dixi Carrillo. Courtesy The SWA Group.

Figure 140: Courtesy The SWA Group.

Figure 141: Photo by Joshua Freiwald. Courtesy The SWA Group.

Figure 142: Photo by Daisy Palau. Courtesy The SWA Group.

Figure 143: Photo by Dixi Carrillo. Courtesy The SWA Group.

Figure 144: Photo by Gerald Campbell. Courtesy The SWA Group.

and Standard Oil Rod and Gun Club, 141

Ecole des Beaux-Arts, design tradition of, 29, 40, 99, 122, 211, 225, 281

Ecology, and landscape architecture, 161–163, 204, 209, 261–265, 305–306

EDAW, Inc. (firm), 119, 285, 296
and Minnesota Power Plant study, 286–287 (see also Eckbo, Dean, Austin and Williams)

Edward McCleod & Associates (firm), 159

Eero Saarinen and Associates (firm), 236–237, Plate 10

Einstein, Albert, 198

Eiseley, Loren, 270

Eliot, Charles, 30, 261

Emerson, Ralph Waldo, 37, 177, 181

Employee Stock Ownership Program, 301

Enerson, Jon, 121

England, landscape gardens and parks of, 14–16, 63, 235, 243, 276

Entenza, John, 132, 139

Environment, total, and architectural design, 291–293

Environmentalism, and art, 66

Environmental Planning & Design (firm), 285

Environmental Simulation Laboratory, 121

Ernest J. Kump and Associates (firm), 240–242, Plate 11

Esherick, Joseph, 102, 163

Estern, Neil, 161

Evans, John, 280

Exhibitions
Armory Show, 29
International Style, 29
in San Francisco, 138–139

Exposition
Centennial, in Philadelphia, 25
Louisiana, in St. Louis, 38
Panama California International, in San Diego, 40, 41
Panama-Pacific, in San Francisco, 138
World's Columbian, in Chicago, 21–24, 180, 281

Expressionism, 57, 157

Farmer, as landscape designer, 185

Farm Security Administration (FSA), 125–127

Farrand, Beatrix, 30

Fein, Albert, 287–291

Fisher and Davis (firm), 252, 255

Fisher-Friedman Associates (firm), 304–306

Fitch, James Marston, 184, 287

Fleming, Bryant, 207

France, gardens of, 122, 175, 186, 188, 191, 243

Frank O. Gehry Associates (firm), 307

Freeman, Allen, 164

French, Daniel Chester, 22

Friedberg, M. Paul, 140, 165, 331–332n23

Fuller, R. Buckminster, 80

Funk, John, 131

Furtado, John, 263, 265

Gabo, Naum, 135

Gallagher, Percival, 207

Garden city
definition of, 45
and evolutionary change, 36
landscape in, 33, 49–52
as objet d'art, 53
as organism, 35
and revolutionary ideals, 32, 35–36

Garden city movement, 30–33, 35–36, 49

Geddes, Patrick, 35, 42